Sociology and M Problems

Charles A. Ellwood

Alpha Editions

This edition published in 2023

ISBN : 9789357962612

Design and Setting By
Alpha Editions
www.alphaedis.com
Email - info@alphaedis.com

Contents

PREFACE

This book is intended as an elementary text in sociology as applied to modern social problems, for use in institutions where but a short time can be given to the subject, in courses in sociology where it is desired to combine it with a study of current social problems on the one hand, and to correlate it with a course in economics on the other. The book is also especially suited for use in University Extension Courses and in Teachers' Reading Circles.

This book aims to teach the simpler principles of sociology concretely and inductively. In Chapters I to VIII the elementary principles of sociology are stated and illustrated, chiefly through the study of the origin, development, structure, and functions of the family considered as a typical human institution; while in Chapters IX to XV certain special problems are considered in the light of these general principles.

Inasmuch as the book aims to illustrate the working of certain factors in social organization and evolution by the study of concrete problems, interpretation has been emphasized rather than the social facts themselves. However, the book is not intended to be a contribution to sociological theory, and no attempt is made to give a systematic presentation of theory. Rather, the student's attention is called to certain obvious and elementary forces in the social life, and he is left to work out his own system of social theory.

To guide the student in further reading, a brief list of select references in English has been appended to each chapter. Methodological discussions and much statistical and historical material have been omitted in order to make the text as simple as possible. These can be found in the references, or the teacher can supply them at his discretion.

The many authorities to whom I am indebted for both facts and interpretations of facts cannot be mentioned individually, except that I wish to express my special indebtedness to my former teachers, Professor Willcox of Cornell and Professors Small and Henderson of the University of Chicago, to whom I am under obligation either directly or indirectly for much of the substance of this book. The list of references will also indicate in the main the sources of whatever is not my own.

CHARLES A. ELLWOOD.

UNIVERSITY OF MISSOURI.

CHAPTER I

THE STUDY OF SOCIETY

What is Society?—Perhaps the great question which sociology seeks to answer is this question which we have put at the beginning. Just as biology seeks to answer the question "What is life?"; zoölogy, "What is an animal?"; botany, "What is a plant?"; so sociology seeks to answer the question "What is society?" or perhaps better, "What is association?" Just as biology, zoölogy, and botany cannot answer their questions until those sciences have reached their full and complete development, so also sociology cannot answer the question "What is society?" until it reaches its final development. Nevertheless, some conception or definition of society is necessary for the beginner, for in the scientific discussion of social problems we must know first of all what we are talking about. We must understand in a general way what society is, what sociology is, what the relations are between sociology and other sciences, before we can study the social problems of to-day from a sociological point of view.

The word "society" is used scientifically to designate the reciprocal relations between individuals. More exactly, and using the term in a concrete sense, a society is any group of individuals who have more or less conscious relations to each other. We say conscious relations because it is not necessary that these relations be specialized into industrial, political, or ecclesiastical relations. Society is constituted by the mental interaction of individuals and exists wherever two or three individuals have reciprocal conscious relations to each other. Dependence upon a common economic environment, or the mere contiguity in space is not sufficient to constitute a society. It is the interdependence in function on the mental side, the contact and overlapping of our inner selves, which makes possible that form of collective life which we call society. Plants and lowly types of organisms do not constitute true societies, unless it can be shown that they have some degree of mentality. On the other hand, there is no reason for withholding the term "society" from many animal groups. These animal societies, however, are very different in many respects from human society, and are of interest to us only as certain of their forms throw light upon human society.

We may dismiss with a word certain faulty conceptions of society. In some of the older sociological writings the word society is often used as nearly synonymous with the word nation. Now, a nation is a body of people politically organized into an independent government, and it is manifest that it is only one of many forms of human society. Another conception of society, which some have advocated, is that it is synonymous with the cultural group. That is, a society is any group of people that have a common civilization, or that are bearers of a certain type of culture. In this case Christendom, for example, would constitute a single society. Cultural groups no doubt are, again, one of the forms of human society, but only one among many. Both the cultural group and the nation are very imposing forms of society and hence have attracted the attention of social thinkers very often in the past to the neglect of the more humble forms. But it is evident that all forms of association are of equal interest to the sociologist, though, of course, this is not saying that all forms are of equal practical importance.

Any form of association, or social group, which may be studied, if studied from the point of view of origin and development, whether it be a family, a neighborhood group, a city, a state, a trade union, or a party, will serve to reveal many of the problems of sociology. The natural or genetic social groups, however, such as the family, the community, and the nation, serve best to exhibit sociological problems. In this text we shall make particular use of the family, as the simplest and, in many ways, the most typical of all the forms of human association, to illustrate concretely the laws and principles of social development. Through the study of the simple and primary forms of association the problems of sociology can be much better attacked than through the study of society at large, or association in general.

From what has been said it may be inferred that *society* as a scientific term means scarcely more than the abstract term *association*, and this is correct. Association, indeed, may be regarded as the more scientific term of the two; at any rate it indicates more exactly what the sociologist deals with. A word may be said also as to the meaning of the word *social*. The sense in which this word will generally be used in this text is that of a collective adjective, referring to all that pertains to or relates to society in any way. The word social, then, is much broader than the words industrial, political, moral, religious, and embraces them all; that is, social phenomena are all phenomena which involve the interaction of two or more individuals. The word social, then, includes the economic, political, moral, religious, etc., and must not be thought of as something set in opposition to, for instance, the industrial or the political.

Society and its Products.—Beneath all the forms and processes of human society lies the fact of association itself. Industry, government, and civilization itself must be regarded as expressions of collective human life rather than *vice versa*. Industry, for example, is one side or aspect of man's social life, and must not be mistaken for society itself. Industry, government, religion, education, art, and the like, are all products of the social life of man. Among these coördinate expressions of collective human life, industry, being concerned with the satisfying of the material needs of men, is perhaps fundamental to the rest. But this must not lead to the mistaken view that the social life of man can be interpreted completely through his industrial life; for, as has just been said, beneath industry and all other aspects of man's collective life lies the biological and psychological fact of association. This is equivalent to saying that industry itself must be interpreted in terms of the biology and psychology of human association. In other words, industrial problems, political problems, educational problems, and the like must be viewed from the collective or social standpoint rather than simply as detached problems by themselves. We must understand the biological and psychological aspects of man's social life before we can understand its special phases.

The Origin of Society.—From the definition of society that we have given it is evident that society is something which springs from the very processes of life itself. It is not something which has been invented or planned by individuals. Life, in its higher forms at least, could not exist without association. From the very beginning the association of the sexes has been necessary for reproduction and for the care and rearing of offspring, and it has been not less necessary for the procuring of an adequate food supply and for protection against enemies. From the association necessary for reproduction has sprung family life and all the altruistic institutions of human society, while from the association for providing food supply have sprung society's industrial institutions. Neither society nor industry, therefore, has had a premeditated, reflective origin, but both have sprung up spontaneously from the needs of life and both have developed down to the present time at least with but little premeditated guidance. It is necessary that the student should understand at the outset that social organization is not a fabrication of the human intellect to any great degree, and the old idea that individuals who existed independently of society came together and deliberately planned a certain type of social organization is utterly without scientific validity. The individual and society are correlatives. We have no knowledge of individuals apart from society or society apart from individuals. What we do know is that human life everywhere is a collective or associated life, the individual being on the one hand largely an expression of the social life surrounding him and on the other hand society being largely an expression of individual character. The reasons for these assertions will appear later as we develop our subject.

What is Sociology?—The science which deals with human association, its origin, development, forms, and functions, is sociology. Briefly, sociology is a science which deals with society as a whole and not with its separate aspects or phases. It attempts to formulate the laws or principles which govern social organization and social evolution. This means that the main problems of sociology are those of the organization of society on the one hand and the evolution of society on the other. These words, *organization* and *evolution*, however, are used in a broader sense in sociology than they are generally used. By organization we mean any relation of the parts of society to each other. By evolution we mean, not necessarily change for the better, but orderly change of any sort. Sociology is, therefore, a science which deals with the laws or principles of social organization and of social change. Put in more exact terms this makes sociology, as we said at the beginning, the science of the origin, development, structure, and function of the forms of association. We may pass over very rapidly certain faulty conceptions of sociology. The first of these is that it is the study of social evils and their remedies. This conception is faulty because it makes sociology deal primarily with the abnormal rather than the normal conditions in society, and secondly, it is to be criticized because it makes sociology synonymous with scientific philanthropy. It is rather the science of philanthropy, which is an applied science resting upon sociology, that studies social evils and their remedies. This is not saying, of course, that sociology does not consider social evils, but that it considers them as incidents in the normal processes of social evolution rather than as its special matter. A second conception of sociology which is to be dismissed as inadequate is the conception that it is the science of social phenomena. This conception is not incorrect, but is somewhat vague, as there are manifestly other sciences of social phenomena, such as economics and political science. Such a conception of sociology would make it include everything in human society. A third faulty conception is that it is the science of human institutions. This is faulty because it again is too narrow. An institution is a *sanctioned* form of human association, while sociology deals with the ephemeral and unsanctioned forms, such as we see in the phenomena of mobs, crazes, fads, fashions, and crimes, as well as with the sanctioned forms. A fourth conception which might be criticized is that sociology is the science of social organization. This makes sociology deal with the laws or principles of the relations of individuals to one another, and of institutions to one another. It is to be criticized as faulty because it fails to emphasize the evolution of those relations. All science is now evolutionary in spirit and in method and believes that things cannot be understood except as they are understood in their genesis and development. It would, therefore, perhaps be more correct to define sociology as the science of the evolution of human interrelations than to define it simply as the science of social organization.

The Problems of Sociology.—The problems of sociology fall into two great classes; first, problems of the organization of society, and second, problems of the evolution of society. The problems of the organization of society are problems of the relations of individuals to one another and to institutions. Such problems are, for example, the influence of various elements in the physical environment upon the social organization; or, again, the influence of various elements in human nature upon the social order. These problems are, then, problems of society in a hypothetically stationary condition or at rest. For this reason Comte, the founder of modern sociology, called the division of sociology which deals with such problems *Social Statics*. But the problems which are of most interest and importance in sociology are those of social evolution. Under this head we have the problem of the origin of society in general and also of various forms of association. More important still are the problems of social progress and social retrogression; that is, the causes of the advancement of society to higher and more complex types of social organization and the causes of social decline. The former problem, social progress, is in a peculiar sense the central problem of sociology. The effort of theoretical sociology is to develop a scientific theory of social progress. The study of social evolution, then, that is, social changes of all sorts, as we have emphasized above, is the vital part of sociology; and it is manifest that only a general science of society like sociology is competent to deal with such a problem. Inasmuch as the problems of social evolution are problems of change, development, or movement in society, Comte proposed that this division of sociology be called *Social Dynamics*.

The Relations of Sociology to Other Sciences. [Footnote: For a fuller discussion of the relations of sociology to other sciences and to philosophy see my article on "Sociology: Its Problems and Its Relations" in the *American Journal of Sociology* for November, 1907.]—(A) *Relations to Biology and Psychology*. In attempting to give a scientific view of social organization and social evolution, sociology has to depend upon the other natural sciences, particularly upon biology and psychology. It is manifest that sociology must depend upon biology, since biology is the general science of life, and human society is but part of the world of life in general. It is manifest also that sociology must depend upon psychology to explain the interactions between individuals because these interactions are for the most part interactions between their minds. Thus on the one hand all social phenomena are vital phenomena and on the other hand nearly all social phenomena are mental phenomena. Every social problem has, in other words, its psychological and its biological sides, and sociology is distinguished from biology and psychology only as a matter of convenience. The scientific division of labor necessitates that certain scientific workers concern themselves with certain problems. Now, the problems with which the biologist and the psychologist deal are not the problems of the organization and evolution of society. Hence, while the sociologist borrows his principles of interpretation from biology and psychology, he has his own distinctive problems, and it is this fact which makes sociology a distinct science.

Sociology is not so easily distinguished from the special social sciences like politics, economics, and others, as it is from the other general sciences. These sciences occupy the same field as sociology, that is, they have to do with social phenomena. But in general, as has already been pointed out, they are concerned chiefly with certain very special aspects or phases of the social life and not with its most general problems. If sociology, then, is dependent upon the other general sciences, particularly upon biology and psychology, it is obvious that its relation to the special sciences is the reverse, namely, these sciences are dependent upon sociology. This is only saying practically the same thing as was said above when we pointed out that industry, government, and religion are but expressions of human social life. In other words, sociology deals with the more general biological and psychological aspects of human association, while the special sciences of economics, politics, and the like, generally deal with certain products or highly specialized phases of society.

(B) *Relations to History.* [Footnote: For a discussion of the practical relations between the teaching of history and of sociology, see my paper on "How History can be taught from a Sociological Point of View," in Education for January, 1910.] A word may be said about the relation of sociology to another science which also deals with human society in a general way, and that is history. History is a concrete, descriptive science of society which attempts to construct a picture of the social past. Sociology, however, is an abstract, theoretical science of society concerned with the laws and principles which govern social organization and social change. In a sense, sociology is narrower than history inasmuch as it is an abstract science, and in another sense it is wider than history because it concerns itself not only with the social past but also with the social present. The facts of contemporary social life are indeed even more important to the sociologist than the facts of history, although it is impossible to construct a theory of social evolution without taking into full account all the facts available in human history, and in this sense history becomes one of the very important methods of sociology. Upon its evolutionary or dynamic side sociology may be considered a sort of philosophy of history; at least it attempts to give a scientific theory which will explain the social changes which history describes concretely.

(C) Relations to Economics. Economics is that special social science which deals with the wealth-getting and wealth-using activities of man. In other words, it is concerned with the commercial and industrial activities of man. As has already been implied, economics must be considered one of the most important of the special social sciences, if not the most important. Yet it is evident that the wealth-getting and wealth-using activities of man are strictly an outgrowth of his social life, and that economics as a science of human industry must rest upon sociology. Sometimes in the past the mistake has been made of supposing that economics dealt with the most fundamental social phenomena, and even at times economists have spoken of their science as alone sufficient to explain all social phenomena. It cannot be admitted, however, that we can explain social organization in general or social progress in terms of economic development. A theory of progress, for example, in which the sole causes of human progress were found in economic conditions would neglect political, religious, educational, and many other conditions. Only a very one-sided theory of society can be built upon such a basis. Economics should keep to its own sphere of explaining the commercial and industrial activities of man and not attempt to become a general science dealing with social evolution. This is now recognized by practically all economists of standing, and the only question which remains is whether economics is independent of sociology or whether it rests upon sociology.

The view which has been presented thus far and which will be adhered to is that economics should rest upon sociology. That economics does rest upon sociology is shown by many considerations. The chief problem of theoretical economics is the problem of economic value. But economic value is but one sort of value which is recognized in society, moral and aesthetic values being other examples of the valuing process, and all values must express the collective judgment of some human group or other. The problem of economic value, in other words, reduces itself to a problem in social psychology, and when this is said it is equivalent to making economics dependent upon sociology, for social psychology is simply the psychological aspect of sociology. Again, industrial organization and industrial evolution are but parts or phases of social evolution in general, and it is safe to say that industry, both in its organization and evolution, cannot be understood apart from the general conditions, psychological and biological, which surround society. Again, many non-economic forces continually obtrude themselves upon the student of industrial conditions, such as custom, invention, imitation, standards, ideals, and the like. These are general social forces which play throughout all phases of human social life and so show the dependence of industry upon society in general, and, therefore, of economics upon sociology. Much more might be said in the way of concretely illustrating these statements, but the purpose of this text precludes anything but the briefest and most elementary statement of these theoretical facts.

(D) *Relations to Politics*. We have already said that the state is one of the chief forms of human association. The science which treats of the state or of government is known as political science or politics. It is one of the oldest of the social sciences, having been more or less systematized by Aristotle. The problems of politics are those of the origin, nature, function, and development of government. It is manifest that politics, both on its practical and theoretical sides, has many close relations to sociology. While the state or nation must not be confused with society in general, yet because the state is the most imposing, if not the most important, form of human association, the relations of politics and sociology must be very intimate. On the one hand, political scientists can scarcely understand the origin, nature, and proper functions of government without understanding more or less about the social life generally; and, on the other hand, the sociologist finds that one of the most important facts of human society is that of social control, or of authority. While political science deals only with the organized authority manifested in the state, which we call government, yet inasmuch as this is the most important form of social control, and inasmuch as political organization is one of the chief manifestations of social organization, the sociologist can scarcely deal adequately with the great problems of social organization and evolution without constant reference to political science.

An important branch of political science is jurisprudence, or the science of law. This, again, is closely related with sociology, on both its theoretical and practical sides. Law is, perhaps, the most important means of social control made use of by society, and the sociologist needs to understand something of the principles of law in order to understand the nature of the existing social order. On the other hand, the jurist needs to know the principles of social organization and evolution in general before he can understand the nature and purpose of law.

(E) *Relations to Ethics.* [Footnote: For a full statement of my views regarding the relations of sociology and ethics, see my article on "The Sociological Basis of Ethics," in the *International Journal of Ethics* for April, 1910.] Ethics is the science which deals with the right or wrong of human conduct. Its problems are the nature of morality and of moral obligation, the validity of moral ideals, the norms by which conduct is to be judged, and the like. While ethics was once considered to be a science of individual conduct it is now generally conceived as being essentially a social science. The moral and the social are indeed not clearly separable, but we may consider the moral to be the ideal aspect of the social.

This view of morality, which, for the most part, is indorsed by modern thought, makes ethics dependent upon sociology for its criteria of rightness or wrongness. Indeed, we cannot argue any moral question nowadays unless we argue it in social terms. If we discuss the rightness or wrongness of the drink habit we try to show its social consequences. So, too, if we discuss the rightness or wrongness of such an institution as polygamy we find ourselves forced to do so mainly in social terms. This is not denying, of course, that there are religious and metaphysical aspects to morality,—these are not necessarily in conflict with the social aspects,—but it is saying that modern ethical theory is coming more and more to base itself upon the study of the remote social consequences of conduct, and that we cannot judge what is right or wrong in our complex society unless we know something of the social consequences.

Ethics must be regarded, therefore, as a normative science to which sociology and the other social sciences lead up. It is, indeed, very difficult to separate ethics from sociology. It is the business of sociology to furnish norms and standards to ethics, and it is the business of ethics as a science to take the norms and standards furnished by the social sciences, to develop them, and to criticize them. This text therefore, will not attempt to exclude ethical implications and judgments from sociological discussions, because that would be futile and childish.

(F) *Relations to Education.* Among the applied sciences, sociology is especially closely related to education, for education is not simply the art of developing the powers and capacities of the individual; it is rather the fitting of individuals for efficient membership, for proper functioning, in social life. On its individual side, education should initiate the individual into the social life and fit him for social service. It should create the good citizen. On the social or public side, education should be the chief means of social progress. It should regenerate society, by fitting the individual for a higher type of social life than at present achieved. We must have a socialized education if our present complex civilization is to endure. Social problems touch education on every side, and, on the other hand, education must bear upon every social problem. It is evident, therefore, that sociology has a very great bearing upon the problems of education; and the teacher who comes to his task equipped with a knowledge of social conditions and of the laws and principles of social organization and evolution will find a significance and meaning in his work which he could hardly otherwise find.

(G) *Relations to Philanthropy.*[Footnote: This topic is more fully discussed in my article on "Philanthropy and Sociology" in The Survey for June 4, 1910.] The great science which deals directly with the depressed classes in society and with their uplift may be called the science of philanthropy. It may be regarded as an applied department of sociology. The science of philanthropy is especially concerned with the prevention, as well as with the curative treatment, of dependency, defectiveness, and delinquency. That part which deals with the social treatment of the criminal class is generally called penology, while the subdivision which treats of dependents and defectives is generally known as "charities" or "charitology."

It is evident that there are very close relations between the science of philanthropy and sociology. The elimination of hereditary defects, the overcoming of the social maladjustment of individuals, and the correction of defective social conditions, the three great tasks of scientific philanthropy, all require great knowledge of human society. The social or philanthropic worker, therefore, requires thorough equipment in sociology that he may approach his tasks aright.

The Relation of Sociology to Socialism.—Curiously enough sociology is often confused with socialism by those who pay but little attention to scientific matters. This comes from the fact that some of the adherents of socialism claim that socialism is a science. As a matter of fact, socialism is primarily a party program. It is the platform of a social and political party that has as the main tenet of its creed the abolition of private property in the means of production. Socialism, in other words, is a scheme to revolutionize the present order of society. It cannot claim to be a science in any sense, though it may rest upon theories which its adherents believe to be scientific. Sociology, on the other hand, is a science, and is concerned not with revolutionizing the social order, but with studying and understanding social conditions, especially the more fundamental conditions upon which social organization and social changes depend. As a science it aims simply at understanding society, at getting at the truth. It is no more related logically to socialism than to the platform of the Republican or the Democratic party.

The theories upon which revolutionary socialism rest may be proved or disproved by scientific sociology. It is perhaps too early to say finally whether sociology will pronounce the theoretical assumptions of socialism correct or incorrect; but so far as we can see it seems probable that the theories of social evolution advocated by the Marxian socialists at least will be pronounced erroneous. In any case, there is no logical connection between sociology as a science and socialism as a program for social reconstruction.

Nevertheless, there has been a close connection between sociology and socialism historically. It has been largely the agitations of the socialists and other radical social reformers which have called attention to the need of a scientific understanding of human society. The socialists and other radical reformers, in other words, have very largely set the problem which sociology attempts to solve. Practically, moreover, the indictments and charges of the socialists and anarchists against the present social order have made necessary some study of that order to see whether these charges were well founded or not. In this sense sociology may be said to be a scientific answer to socialism, not in the sense that sociology is devoted to refuting socialism, but in the sense that sociology has been devoted very largely to inquiring into many of the theoretical assumptions which revolutionary socialism makes.

The further relations of sociology to socialism will be taken up later. Here we are only concerned to have the reader see that there is a sharp distinction between the sociological movement on the one hand, that is, the movement to obtain fuller and more accurate knowledge concerning human social life, and the socialist movement, the movement to revolutionize the present social and economic order. Moreover, it may be remarked that while socialism seems to be mainly an economic program, it involves such total and radical reconstruction of social organization that in the long run the claims of socialism to a scientific validity must be passed upon by sociology rather than by economics.

The Relation of Sociology to Social Reform.—From what has been said it is also evident that sociology must not be confused with any particular social reform movement or with the movement for social reform in general. Sociology, as a science, cannot afford to be developed in the interest of any social reform. Certain social reforms, sociology may give its approval to; others it may designate as unwise; but this approval or disapproval will be simply incidental to its discovery of the full truth about human social relations. This is not saying, of course, that social theory should be divorced from social practice, or that the knowledge which sociology and the other social sciences offer concerning human society has no practical bearing upon present social conditions. On the contrary, while all science aims abstractly at the truth, all science is practical also in a deeper sense. No science would ever have been developed if it were not conceived that the knowledge which it discovers will ultimately be of benefit to man. All science exists, therefore, to benefit man, to enable him to master his environment, and the social sciences not less than the other sciences. The physical sciences have already enabled man to attain to a considerable mastery over his physical environment. When the social sciences have been developed it is safe to say that they will enable man not less to master his social environment. Therefore, while sociology and the special social sciences present as yet no program for action, aiming simply at the discovery of the abstract truth, they will undoubtedly in time bring about vast changes for the betterment of social conditions.

SELECT REFERENCES

For Brief Reading:

WARD, *Outlines of Sociology*, Chaps. I-VIII.
ROSS, *The foundations of Sociology*, Chaps. I and II.
DEALEY, *Sociology, Its simpler Teachings and Applications*, Chap. I.

For More Extended Reading:

GIDDINGS, *The Principles of Sociology,* 3d edition.
SMALL, *General Sociology.*
SPENCER, *The Study of Sociology.*
STUCKENBERG, *Sociology: The Science of Human Society.*
WARD, *Pure Sociology.*
American Journal of Sociology, many articles.
For a fairly extensive bibliography on sociology, consult Howard's
    General Sociology: An Analytical Reference Syllabus.

CHAPTER II

THE BEARING OF THE THEORY OF EVOLUTION UPON SOCIAL PROBLEMS

Since Darwin wrote his *Origin of Species* all the sciences in any way connected with biology have been profoundly influenced by his theory of evolution. It is important that the student of sociology, therefore, should understand at the outset something of the bearing of Darwin's theory upon social problems.

We may note at the beginning, however, that the word *evolution* has two distinct, though related, meanings. First, it usually means Darwin's doctrine of descent; secondly, it is used to designate Spencer's theory of universal evolution. Let us note somewhat in detail what evolution means in the first of these senses.

The Darwinian Theory of Descent.—Darwin's theory of descent is the doctrine that all forms of life now existing or that have existed upon the earth have sprung from a few simple primitive types. According to this theory all forms of animals and plants have sprung from a few primitive stocks, though not necessarily one, because even in the beginning there may have existed a distinction at least between the plant and the animal types. So far as the animal world is concerned, then, this theory amounts to the assertion of the kinship of all life. From one or more simple primitive unicellular forms have arisen the great multitude of multicellular forms that now exist. Popularly, Darwin's theory is supposed to be that man sprang from the apes, but this, strictly speaking, is a misconception. Darwin's theory necessitates the belief, not that man sprang from any existing species of ape, but rather that the apes and man have sprung from some common stock. It is equally true, however, that man and many other of the lower animals, according to this theory, have come from a common stock. As was said above, the theory is not a theory of the descent of man from any particular animal type, but rather the theory of the kinship, the genetic relationship, of all animal species.

It is evident that if we assume Darwin's theory of descent in sociology we must look for the beginnings of many peculiarly human things in the animal world below man. Human institutions, according to this theory, could not be supposed to have an independent origin, or human society in any of its forms to be a fact by itself, but rather all human things are connected with the whole world of animal life below man. Thus if we are, according to this theory, to look for the origin of the family, we should have to turn first of

- 14 -

all to the habits of animals nearest man. This is only one of the many bearings which Darwin's theory has upon the study of social problems; but it is evident even from this that it revolutionizes sociology. So long as it was possible to look upon human society as a distinct creation, as something isolated, by itself in nature, it was possible to hold to intellectualistic views of the origin of human institutions.

But some one may ask: Why should the sociologist accept Darwin's theory? What proofs does it rest upon? What warrant has a student of sociology for accepting a doctrine of such far-reaching consequences? The reply is, that biologists, generally, during the last fifty years, after a careful study of Darwin's arguments and after a careful examination of all other evidence, have come substantially to agree with him. There is no great biologist now living who does not accept the essentials of the doctrine of descent. Five lines of proof may be offered in support of Darwin's theories, and it may be well for us, as students of sociology, briefly to review these.

(1) The homologies or similarities of structure of different animals. There are very striking similarities of structure between all the higher animals. Between the ape and man, for example, there are over one hundred and fifty such anatomical homologies; that is, in the ape we find bone for bone, and muscle for muscle, corresponding to the structure of the human body. Even an animal so remotely related to man as the cat has many more resemblances to man in anatomical structure than dissimilarities. Now, the meaning of these anatomical homologies, biologists say, is that these animals are genetically related, that is, they had a common ancestry at some remote period in the past.

(2) The presence of vestigial organs in the higher animals supplies another argument for the belief in common descent. In man, for example, there exist over one hundred of these vestigial or rudimentary organs, as the vermiform appendix, the pineal gland, and the like. Many of these vestigal organs, which are now functionless in man, perform functions in lower animals, and this is held to show that at some remote period in the past they also functioned in man's ancestors.

(3) The facts of embryology seem to point to the descent of the higher types of animals from the lower types. The embryo or fetus in its development seems to recapitulate the various stages through which the species has passed. Thus the human embryo at one stage of its development resembles the fish; at another stage, the embryo of a dog; and for a long time it is impossible to distinguish between the human embryo and that of one of the larger apes. These embryological facts, biologists say, indicate genetic relation between the various animal forms which the embryo in its different stages simulates.

(4) The fossil remains of extinct species of animals are found in the earth's crust which are evidently ancestors of existing species. Until the doctrine of descent was accepted there was no way of explaining the presence of these fossil remains of extinct animals in the earth's crust. It was supposed by some that the earth had passed through a series of cataclysms in which all forms of life upon the earth had been many times destroyed and many times re-created. It is now demonstrated, however, that these fossils are related to existing species, and sometimes it is possible to trace back the evolution of existing forms to very primitive forms in this way. For example, it is possible to trace the horse, which is now an animal with a single hoof, walking on a single toe, back to an animal that walked upon four toes and had four hoofs and was not much larger than a fox. It is not so generally known that it is also possible to trace man back through fossil human remains that have been discovered in the earth's crust to the time when he is apparently just emerging from some apelike form. The latest discovery of the fossil remains of man made by Dr. Dubois in Java in 1894 shows a creature with about half the brain capacity of the existing civilized man and with many apelike characteristics. Thus we cannot except even man from the theory of evolution and suppose that he was especially created, as Alfred Russel Wallace, Darwin's contemporary and colaborer, and others, have supposed.

(5) The last line of argument in favor of the belief that all existing species have descended from a few simple primitive forms is found in the fact of the variation of animals through artificial selection under domestication. For generations breeders have known that by carefully selecting the type of animal or plant which they have desired, it is possible to produce approximately that type. Thus have originated all the breeds or varieties of domestic plants and animals. Now, Darwin conceived that nature also exercises a selection by weeding out those individuals that are not adapted to their environment. In other words, nature, though unconscious, selects in a negative way the stronger and the better adapted. Animals vary in nature as well as under domestication from causes not yet well understood. The variations that were favorable to survival, Darwin argued, would secure the survival, through the passing on of these variations by heredity of the better adapted types of plants and animals. The natural process of weeding out the inferior or least adapted through early death, or through failure to reproduce, Darwin called "natural selection", and likened it in its effect upon organisms to the artificial selection which breeders consciously use to secure types of plants or animals that they desire. The only great addition to Darwin's theories which has been made since he wrote is that of the Dutch botanist, Hugo de Vries, who has shown that the variations which are fruitful for the production of new species are probably great or discontinuous variations, which he terms "mutations," instead of the small

fluctuating variations which Darwin thought were probably most important in the production of new species. De Vries' theory in no way affects the doctrine of descent, nor does it take away from the importance of natural selection in fixing the variations. Darwin's theory, therefore, stands in all of its essentials to-day unquestioned by men of science, and it must be assumed by the student of sociology in any attempt to explain social evolution.

Spencer's Theory of Universal Evolution.—A second meaning given to the word *evolution* is that which Spencer popularized in his *First Principles*. This is a philosophical theory of the universe which asserts that not only have species of animals come to be what they are through a process of development, but everything whatsoever that exists, from molecules of matter to stars and planets. It is the view that the universe is in a process of development. Evolution in this wider sense includes all existing things whatsoever, while evolution in the sense of Darwin's theory is confined to the organic world. While the theory that all things existing have through a process of orderly change come to be what they are, is a very old one, yet it was undoubtedly Spencer's writings which popularized the theory, and to Spencer we also owe the attempt in his Synthetic Philosophy to trace the working of evolution in all the different realms of phenomena. The belief in universal evolution which Spencer popularized has also come to be generally accepted by scientific and philosophical thinkers. While Spencer's particular theories of evolution may not be accepted, some form of universal evolution is very generally believed in. The thought of evolution now dominates all the sciences,—physical, biological, psychological, and sociological. It is evident that the student of society, if he accepts fully the modern scientific spirit, must also assume evolution in this second or universal sense.

The Different Phases of Universal Evolution.—It may be well, in order to correlate our knowledge of social evolution with knowledge in general, to note the different well-marked phases of universal evolution.

(1) *Cosmic Evolution.* This is the phase the astronomer and the geologist are particularly interested in. It deals with the evolution of worlds. In this phase we are dealing merely with physical matter, and it is supposed that the active principle which works in this phase of evolution is the attraction of particles of matter for one another. This leads to the condensation of matter into suns and their planets, and the geological evolution of the earth, for example. Laplace's nebular hypothesis is an attempt to give an adequate statement of the cosmic phase of evolution. While this hypothesis has been much criticized of late, in its essentials it seems to stand. We are not, however, as students of society, concerned with this phase of evolution.

(2) *Organic Evolution.* This is the phase of evolution with which Darwin dealt and which biology, as a science of evolution of living forms, deals with. The great merit of Darwin's work was that he showed that the active principle in this phase of evolution is natural selection; that is, the extermination of the unadapted through death or through failure to reproduce. Types unsuited to their environment thus die before reproduction. The stronger and better fitted survive, and thus the type is raised. Natural selection may be regarded, then, as essentially the creative force in this phase of evolution.

(3) *The Evolution of Mind.* This might be included in organic evolution, but all organisms do not apparently have minds. It is evident that among animals those that would stand the best chance of surviving would not be simply those that have the strongest brute strength, but rather those that have the keenest intelligence and that could adapt themselves quickly to their environment, that could see approaching danger and escape it. Natural selection has, therefore, favored in the animal world the survival of those animals with the highest type of intelligence. It cannot be said, however, that natural selection is the only force which has created the mind in all its various expressions.

(4) *Social Evolution.* By social evolution we mean the evolution of groups, or, in strict accordance with our definition of society, groups of psychically interconnected individuals. Groups are to be found throughout the animal world, and it is in the human species, as we have already seen, that the highest types of association are found. This is not an accident. Association, or living together in groups, has been one of the devices by which animal species have been enabled to survive. It is evident that not only would intelligence help an animal to survive more than brute strength, but that ability to cooperate with one's fellows would also help in the same way. Consequently we find a degree of combination or coöperation almost at the very beginning of life, and it is without doubt through coöperation that man has become the dominant and supreme species upon the planet. Man's social instincts, in other words, have been perhaps even more important for his survival than his intelligence. The man who lies, cheats, and steals, or who indulges in other unsocial conduct sets himself against his group and places his group at a disadvantage as compared with other groups. Now, natural selection is continually operating upon groups as well as upon individuals, and the group which can command the most loyal, most efficient membership, and has the best organization, is, other things being equal, the group which survives. Natural selection is, then, active in social evolution as well as in general organic evolution. But the distinctive principle of social evolution is coöperation. In other words, it is sympathetic feeling, altruism, which has made the higher types of social evolution possible.

While the same factors are at work in the higher phases of evolution which are at work in the lower phases, yet it is evident that the higher phases have new and distinct factors. Sociology, being especially concerned with social evolution, has a new and distinct factor at work which we may call association, coöperation, or combination, and this it is which gives sociology its distinct place in the list of general sciences.

Factors In Organic Evolution.—As has already been said, the factors which are at work in organic evolution generally are also at work in social evolution. We need, therefore, to note these factors carefully and to see how they are at work in human society as well as in the animal world below man. While these factors are not all of the factors which are at work in social evolution, still they are the primitive factors, and are, therefore, of fundamental importance. Let us see what these factors are.

(1) *The Multiplication of Organisms in Some Geometric Ratio through Reproduction.* It is a law of life that every species must increase so that the number of offspring exceeds the number of parents if the species is to survive. If the offspring only equal in number the parents, some of them will die before maturity is reached or will fail to reproduce, and so the species will gradually become extinct. Every species normally increases, therefore, in some geometric ratio. Now, this tendency to reproduce in some geometric ratio, which characterizes all living organisms, means that any species, if left to itself, would soon reach such numbers as to occupy the whole earth. Darwin showed, for example, that though the elephant is the slowest breeding of all animals, if every elephant lived its normal length of life (one hundred years) and to every pair were born six offspring, then, at the end of seven hundred years there would be nineteen million living elephants descended from a single pair. This illustration shows the enormous possibilities of any species reproducing in geometric ratio, as all species in order to survive must do.

That this tendency to increase in some geometric ratio applies also to man is evident from all of the facts which we know concerning human populations. It is not infrequent for a people to double its numbers every twenty-five years. If this were continued for any length of time, it is evident that a single nation could soon populate the whole earth.

(2) *Heredity.* Heredity in organic evolution secures a continuity of the species or racial type. By heredity is meant the resemblance between parent and offspring. It is the law that like begets like. Offspring born of a species belong to that species, and usually resemble their parents more closely even than other members of the species.

It is evident that heredity is at work also in human society as well as in the animal world. We do not expect that the children born of parents of one race, for example, will belong to another race. Racial heredity is one of the most significant facts of human society, and even family heredity counts in its influence far more than some have supposed.

(3) *Variation.* This factor in organic evolution means that no two individuals, even though born of the same parents, are exactly like each other. Neither are they of a type exactly between their two parents, as theoretically they should be, since inheritance is equal from both parents. Every new individual born in the organic world, while it resembles its parents and belongs to its species or race, varies within certain limits. This variation so runs through organic nature that we are told that there are no two leaves on a single tree exactly alike. The result of this variation, the causes of which are not yet well understood, is that some individuals vary in favorable directions, others in unfavorable directions. Some are born strong, some weak; some inferior, some superior.

It is evident that variation characterizes the human species quite as much as other species, and indeed the limits of variation are wider, probably, in the human species than in any other species. Man is the most variable of all animals, and human individuality and personality owe not a little of their distinctiveness to this fact.

(4) *The Struggle for Existence.* Individuals in all species, as we have seen, are born in larger numbers than is necessary. The result is that a competition is entered into between species and individuals within the species for place and for existence. This competition or struggle results in the dying out of the inferior, that is, of those who are not adapted to their environment. The gradual dying out of the inferior or unadapted through competition results in the survival of the superior or better adapted, and ultimately in the survival of the fittest or those most adapted. Thus the type is raised, and we have evolution through natural selection, that is, through the elimination of the unfit.

Some have thought that this struggle for existence which is so evident in the animal world does not take place in human society. This, however, is a mistake. The struggle for existence in human society is not an unmitigated one, as it seems to be very often in the animal world, but it is nevertheless a struggle which has the same consequences. In the human world the competition, except in the lower classes, is not so much for food, as it is for position and for supremacy. But this struggle for place and power results in human society in the weak and inferior going to the wall, and therefore ultimately in their elimination. In all essential respects, then, the struggle for existence goes on in human society as it does in the animal world. This means that in society, as in the animal world, progress comes primarily through the elimination of unfit individuals. The unfit in human society, as we shall see, are especially those who cannot adapt themselves to their social environment. Progress in society, in a certain sense, waits upon death, as it does in all the rest of the animal world. Death is the means by which the stream of life is purged from its inferior and unfit elements.

(5) *Another Factor in Organic Evolution is Coöperation*, or altruism, as we have already called it. As Henry Drummond has said, this is the struggle not for one's own life but for the lives of others. Really, however, it is a device which enables a group of individuals to struggle more successfully with the adverse factors in their environment. Something of coöperation,—that is, a group of individuals carrying on a common life,—is found almost at the beginning of life, and, as we rise in the scale of animal creation, the amount of coöperation and of altruistic feelings which accompany it very greatly increases. Perhaps the chief source of this coöperation is to be found in the rearing of offspring. The family group, even in the lower animals, seems to be the chief source of altruism. At any rate, sympathetic or altruistic instincts grow up in all animals, probably chiefly through the necessities of reproduction.

It is only in human social life that coöperation, or altruism, attains its full development. Human society is characterized by the protection it affords to its weaker members, and in human society the natural process of eliminating the inferior often seems reversed. As Huxley has pointed out, human society tries to fit as many as possible to survive, and we may add, not only to survive, but to live well. Altruism and its resulting coöperation have come especially to characterize human social evolution. To some extent this is due, no doubt, to the necessities of group survival; for only that nation, for example, can survive that can maintain the most loyal citizenship, the best institutions, and the largest spirit of self-sacrifice in its members. Human social groups, therefore, try to fit as many individuals as possible for the most efficient membership, and this necessitates caring for the temporarily weak, and also for the permanently incapacitated, in order that the sentiments of social solidarity may be strengthened to their utmost.

It is evident, then, that all the factors at work in organic evolution are at work also in social evolution, though in some part modified and varying in degree. The struggle for existence in human society, for example, has been greatly modified from the condition in the early animal world, while coöperation, or altruism, is much more highly developed. Nevertheless, these factors of organic evolution are at work in social evolution and must be taken into full account by the student of social problems. Social evolution rests upon organic evolution.

Some Effects upon Industry.—These factors in organic evolution express themselves more or less in the industrial phase of human society. Thus, the first factor, the multiplication of organisms through reproduction in some geometric ratio, was first studied by Malthus, an economist in the beginning of the nineteenth century, and exclusively with reference to its effect upon economic conditions. Malthus perceived the tendency for human beings to multiply in some geometric ratio where food supply was sufficiently abundant, and argued from this that if better wages, and so a larger food supply, were given the lower classes, they would multiply so much more rapidly that worse poverty would result than before. There is no doubt that in certain classes of human society there is a tendency for population to press against food supply, and it is in these classes that the struggle for existence takes on its most animal-like forms.

Again, the struggle for existence is continually illustrated in the world of human industry. Not only do individuals lose place and power because they are unadapted to their environment, but also economic groups, such as corporations, show the natural competition or struggle for existence sometimes in its most intense form. The result in all cases is the dying out of the least adapted and the survival of the better adapted. Thus, through competition and the survival of the better adapted we secure in industry the evolution of higher types of industrial organization, industrial methods, and the like, just as higher types are secured in the same way in the animal world. Again, in economic matters, as in other social affairs, coöperation continually comes in to modify competition and to lift it to a higher plane. Just as the higher type of societies has been characterized by higher types of coöperation, so it is safe to say that the higher types of industry are characterized by higher types of coöperation. And while, as we shall see later, coöperation can never displace competition in industry any more than elsewhere in life, yet increasing coöperation characterizes the higher types of industry as well as the higher types of society.

A word of caution is perhaps necessary against confusing the economic struggle as it exists in modern society with the natural struggle under primitive conditions. It is evident that in present society the economic struggle has been greatly changed in character from the primitive struggle, and therefore can no longer have the same results. Laws of inheritance, of taxation, and many other artificial economic conditions, have greatly interfered with the natural struggle. The rich and economically successful are therefore by no means to be confused with the biologically fit. On the contrary, many of the economically successful are such simply through artificial advantageous circumstances, and from the standpoint of biology and sociology they are often among the less fit, rather than the more fit, elements of society.

A Brief Survey of Social Evolution from the Biological Standpoint.—In order to sum up and make clear some of the principal applications to social evolution of the biological principles just stated we shall endeavor to state in a brief way some of the salient features of social evolution from the biological standpoint.

From the very beginning there has been no such thing as unmitigated individual struggle among animals. Nowhere in nature does pure individualism exist in the sense that the individual animal struggles alone, except perhaps in a few solitary species which are apparently on the way to extinction. The assumption of such a primitive individual struggle has been at the bottom of many erroneous views of human society. The primary conflict is between species. A secondary conflict, however, is always found between the members of the same species. Usually this conflict within the species is a competition between groups. The human species exactly illustrates these statements. Primitively its great conflict was with other species of animals. The supremacy of man over the rest of the animal world was won only after an age-long conflict between man and his animal rivals. While this conflict went on there was apparently but little struggle within the species itself. The lowest groups of which we have knowledge, while continually struggling against nature, are rarely at war with one another. But after man had won his supremacy and the population of groups came to increase so as to encroach seriously upon food supply, and even on territorial limits of space, then a conflict between human groups, which we call war, broke out and became almost second nature to man. It needs to be emphasized, however, that the most primitive groups are not warlike, but only those that have achieved their supremacy over nature and attained considerable size. In other words, the struggle between groups which we call war was occasioned very largely by numbers and food supply. To this extent at least war primitively arose from economic conditions, and it is remarkable how economic conditions have been instrumental in bringing about all the great wars of recorded human history.

The conflict among human groups, which we call war, has had an immense effect upon human social evolution. Five chief effects must be noted.

(1) Intergroup struggle gave rise to higher forms of social organization, because only those groups could succeed in competition with other groups that were well organized, and especially only those that had competent leadership.

(2) Government, as we understand the word, was very largely an outcome of the necessities of this intergroup struggle, or war. As we have already seen, the groups that were best organized, that had the most competent leadership, would stand the best chance of surviving. Consequently the war leader or chief soon came, through habit, to be looked upon as the head of the group in all matters. Moreover, the exigencies and stresses of war

frequently necessitated giving the war chief supreme authority in times of danger, and from this, without doubt, arose despotism in all of its forms. The most primitive tribes are republican or democratic in their form of government, but it has been found that despotic forms of government rapidly take the place of the primitive democratic type, where a people are continually at war with other peoples.

(3) A third result of war in primitive times was the creation of social classes. After a certain stage was reached groups tried not so much to exterminate one another as to conquer and absorb one another. This was, of course, after agriculture had been developed and slave labor had reached a considerable value. Under such circumstances a conquered group would be incorporated by the conquerors as a slave or subject class. Later, this enslaved class may have become partially free as compared with some more recently subjugated or enslaved classes, and several classes in this way could emerge in a group through war or conquest. Moreover, the presence of these alien and subject elements in a group necessitated a stronger and more centralized government to keep them in control, and this was again one way in which war favored a development of despotic governments. Later, of course, economic conditions gave rise to classes, and to certain struggles between the classes composing a people.

(4) Not only was social and political organization and the evolution of classes favored by intergroup struggle, but also the evolution of morality. The group that could be most efficiently organized would be, other things being equal, the group which had the most loyal and most self-sacrificing membership. The group that lacked a group spirit, that is, strong sentiments of solidarity and harmonious relations between its members, would be the group that would be apt to lose in conflict with other groups, and so its type would tend to be eliminated. Consequently in all human groups we find recognition of certain standards of conduct which are binding as between members of the same group. For example, while a savage might incur no odium through killing a member of another group, he was almost always certain to incur either death or exile through killing a member of his own group. Hence arose a group code of ethics founded very largely upon the conceptions of kinship or blood relationship, which bound all members of a primitive group to one another.

(5) A final consequence of war among human groups has been the absorption of weaker groups and the growth of larger and larger political groups, until in modern times a few great nations dominate the population of the whole world. That this was not the primitive condition, we know from human history and from other facts which indicate the disappearance of a vast number of human groups in the past. The earth is a burial ground of tribes and natrons as well as of individuals. In the competition between

human groups, only a few that have had efficient organization and government, loyal membership and high standards of conduct within the group, have survived. The number of peoples that have perished in the past is impossible to estimate. But we can get some inkling of the number by the fact that philologists estimate that for every living language there are twenty dead languages. When we remember that a language not infrequently stands for several groups with related cultures, we can guess the immense number of human societies that have perished in the past in this intergroup competition.

Even though war passes away entirely, nations can never escape this competition with one another. While the competition may not be upon the low and brutal plane of war, it will certainly go on upon the higher plane of commerce and industry, and will probably be on this higher plane quite as decisive in the life of peoples in future as war was in the past.

While the primary struggle within the human species has been in the historic period between nations and races, this is not saying, of course, that struggle and competition have not gone on within these larger groups. On the contrary, as has already been implied, a continual struggle has gone on between classes, first perhaps of racial origin, and later of economic origin. Also there is within the nation a struggle between parties and sects, and sometimes between "sections" and communities. Usually, however, the struggle within the nation is a peaceful one and does not come to bloodshed.

Again, within each of these minor groups that we have mentioned struggle and competition in some modified form goes on between its members. Thus within a party or class there is apt to be a struggle or competition between factions. There is, indeed, no human group that is free from struggle or competition between its members, unless it be the family. The family seems to be so constituted that normally there is no competition between its members,—at least, there is good ground for believing that competition between the members of a family is to be considered exceptional, or even abnormal.

From what has been said it is evident that competition and coöperation are twin principles in the evolution of social groups. While competition characterizes in the main the relation between groups, especially independent political groups, and while coöperation characterizes in the main the relation of the members of a given group to one another, still competition and coöperation are correlatives in practically every phase of the social life. Some degree of competition, for example, has to be maintained by every group between its members if it is going to maintain high standards of efficiency or of loyalty. If there were no competition with respect to the matters that concern the inner life of groups, it is evident that the groups would soon lose efficiency in leadership and in membership and would sooner or later be eliminated. Consequently society, from certain points of view, presents itself to the student at the present time as a vast competition, while from other standpoints it presents itself as a vast coöperation.

It follows from this that competition and coöperation are both equally important in the life of society. It has been a favorite idea that competition among human beings should be done away with, and that coöperation should be substituted to take its place entirely. It is evident, however, that this idea is impossible of realization. If a social group were to check all competition between its members, it would stop thereby the process of natural selection or of the elimination of the unfit, and, as a consequence, would soon cease to progress. If some scheme of artificial selection were substituted to take the place of natural selection, it is evident that competition would still have to be retained to determine who were the fittest. A society that would give positions of trust and responsibility to individuals without imposing some competitive test upon them would be like a ship built partially of good and partially of rotten wood,—it would soon go to pieces.

This leads us to emphasize the continued necessity of selection in society. No doubt natural selection is often a brutal and wasteful means of eliminating the weak in human societies, and no doubt human reason might devise superior means of bringing about the selection of individuals which society must maintain. To some extent it has done this through systems of education and the like, which are, in the main, selective processes for picking out the most competent individuals to perform certain social functions. But the natural competition, or struggle between individuals, has not been done away with, especially in economic matters, and it is evidently impossible to do away with it until some vast scheme of artificial selection can take its place. Such a scheme is so far in the future that it is hardly worth talking about. The best that society can apparently do at the present time is to regulate the natural competition between individuals, and this it is doing increasingly.

What people rightfully object to is, not competition, but unregulated or unfair competition. In the interest of solidarity, that is, in the interest of the life of the group as a whole, all forms of competition in human society should be so regulated that the rules governing the competition may be known and the competition itself public. It is evident that in politics and in business we are very far from this ideal as yet, although society is unquestionably moving toward it.

A word in conclusion about the nature of moral codes and standards from the social point of view. It is evident that moral codes from the social point of view are simply formulations of standards of conduct which groups find it convenient or necessary to impose upon their members. Even morality, in an idealistic sense, seems from a sociological standpoint to be those forms of conduct which conduce to social harmony, to social efficiency, and so to the survival of the group. Groups, however, as we have already pointed out, cannot do as they please. They are always hard-pressed in competition by other groups and have to meet the standards of efficiency which nature imposes. Morality, therefore, is not anything arbitrarily designed by the group, but is a standard of conduct which necessities of social survival require. In other words, the right, from the point of view of natural science, is that which ultimately conduces to survival, not of the individual, but of the group or of the species. This is looking at morality, of course, from the sociological point of view, and in no way denies the religious and metaphysical view of morality, which may be equally valid from a different standpoint.

Finally, we need to note that natural selection does not necessitate in any mechanical sense certain conduct on the part of individuals or groups. Rather, natural selection marks the limits of variation which nature permits, and within those limits of variation there is a large amount of freedom of choice, both to individuals and to groups. Human societies, therefore, may be conceivably free to take one of several paths of development at any particular point. But in the long run they must conform to the ultimate conditions of survival; and this probably means that the goal of their evolution is largely fixed for them. Human groups are free only in the sense that they may go either backward or forward on the path which the conditions of survival mark out for them. They are free to progress or to perish. But social evolution in any case, in the sense of social change either toward higher or toward lower social adaptation, is a necessity that cannot be escaped. Sociology and all social science is, therefore, a study not of what human groups would like to do, but of what they must do in order to survive, that is, how they can control their environment by utilizing the laws which govern universal evolution.

From this brief and most elementary consideration of the bearings of evolutionary theory upon social problems it is evident that evolution, in the sense of what we know about the development of life and society in the past, must be the guidepost of the sociologist. Human social evolution, we repeat, rests upon and is conditioned by biological evolution at every point. There is, therefore, scarcely any sanity in sociology without the biological point of view.

SELECT REFERENCES

For brief reading:

FAIRBANKS, *Introduction to Sociology,* Chaps. XIV.-XV.
JORDAN, *Foot-Notes to Evolution,* Chaps. I.-III.
ELY, *Evolution of Industrial Society.* Part II, Chaps. I.-III.

For more extended reading:

DARWIN, *Descent of Man.*
FISKE, *Outlines of Cosmic Philosophy.*
WALLACE, *Darwinism.*

On the religious aspects of evolution:

DRUMMOND, *Ascent of Man.*
FISKE, *The Destiny of Man.*
FISKE, *Through Nature to God.*

CHAPTER III

THE FUNCTION OF THE FAMILY IN SOCIAL ORGANIZATION

Instead of continuing the study of social evolution in general it will be best now, before we take up some of the problems of modern society, to study the evolution of some important social institution, because in so doing we can see more clearly the working of the biological and psychological forces which have brought about the evolution of human institutions. An institution, as has already been said, is a sanctioned grouping or relation in society. Now, there can be scarcely any doubt that the two most important institutions of human society are the family and property. In Western civilization these take the form of the monogamic family and of private property. It is upon these two institutions that our civilization rests. The state is a third very important institution in society, but it exists largely for the sake of protecting the family and property.

Of the two institutions, the family and property, the family is without doubt prior in time and more fundamental,—more important in human association. We shall, therefore, study very briefly the origin and development of the family as a human institution in order to illustrate some of the principles of social evolution in general. But before we can take up the question of the origin of the family it will be well for us to see just what the function of this institution is in the human society of the present, in order to justify the assertion just made that it is the most important and fundamental institution of humanity.

The Family the Primary Social Institution.—Let us note first of all that in society, as it exists at present, the family is the simplest group capable of maintaining itself. It is, therefore, we may say, the primary social structure. Because it contains both sexes and all ages it is capable of reproducing itself, and so of reproducing society. For the same reason it contains practically all social relations in miniature. It has therefore often been called, and rightly, "the social microcosm". The relations of superiority, subordination, and equality, which enter so largely into the structure of all social institutions, are especially clearly illustrated in the family in the relations of parents to children, of children to parents, of parents to each other, and of children to one another. Comte, for this reason, claimed that the family was the unit of social organization, not the individual. However this may be, it is evident that families do enter, as units, very largely into our social and industrial life. While the tendency may be to make the individual the unit of modern society, it is nevertheless true that the family remains the simplest social structure in society, and from it, in some sense, all other social relations whatsoever are evolved.

The Family Differs from All Other Social Institutions, however, in two respects: First, its members have their places fixed in the family group by their organic natures, that is, the relations of husband and wife, parent and child, rest upon biological differences and relations, so that one may say that the family is almost as much a biological structure as it is a social structure. This is not, to any extent, true of other institutions. Secondly, the family is not a product, so far as we can see, of other forms of association, but rather it itself produces these other forms of association. The family, in other words, is not a result of social organization in general, but seems rather to antedate both historically and logically the forms of social life. It is not a product of society, but it itself produces society.

THE PRIMARY FUNCTION OF THE FAMILY is continuing the life of the species; that is, the primary function of the family is reproduction in the sense of the birth and rearing of children. While other functions of the family have been delegated in a large measure to other social institutions, it is manifest that this function cannot be so delegated. At least we know of no human society in which the birth and rearing of children has not been the essential function of the family. From a sociological point of view the childless family is a failure. While the childless family may be of social utility to the individuals that form it, nevertheless from the point of view of society such a family has failed to perform its most important function and must be considered, therefore, socially a failure.

The Function of the Family in Conserving the Social Order.—The family is still the chief institution in society for transmitting from one generation to another social possessions of all sorts. Property in the form of land or houses or personal property, society permits the family to pass along from generation to generation. Thus, also, the material equipment for industry, that is capital, is so transmitted. While it is obvious that the material goods of society are thus transmitted by the family from one generation to another, it is perhaps not quite so obvious, but equally true, that the spiritual possessions of the race are also thus transmitted. For example, language is very largely transmitted in the family, and students tell us that each family has its own peculiar dialect. Literature, ideas, beliefs on government, law, religion, moral standards, artistic tastes and appreciation—all of these are still largely transmitted in society from one generation to another through the family. While public institutions, such as libraries, art galleries, universities, scientific museums, and the like, are often adopted to conserve and transmit these spiritual possessions of the race, yet it is safe to say that if it were possible for society to depend upon these institutions to transmit knowledge, artistic standards, and moral ideals, there would be great discontinuity in social life. The family has been in the past, and is still, the great conserving agency in human society, preserving and transmitting from generation to generation both the material and spiritual possessions of the race.

The Function of the Family in Social Progress.—While the conservative function of the family is very obvious, its function in furthering social progress is perhaps not so obvious. Nevertheless, this is one of the greatest functions of the family life, because the family is the chief or almost sole generator of altruism in human society, and it is upon altruism that society depends for every upward advance in coöperation. It is in the family that children learn to love and obey, to be of service, and to respect one another's rights. The amount of altruism in a given group has a very close relation to the quality of its family life. If the family fails to teach the spirit of service and self-sacrifice to its members, it is hardly probable that they will get very much of that spirit from society at large. The ideal of a human brotherhood has no meaning unless family affection gives it meaning. If the family is the chief generator of altruism in human society and if society depends upon altruism for each forward step in moral progress, then the family is the chief source of social progress.

What we have said is a brief presentation of the claims of the family in modern society to count not only as the primary but also as the most important human institution. The family, it is evident, is charged by society with the most important task, not only of producing the new individuals in society, but of training each individual as he comes on the stage of life, adjusting him to society in all of its aspects, such as industry, government, and religion. If the family fails to perform these important functions the chances are that unsocialized individuals will take important places in society, and this means ultimately social anarchy.

The Family Life may be regarded as a School for Socializing the Individual. We need not trace in detail how the family does this for the child. It is evident that the rudiments of morality, of government, of religion, and even of industry and knowledge, must be learned by the child in the family group. If the child fails, for example, to learn morality, to get moral standards and ideals from his family life, he stands but poor chance of getting them later in society. Again, if the child fails to learn what law is and to get proper ideals of the relation of the citizen to the state in his family life, there are good prospects of his being numbered among the lawless elements of society later. In the family, we repeat, the child first experiences all the essential relations of society, learns the meaning of authority, obedience, loyalty, and all the human virtues. Moreover, the family life furnishes the moral and religious concepts which human society has set before it as its goal. The ideal of human brotherhood, for example, is manifestly derived from the family life; so also the religious idea of the Divine Fatherhood. If a nation's family life fails to illustrate these concepts, it is safe to say that they will not have great influence in society generally. The nation whose family life decays, therefore, rots at the core, dries up the springs of all social and civic virtues.

The Family and Industry.—From what has been said in general terms it is evident that the family has a very important relation to the industrial activities of society, and industry a very important bearing upon the family. Primitively all industry centered in the family. Modern industry, as has been well said, is but an enormous expansion of primitive housekeeping; that is, the preparation of food and clothing and shelter by the primitive family group for its own existence is the germ out of which all modern industry has developed. The very word *economics* means the science or the art of the household.

In primitive communities and in newly settled districts the family often carries on all essential industrial activities. It produces all the raw material, manufactures the finished products, and consumes the same. But with the growth of complex societies there has come a great industrial division of labor, and the family has delegated industrial activity after activity to some other institution until at the present time the modern family performs scarcely any industrial activities, except the preparation of food for immediate consumption. Even this, however, in modern cities seems about to be delegated to some other institution.

All that need be said at present about the delegation of the industrial activities of the family to other industrial institutions is that the movement is not one which need cause any anxiety so long as it does not interfere with the essential function of the family, namely, the birth and rearing of children. Even though children can no longer learn the rudiments of industry in their home life, still it is possible through manual and industrial training in our public schools to teach all children this. And the removal of industries from the home, even such essential industries as the preparation of food, is to be regarded as a boon if it gives more time to the parents, especially to the mother, for the proper care and bringing up of their children.

But the removal of industries from the family group has not always had the beneficent effect of simply giving more time to the parents for the proper care of their children. On the contrary, the removal of these industries has often been followed by the removal of the parents themselves from the home and the practical disintegration of the family. This has been particularly the case where married women have gone into factories. Under such circumstances children have often been neglected, allowed to grow up on the streets, and to grow up as unsocialized individuals in general. It would seem that the labor of married women outside of the home should be forbidden by the state, except in certain instances, with a view to assuring to the state itself a better citizenship. The labor of children in factories and other industrial institutions has sprung very largely from the same general causes. While child labor may have the merit of giving the child some industrial training, still it has been shown that it dwarfs the child in body and mind, produces a one-sided development, fails to prepare for citizenship in the higher sense, and so must be regarded as altogether an evil. Even the labor of the young unmarried women in factories and shops, when they should be preparing for the duties of wifehood and motherhood, is to some extent an evil in society, though not by any means of the same proportions as the labor of married women.

The Subordination of Industry to the Family Life is necessary, therefore, from a social point of view. Industry, as we have seen, was primitively an adjunct of the family life, and all modern industry, if rightfully developed, should be but an adjunct to the family life. Industrial considerations must be, therefore, subordinate to domestic considerations, that is, to considerations of the welfare of parents and their children in the family group. One trouble with modern society is that industry has come to dominate as an independent interest that oftentimes does not recognize its reasonable and socially necessary subordination to the higher interests of society. There can be no sane and stable family life until we are willing to subordinate the requirements of industry, that is, of wealth-getting, to the requirements of the family for the good birth and proper rearing of children.

SELECT REFERENCES

For brief reading:

HENDERSON, *Social Elements*, Chap. IV.
DEWEY AND TUFTS, *Ethics*, Chap. XXVI.
ADLER, *Marriage and Divorce*, Lecture I.

For more extended reading:

BOSANQUET, *The Family*.
SALEEBY, *Parenthood and Race Culture*.

CHAPTER IV

THE ORIGIN OF THE FAMILY

We must understand the biological roots of the family before we can understand the family as an institution, and especially before we can understand its origin. Let us note, then, briefly the chief biological facts connected with the family life.

The Biological Foundations of the Family.—(1) *The Family rests upon the Great Biological Fact of Sex.* While sex does not characterize all animal forms, still it does characterize all except the simplest forms of animal life. These simplest forms multiply or reproduce by fission, but such asexual reproduction is almost entirely confined to the unicellular forms of life. It may be inferred, therefore, that the higher animal types could not have been evolved without sexual reproduction, and something of the meaning or significance of sex in the whole life process will, therefore, be helpful in understanding all of the higher forms of evolution. Biologists tell us that the meaning or purpose of sexual reproduction is to bring about greater organic variation. Now variation, as we have seen, is the raw material upon which natural selection acts to create the higher types. The immense superiority of sexual reproduction over asexual reproduction is due to the fact that it multiplies so greatly the elements of heredity in each new organism, for under sexual reproduction every new organism has two parents, four grandparents, and so on, each of which perhaps contributes something to its heredity. The biological meaning of sex, then, is that it is a device of nature to bring about organic variation. From the point of view of the social life we may note also that sex adds greatly to its variety, enriching it with numerous fruitful variations which undoubtedly further social evolution. The bareness and monotony of a social life without sex can readily be imagined.

While the differences between the sexes have been mainly elaborated through the differences of reproductive function, yet these differences have come to be fundamental to the whole nature of the organism. In the higher animals, therefore, the sexes differ profoundly in many ways from each other. Biologists tell us that the chief difference between the male and female organism is a difference in metabolism, that is, in the rapidity of organic change which goes on within the body. In the male metabolism is much more rapid than in the female; hence the male organism is said to be more katabolic. In the female the rapidity of organic change is less; hence the female is said to be more anabolic. Put in more familiar terms, the male tends to expend energy, is more active, hence also stronger; the female tends more to store up energy, is more passive, conservative, and weaker. These fundamental differences between the sexes express themselves in many ways in the social life. The differences between man and woman, therefore, are not to be thought of as due simply to social customs and usages, the different social environment of the two sexes, but are even more due to a radical and fundamental difference in their whole nature. The belief that the two sexes would become like each other in character if given the same environment is, therefore, erroneous. That these differences are original, or inborn, and not acquired, may be readily seen by observing children of different sex. Even from their earliest years boys are more active, restless, energetic, destructive, untidy, and disobedient, while little girls are quieter, less restless, less destructive, neater, more orderly, and more obedient. These different innate qualities fit the sexes naturally for different functions in human society, and there is, therefore, a natural division of labor between them from the first. Indeed, the division of labor between the two sexes may be said to be the fundamental division of labor in human society.

The causes which produce sex in the individual are not known to any extent and are probably beyond the control of man. In each species the relative number of the two sexes is fixed by nature, probably through some obscure working of natural selection, and in practically all of the higher species of animals, man included, the number of the two sexes is relatively equal. In human society much depends upon this relative numerical equality of the two sexes. Hence it can be readily seen that it is fortunate that man does not know how to control the sex of offspring, for if he did the numerical equality of the two sexes might be disturbed and serious social results would follow.

(2) *The Influence of Parental Care.* Sex alone could never have produced the family in the sense of a relatively permanent group of parents and offspring. We do not begin to find the family until we get to those higher types where we find some parental care. In the lowest types the relation between the sexes is momentary and the survival of offspring is secured simply through the production of enormous numbers. Thus the sturgeon, a low type of fish, produces between one and two million of eggs at a single spawning, from which it is estimated that not more than a dozen individuals survive till maturity is reached. Thus sexual reproduction of itself necessitates no parental care and in itself could give rise in no way to the family; but quite low in the scale of life we begin to find some parental care as a device to protect immature offspring and secure their survival without the expenditure of such an enormous amount of energy in mere physiological reproduction. Even among the fishes we find some that watch over the

eggs after they are spawned and care for their young by leading them to suitable feeding grounds. In such cases a much smaller number of young need to be produced in order that a few may survive until maturity is reached. In the mammals the mother, obviously, must care for the young for some time, since mammals are animals that suckle their young. But this care of the young by a single parent only foreshadows the family as we understand it. Among the mammals it is not until we reach the higher types that we find care of offspring by both parents,—a practice, however, which is common among the birds. It is evident that as soon as both parents are concerned in the care of the offspring they have a much better chance of survival. Hence, natural selection favors the growth of this type of group life and develops powerful instincts to keep male and female together till after the birth and rearing of offspring. Such we find to be the condition among many of the higher mammals, such as some of the carnivora, and especially among the monkeys and apes and man.

If it is allowable at this point to generalize from the facts given, it must be said that the family life is essentially a device of nature for the preservation of offspring through a more or less prolonged infancy. The family group and the instincts upon which it rests were undoubtedly, therefore, instituted by natural selection. Summing up, we may say, then, the animal family group owes its existence, first, to the production of child or immature forms that need more or less prolonged care; secondly, to the prolongation of this period of immaturity in the higher animals, and especially in man; thirdly, to the development, parallel with these two causes, of parental instincts which keep male and female together for the care of the offspring. It is evident, then, that the family life rests, not upon sex attraction, but upon the fact of the child and the corresponding psychological fact of parental instinct. The family, then, has been created by the very conditions of life itself and is not a man-made institution.

The Origin of the Family in the Human Species.—Two great theories of the origin of the family in the human species have in the past been more or less accepted, and these we must now examine and criticize. First, the traditional theory that the human family life was from the beginning a pure monogamy. Secondly, the so-called evolutionary theory that the human family life arose from confused if not promiscuous sex relations. The first of these theories, favored both by the Bible and Aristotle, held undisputed sway down to the middle of the nineteenth century. Then, after the publication of Darwin's *Origin of Species* in 1859, certain social theorists began to put forward the second theory in the name of evolution. In order that we may see precisely what the origin of the human family life was, and its primitive form, we must now proceed to criticize these two theories, especially the last, which is known as the hypothesis of a primitive state of promiscuity.

The Habits of the Higher Animals. We have already spoken of the origin of the family group in the animal world generally, but it must be admitted that there are some difficulties in arguing directly from the lower animals to man. Man is so separated from the lower animals through having passed through many higher stages of an independent evolution that in many respects his life is peculiar to itself. This is true especially of his family life. If we survey the whole range of animal life and then the whole range of human life, we find that there are but two or three striking similarities between the family life of man and that of the brutes, but a great many striking dissimilarities. The similarities may be summed up by saying that man exhibits in common with all the animals the phenomena of courtship, that is, of the male seeking to win the female, also the phenomenon of male jealousy, and we may perhaps add an instinctive aversion to crossing with the other species. These characteristics of his family life man shares with the brutes below him. There are, however, many things peculiar to the human family life that are found in no animal species below man. The most striking of these differences may be mentioned. (1) Man has no pairing season, as practically all other animals have. (2) The number of young born in the human species is on the whole much smaller than in any other animal species. (3) The dependence of offspring upon parents is far longer in the human species than in any other species. (4) Man has an antipathy to incest or close inbreeding which seems to be instinctive. This is not found clearly in any animal species below man. (5) There is a tendency among human beings to artificial adornment during the period of courtship, but not to natural ornament to any extent, as among many animal species. (6) The indorsement of society is almost invariably sought, both among uncivilized and civilized peoples, before the establishment of a new family—usually through the forms of a religious marriage ceremony. (7) Chastity in women, especially married women, is universally insisted upon, both among uncivilized and civilized peoples, as the basis of human family life. (8) There is a feeling of modesty or of shame as regards matters of sex among the human beings. (9) In humanity we find, besides animal lust, spiritual affection, or love, as a bond of union between the two sexes.

None of these peculiarities of human family life are found in the family life of any animal species below man. It might seem, therefore, that man's family life must be regarded as a special creation unconnected with the family life of the brutes below him. But this view is hardly probable, rather is impossible from the standpoint of evolution. We must say that these peculiarities of human family life are to be explained through the fact that man has passed through many more stages of evolution, particularly of intellectual evolution, than any of the animals below him. If we examine these peculiarities of man's family life carefully, we will see that they all can be explained through natural selection and man's higher intellectual development. That man has no pairing season, has fewer offspring born, and a longer period of dependence of the offspring upon parents, and the like, is directly to be explained through natural selection; while seeking the indorsement of society before forming a new family, sexual modesty, tendencies to artificial adornment, and the like, are to be explained through man's self-consciousness and higher intellectual development, also through the fuller development of his social instincts. The gap between the human family life and brute family life is, therefore, not an unbridgeable one.

That this is so, we see most clearly when we consider the family life of the anthropoid or manlike apes—man's nearest cousins in the animal world. All of these apes, of which the chief representatives are the gorilla, orangutan, and the chimpanzee, live in relatively permanent family groups, usually monogamous. These family groups are quite human in many of their characteristics, such as the care which the male parent gives to the mother and her offspring, and the seeming affection which exists between all members of the group. Such a group of parents and offspring among the higher apes is, moreover, a relatively permanent affair, children of different ages being frequently found along with their parents in such groups. So far as the evidence of animals next to man, therefore, goes, there is no reason for supposing that the human family life sprang from confused or promiscuous sex relations in which no permanent union between male and female parent existed. On the contrary, there is every reason to believe, as Westermarck says, that human family life is an inheritance from man's apelike progenitor.

The Evidence from the Lower Human Races.—The evidence afforded by the lowest peoples in point of culture even more clearly, if anything, refutes the hypothesis of a primitive state of promiscuity. The habits or customs of the lowest peoples were not well known previous to the nineteenth century. Therefore it was possible for such a theory as the patriarchal theory of the primitive family to remain generally accepted, as we have already said, down to the middle of the nineteenth century. This was the theory that the oldest or most primitive type of human family life is that depicted in the opening pages of the Book of Genesis, namely, a family life in which the father or eldest male of the family group is the absolute ruler of the group and practically owner of all persons and property. The belief that this was the primitive type of the human family life was first attacked by a German-Swiss philologist by the name of Bachofen in a work entitled *Das Mutterrecht* (The Matriarchate), published in 1861, in which he argued that antecedent to the patriarchal period was a matriarchal period, in which women were dominant socially and politically, and in which relationships were traced through mothers only. Bachofen got his evidence for this theory from certain ancient legends, such as that of the Amazons, and other remains in Greek and Roman literature, which seemed to point to a period antecedent to the patriarchal.

In 1876 Mr. J.F. McLennan, a Scotch lawyer, put forth, independently, practically the same theory, basing it upon certain legal survivals which he found among many peoples. With Bachofen, he argued that this matriarchal period must have been characterized by promiscuous relations of the sexes. In 1877 Mr. Lewis H. Morgan, an American ethnologist and sociologist, put forth again, independently, practically the same theory, basing it upon an extensive study of the North American Indian tribes. Morgan had lived among the Iroquois Indians for years and had mastered their system of relationship, which previously had puzzled the whites. He found that they traced relationship through mothers only, and not at all along the male line. This method of reckoning relationship, moreover, he found also characterized practically all of the North American Indian tribes, and he argued that the only explanation of it was that originally sexual relations were of such an unstable or promiscuous character that they would not permit of tracing descent through fathers.

From these theories sociological writers put forth the conclusion that the primitive state was one of promiscuity, or, as Sir John Lubbock called it in his *Origin of Civilization*, one of "communism in women." Post, a German student of comparative jurisprudence, for example, summed up the theory by saying that "monogamous marriage originally emerged everywhere from pure communism in women, through the intermediate stages of limited communism in women, polyandry, and polygyny." Even Herbert Spencer in his *Principles of Sociology*, while he avoided accepting such an extreme theory, asserted that in the beginning sex relations were confused and unregulated, and that all forms of marriage—polyandry, polygyny, monogamy, and promiscuity— existed alongside of one another and that monogamy survived through its being the superior form.

Before giving a criticism in detail of this theory let us note whether the evidence from the lowest peoples confirms it. The lowest peoples in point of culture are not the North American Indians nor the African Negroes, but certain isolated groups that live almost in a state of nature, without any attempt to cultivate the soil or to control nature in other respects. Such are the Bushmen of South Africa, the Australian Aborigines, the Negritos of the Philippine Islands and of the Andaman Islands, the Veddahs of Ceylon, and the Fuegians of South America. Now all of these peoples, with a possible exception, practice monogamy and live in relatively stable family groups. Their monogamy, however, is not of the type which we find in patriarchal times or among civilized peoples, but is a simple pairing monogamy, husband and wife remaining together indefinitely if children are born, but if no children are born, separation may easily take place. Westermarck in his *History of Human Marriage* has reviewed at length all of the evidence from these lower peoples and shows undoubtedly that nothing approaching promiscuity existed among them. Promiscuity is apt to be found at a higher stage of social development, and is especially apt to be found among the nature peoples after the white man has visited them and demoralized their family life. But in all these cases the existence of promiscuity is manifestly something exceptional and abnormal. Perhaps civilized peoples such as the Romans of the decadence have more nearly approximated the condition of promiscuity than any savage people of which we have knowledge. At any rate, one must conclude that the lowest existing savages found in the nineteenth century had definite forms of family life, and that the type usually found was the simple pairing monogamy which we have just mentioned.

Objections to the Hypothesis of a Primitive State of Promiscuity.—We may now briefly sum up the main criticisms of this theory of a primitive state of promiscuity, not only as we may derive them from inductive study of the higher animals and the lower peoples, but also as we may deduce them from known psychological and biological facts or principles.

(1) In the first place, then, the animals next to man, namely, the anthropoid apes, do not show a condition of promiscuity.

(2) The evidence from the lower peoples does not show that such a condition exists or has ever existed among them.

(3) A third argument against this hypothesis may be gained from what we know of primitive economic conditions. Under the most primitive conditions, in which man had no mastery over nature, food supply was relatively scarce, and as a rule only very small groups of people could live together. The smallness of primitive groups, on account of the scarcity of food supply, would prevent anything like promiscuity on a large scale.

(4) A fourth argument of a deductive nature is that the jealousy of the male, which characterizes all higher animals and especially man, would prevent anything like the existence of sexual promiscuity. The tendency of man would have been to appropriate one or more women for himself and drive away all rivals. Long ago Darwin argued that this would prevent anything like the existence of a general state of promiscuity.

(5) A fifth argument against this theory may be got from the general biological fact that sexual promiscuity tends to pathological conditions unfavorable to fecundity, that is, fertility, or the birth of offspring.

Physicians have long ago ascertained this fact, and the modern prostitute gives illustration of it by the fact that she has few or no children. Among the lower animal species, in which some degree of promiscuity obtains, moreover, powerful instincts keep the sexes apart except at the pairing season. Now, no such instincts exist in man. Promiscuity in man would, therefore, greatly lessen the birth rate, and any group that practiced it to any extent would soon be eliminated in competition with other groups that did not practice it.

(6) We have finally the general social fact that promiscuity would lead to the neglect of children. Promiscuity means that the male parent does not remain with the female parent to care for the offspring and, therefore, in the human species it would mean that the care of children would be thrown wholly upon the mother. This means that the children would have less chance of surviving. Not only would promiscuity lead to lessening the birth rate, but it would lead to a much higher mortality in children born. This is found to be a striking fact wherever we find any degree of promiscuity among any people. Hence, promiscuity would soon exterminate any people that practiced it extensively in competition with other peoples that did not practice it.

From all of these lines of argument, without going over the evidence in greater detail, it seems reasonable to conclude with Westermarck "that the hypothesis of a primitive state of promiscuity has no foundation in fact and is essentially unscientific." The facts put forth in support of the theory do not justify the conclusion, Westermarck says, that promiscuity has ever been a general practice among a single people and much less that it was the primitive state. Promiscuity is found, however, more or less in the form of sexual irregularities or immorality among all peoples; more often, however, among the civilized than among the uncivilized, but among no people has it ever existed unqualified by more enduring forms of sex relation. Moreover, because promiscuity breaks up the social bonds, throws the burden of the care of children wholly upon the mother, and lessens the birth rate, we are justified in concluding that promiscuity is essentially an antisocial practice. This agrees with the facts generally shown by criminology and sociology, that the elements practicing promiscuity to any great extent in modern societies are those most closely related with the degenerate and criminal elements. Those elements, in other words, in modern society that practice promiscuity are on the road to extinction, and if a people generally were to practice it there is no reason to believe that such a people would meet with any different fate.

The Earliest Form of the Family Life in the Human Species, therefore, is probably that of the simple pairing monogamous family found among many of the higher animals, especially the anthropoid apes, and also found among the lower peoples. This primitive monogamy, however, as we have already seen, was not accompanied by the social, legal, and religious elements that the historic monogamic family has largely rested upon. On the contrary, this primitive monogamy rested solely upon an instinctive basis, and, as we have seen, unless children were born it was apt to be relatively unstable. Permanency in family relations among primitive peoples depended largely upon the birth of children. Thus we find confirmed our conclusion drawn some time ago that family life rests primarily upon the parental instinct. That it still so rests is shown by the fact, as we shall see later, that divorce is many times more common among couples that have no children than among those that have children.

SOME GENERAL CONCLUSIONS, both of theoretical and practical bearing, may here be pointed out. We have seen that the biological processes of life have created the family, and that the family, as an institution, rests upon these biological conditions. Hence it is not too much to say, first, that the family is not a man-made institution; and, secondly, that it rests upon certain fundamental instincts of human nature. Now, both of these statements are also true to a certain extent as to human society in general. There is a sense in which social organization is not wholly man-made, and it is true that all human institutions rest to some extent upon human instincts. This is not saying, of course, that man has not modified and may not modify social organization and human institutions through his reason, but it is saying that the essential elements in human institutions and in the social order must correspond to the conditions of life generally and to the instincts which natural selection has implanted in the species. To attempt to reorganize human society or to reconstruct institutions regardless of the biological conditions of life, or regardless of human instincts, is to meet with certain failure.

A practical conclusion which may be drawn also is that those people who advocate sexual promiscuity in present society, or free love, as they please to style it, are advocating a condition which would result in the elimination of any group that practiced it. Promiscuity, or even great instability in the family life, as we have already seen, would lead to the undermining of everything upon which a higher civilization rests. The people in modern society who advocate such theories as free love, therefore, are more dangerous than the worst anarchist or the most revolutionary socialist. In other words, the modern attack upon the family is more of a menace to all that is worth while in human life than all attacks upon government and property, although it is not usually resented as such; and it is one of the most serious signs of the times that many intellectual people have indorsed such views. We must reemphasize, therefore, the fact that the family is the central institution of human society, that industry and the state must subordinate themselves to its interest. Neither the state nor industry has had much to do with the origin of the family, and neither the state nor industry may safely determine its forms independent of the biological requirements for human survival. Moreover, it is evident that human society from the beginning has in more or less instinctive, and also in more or less conscious, ways attempted to regulate the relations between the sexes with a view to controlling the reproductive process. While material civilization is mainly a control over the food process, moral civilization involves a control over the reproductive process, that is, over the birth and rearing of children; and such control over the reproductive process, which has certainly been one of the aims of all social organization in the past, whether of savage peoples or of civilized peoples, evidently precludes anything like the toleration of promiscuity or even of free love.

SELECT REFERENCES

For brief reading:

WESTERMARCK, *History of Human Marriage*, Chaps. I-VI.
HOWARD, *History of Matrimonial Institutions*, Vol. I, Chaps. I-III
HEINEMAN, *Physical Basis of Civilization*, Chaps. IV-VII.

For more extended reading:

CRAWLEY, *The Mystic Rose: A Study of Primitive Marriage.*
GEDDES AND THOMSON, *Evolution of Sex.*
LETOURNEAU, *The Evolution of Marriage.*
MORGAN, *Ancient Society.*
STARCKE, *The Primitive Family.*
SPENCER, *Principles of Sociology*, Vol. I.

CHAPTER V

THE FORMS OF THE FAMILY

The family as an institution has varied greatly in its forms from age to age and from people to people. This is what we should expect, seeing that all organic structures are variable. Such variations in human institutions are due partially to the influences of the environment, partially to the state of knowledge, and partially to many other causes as yet not well understood. The family illustrates in greater or less degree the working of these causes of variation and of change in human institutions.

The Maternal and Paternal Families.—As regards the general form of the family we have to note first of all the two great forms which we may characterize respectively as "the maternal family" and "the paternal family." As we have already seen, Bachofen, Morgan, and others discovered a condition of human society in which relationship was traced through mothers only, and in which property or authority descended along the female line rather than along the male line. Further investigation and research have shown that up to recent times, say up to fifty years ago, one half of all the peoples of the world, if we reckon them by nations and tribes rather than by numbers, practiced this system of reckoning kinship through mothers only, and passed property and authority down along the female line. Ethnologists and sociologists have practically concluded, from the amount of evidence now collected, that this maternal or metronymic system was the primitive system of tracing relationships, and that it was succeeded among the European peoples by the paternal system so long ago that the transition from the one to the other has been forgotten, except as some trace of it has been preserved in customs, legends, and the like.

Among many tribes of the North American Indians this metronymic or maternal system was peculiarly well-developed. Children took their mother's name, not their father's name; belonged to their mother's clan, not their father's clan; and the chief transmitted his authority, if hereditary, not to his own son, but to his eldest sister's son. The relatives on the father's side, indeed, were quite ignored. Frequently the maternal uncle had more legal authority over the children than their own father, seeing that the children belonged to his clan, that is, to their mother's clan.

Now, Bachofen claimed not only that in this stage was kinship reckoned through mothers only, but that women were dominant socially and politically; that there existed a true matriarchy, or rule of the mothers. Do the facts support Bachofen's theory? Let us see. The Iroquois Indians, among whom Morgan lived, were a typical maternal or metronymic people. Among them, without any doubt, the women had a position of influence socially and even politically which often is not found among peoples of higher culture. For example, among the Iroquois the government of the clan was in the hands of four women councilors (Matrons), who were elected by all the adults in the clan. These four women councilors, however, elected a Peace Sachem, who carried out the will of the clan in all matters pertaining to peace generally. Moreover, the councilors of the several clans, four fifths of whom were women, met together to form the Tribal Council; but in this Tribal Council the women sat separate, not participating in the deliberations, but exercising only a veto power on the decisions of the men. In matters of war, however, government was intrusted to two war chiefs elected from the tribe generally, the women here only having the right to veto the decision of the tribe to enter upon the warpath. Thus we see that while the women of the Iroquois Indians had a great deal of social and political influence, the actual work of government was largely turned over by them to the men, and especially was this true of directing the affairs of the tribe in time of war. There is no doubt, however, that in the maternal stage of social evolution women had an influence in domestic, religious, and social matters much greater than they had at many later stages of social development. Among the Zuni of New Mexico, for example, another well-developed maternal people, marriage is always arranged by the bride's parents. The husband goes to live with his wife, and is practically a guest in his wife's house all his life long, she alone having the right of divorce. Indeed, among all maternal peoples the rule is that the husband goes to live with the wife, and not the wife with the husband, the children, as we have already seen, keeping the mother's name and belonging to her kindred or clan.

Nevertheless we cannot agree with Bachofen that a true matriarchy, or government by women, ever existed. On the contrary, among all of these maternal peoples, while the women may have much influence socially and politically, the men, on account of their superior strength, are intrusted with the work not only of protecting and providing for the families and driving away enemies, but also largely with the work of maintaining the internal government and order of the people. Strictly speaking, therefore, there has never been a matriarchal stage of social evolution, but rather a maternal or metronymic stage.

We have already said that this stage was probably the primitive one. How are we to explain, then, that primitive man reckoned kinship through mothers only? Was this due, as Morgan thought, to a primitive practice of promiscuity which prevented tracing relationships through fathers? The reply is, that among the many maternal peoples now well known, among whom relationships are traced through mothers only, we find no evidence of the practice of general promiscuity now or even in remote times. The North American Indians, for example, had quite definite forms of the family life and were very far removed from the practice of promiscuity, though they traced relationship through mothers only. It is evident that the causes of the maternal family and the maternal system of relationship are not so simple as Morgan supposed. What, then, were the causes of the maternal system? It is probable that man in the earliest times did not know the physiological connection between father and child. The physiological connection between mother and child, on the other hand, was an obvious fact which required no knowledge of physiology to establish; therefore, nothing was more natural than for primitive man to recognize that the child was of the mother's blood, but not of the father's blood. Therefore, the child belonged to the mother's people and not to the father's people. If it be asked whether it is possible that there could be any human beings so ignorant that they do not know the physiological connection between father and child, the reply is, that this is apparently the case among a number of very primitive peoples, even down to recent times. It is not infrequent among these peoples to find conception and childbirth attributed to the influence of the spirits, rather than to relations between male and female. While, therefore, a social connection between the father and the children was recognized, leading the father to provide in all ways for his children, as fathers do whether among civilized or uncivilized peoples, yet the blood relationship between the father and the child could not have been clear in the most primitive times.

Perhaps an even more efficient cause, however, of the maternal system was the fact that the mother in primitive times was the stable element in the family life, the constant center of the family. The husband was frequently away from home, hunting or fighting, and oftentimes failed to return. Nothing was more natural, therefore, than that the child should be reckoned as belonging to the mother, take her name and belong to her kindred or clan. Moreover, after the custom of naming children from mothers and reckoning them as belonging to the mother's clan was established, it could not be displaced by the mere discovery of the physiological connection between the father and the child. On the contrary social habits, like habits in the individual, tend to persist until they work badly. We find, therefore, the maternal system persisting among peoples who for many generations had come fully to recognize the physiological connection of father and child. Indeed, the maternal system could never have been done away with if social evolution had not brought about new and complex conditions which caused the system to break down and to be replaced by the paternal system.

The Paternal or Patriarchal Family. At a certain stage we find, then, that a vast revolution took place in human society, especially in the family life, and the family and society generally came to be organized more definitely in regard to the male element. At a certain period, indeed, we find that the authority of the husband and father in the family has become supreme, and that he is practically owner of all persons and property of the family group, the wife and children being reduced, if not to the position of property, at least to the position of subject persons. This is the patriarchal family, classical pictures of which we find set forth in the pages of the Old Testament. How, then, did the transition take place from the maternal system, in which the mother was so important in the family, to the paternal system, in which the father was so all-important? What were the causes which brought about the breakdown of the maternal system and the gradual development of the patriarchal family? Some of these causes we can clearly make out from the study of social history.

(1) War was unquestionably a cause of the breakdown of the maternal system through the fact that women were captured in war, held as slaves, and made wives or concubines by their captors. These captured wives were regarded as the property of the captor. Any children born to them were, therefore, also regarded as the property of the captor. Furthermore, these captured wives were separated from their kindred, and their children could not possibly belong to any clan except their husband's. Manifestly this cause could not have worked in the earliest times, when slave captives were not valuable; but as soon as slavery became instituted in any form, then women slaves were particularly valued, not only for their labor, but because they might be either concubines or wives. It is evident, then, that war and slavery would thus indirectly tend to undermine the maternal system.

(2) Wife purchase would operate in the same way. Among peoples that had developed a commercial life as well as slavery it early became the practice to purchase wives. It is evident that these purchased wives would be regarded as a sort of property, and the husband would naturally claim the children as belonging to him. Among certain North American Indians we find exactly this state of affairs. If a man married a wife without paying the purchase price for her, then her children took her name and belonged to her clan; but if he had purchased her, say with a number of blankets, then the children took his name and belonged to his clan.

(3) The decisive cause, however, of the breakdown of the maternal system was the development of the pastoral stage of industry. Now, the grazing of flocks and herds requires considerable territory and necessitates small and compact groups widely separated from one another. Hence, in the pastoral stage the wife must go with the husband and be far removed from the influence and authority of her own kindred. This gave the husband greater

power over his wife. Moreover, the care of flocks and herds accentuated the value of the male laborer, while primitively woman had been the chief laborer. In the pastoral stage the man had the main burden of caring for the flocks and herds. Under such circumstances nothing was more natural than that the authority of the owner of the family property should gradually become supreme in all matters, and we find, therefore, among all pastoral peoples that the family is itself a little political unit, the children taking the father's name, property and authority passing down along the male line, while the eldest living male is usually the ruler of the whole group.

(4) After all these causes came another factor—ancestor worship. While ancestor worship exists to some extent among maternal peoples, it is usually not well-developed for some reason or other until the paternal stage is reached. Ancestor worship, being the worship of the departed ancestors as heroes, seems to develop more readily where the line of ancestors are males. It may be suggested that the male ancestor is apt to be a more heroic figure than the female ancestor. At any rate, when ancestor worship became fully developed it powerfully tended to reenforce the authority of the patriarch, because he was, as the eldest living ancestor, the representative of the gods upon earth, therefore his power became almost divine. Religion thus finally came in to place the patriarchal family upon a very firm basis.

Thus we see how each of these two great forms, the maternal family and the paternal family, arose out of natural conditions, and therefore they may be said to represent two great stages in the social evolution of man. It is hardly necessary to point out that civilized societies are now apparently entering upon a third stage, in which there will be relative equality given to the male and the female elements that go to make up the family.

Polyandry.—We must notice now the various forms of marriage by which the family has been constituted among different peoples and in different ages. Marriage, like the family itself, is variable, and an indefinite number of forms may be found among various peoples. We shall notice, however, only the three leading forms,—polyandry, polygyny, and monogamy,—and attempt to show the natural conditions which favor each. It is evident that if we assume that the primitive form of the family was that of a simple pairing monogamy, the burden is laid upon us to show how such different types as polyandry and polygyny arose.

Polyandry, or the union of one woman with several men, is a relatively rare form of marriage and the family, found only in certain isolated regions of the world. It is particularly found in Tibet, a barren and inhospitable plateau north of India and forming a part of the Chinese Empire. It is also found in certain other isolated mountainous regions in India, and down to recent times also in Arabia. In none of these places does it exist exclusively, but rather alongside of monogamy and perhaps other forms of the family. Thus in Tibet the upper classes practice polygyny and monogamy, while among the lower classes we find polyandry and monogamy. In all these regions where polyandry occurs, moreover, it is to be noted that the conditions of life are harsh and severe. Tibet is an exceptionally inhospitable region, with a climate of arctic rigor, the people living mainly by grazing. Under such circumstances it is conceivably difficult for one man to support and protect a family. At any rate, the form of polyandry which we find in Tibet suggests that such economic conditions may have been the main cause of its existence. Ordinarily in Tibet a polyandrous family is formed by an older brother taking a wife, and then admitting his younger brothers into partnership with him. The older brother is frequently absent from home, looking after the flocks, and in his absence one of the younger brothers assumes the headship of the family. Under such circumstances we can see how the natural human instincts which would oppose polyandry under ordinary circumstances, namely, the jealousy of the male, might become greatly modified, or cease to act altogether. Certain other conditions besides economic ones might also favor the existence of polyandry, such as the scarcity of women. Summing up, we can say, then, that this rare form of the family seems to have as its causes: (1) In barren and inhospitable countries the labor of one man is sometimes found not sufficient to support a family. (2) Also there probably exists in such regions an excess of males. This might be due to one of two causes: First, the practice of exposing female infants might lead to a scarcity of women; secondly, in such regions it is found that from causes not well understood a larger number of males are born. It may be noted as a general fact that when the conditions of life are hard in human society, owing to famine, war, or barrenness of the soil, a larger number of male births take place. We may therefore infer that this would disturb the numerical proportion of the sexes in such regions. (3) A third cause may be suggested as having something to do with the matter, namely, that habits of close inbreeding, or intermarriage, might perhaps tend to overcome the natural repugnance to such a relation. Moreover, close inbreeding also, as the experiments of stock-breeders show, would tend to produce a surplus of male births, and so would act finally in the same way as the second cause.

POLYGYNY, [Footnote: The word "polygamy" is too broad in its meaning to use as a scientific term for this form of the family. "Polygamy" comes from two Greek words meaning "much married;" hence it includes "polyandry" (having several husbands) and "polygyny" (having several wives).] or the union of one man with several women, is a much more common form of marriage. It is, in fact, to be found sporadically among all peoples and in all ages. It has perhaps existed at least sporadically from the most primitive times, because we find that at least one of the anthropoid apes, namely, the gorilla, practices it to some extent. It is manifest, however, that it could not have existed to any extent among primitive men, except where food supply was exceptionally abundant. In the main, polygyny is a later development, then, which comes in when some degree of wealth has been accumulated, that is, sufficient food supply to make it possible for one man to support several families. Polygyny came in especially after women came to be captured in war and kept as slaves or wives. The practice of wife capture, indeed, and the honor attached to the custom, had much to do in making the practice of polygyny common among certain peoples. Wherever slavery has existed, we may also note, polygyny, either in its legal form or in its illegal form of concubinage, has flourished. Polygyny, indeed, is closely related with the institution of slavery and is practically coextensive with it. In the ancient world it existed among the Hebrews and among practically all of the peoples of the Orient, and also sporadically among our own Teutonic ancestors. In modern times polygyny still exists among all the Mohammedan peoples and to a greater or less degree among all semicivilized peoples. It exists in China in the form of concubinage. It even exists in the United States, for all the evidence seems to show that the Utah Mormons still practice polygyny to some extent, although it may be doubted whether polygynous unions are being formed among them at the present time.

Two facts always need to be borne in mind regarding polygyny: First, that wherever it is practiced it is relatively confined to the upper and wealthy classes, for the reason that the support of more than one family is something which only the wealthy classes in a given society could assume. Secondly, it follows that under ordinary circumstances only a small minority of a given population practice polygyny, even in countries in which it is sanctioned. In Mohammedan countries like Turkey and Egypt, for example, it is estimated that not more than five per cent of the families are polygynous, while in other regions the percentage seems to be still smaller. The reason for this is not only the economic one just mentioned, but that everywhere the sexes are relatively equal in numbers, and therefore it is impossible for polygyny to become a widespread general custom. If some men have more than one wife it is evident that other men will probably have to forego marriage entirely. This is not saying that under certain circumstances, namely, the importation of large numbers of women, a higher per cent of polygynous families may not exist. It is said that among the negroes on the west coast of Africa the number of polygynous families reaches as high as fifty per cent, owing to the fact that female slaves are largely imported into that district, and that they serve not only as wives, but do the bulk of the agricultural labor, the male negro preferring female slaves, who can do his work and be wives at the same time, to male slaves.

But such cases as these are altogether exceptional and manifestly could not become general.

Summing up, we may say that the causes of polygyny are, then:

(1) First of all, the brutal lust of man. No doubt man's animal propensities have had much to do with the existence of this form of the family. Nevertheless, while male sensuality is at the basis of polygyny, it would be a mistake to think that sensuality is an adequate explanation in all cases. On the contrary, we find many other causes, chiefly, perhaps, economic, operating also to favor the development of polygyny.

(2) One of these is wife capture, as we have already seen. The captured women in war were held as trophies and slaves, and later became wives or concubines. Among all peoples at a certain stage the honor of wife capture has alone been a prolific cause of polygyny.

(3) Another cause, after slavery became developed, was the high value set on women as laborers. Among many barbarous peoples the women do the main part of the work. They are more tractable as slaves, and consequently a high value is set upon their labor. As we have already seen, these female slaves usually serve at the same time as concubines, if not legal wives of their masters.

(4) Another cause which we can perhaps hardly appreciate at the present time is the high valuation set on children. We see this cause operating particularly in the case of the patriarchs of the Old Testament. Under the patriarchal family great value was set upon children as necessary to continue the family line. Where the device of adoption was not resorted to, therefore, in case of barrenness or the birth exclusively of female children, nothing was more natural than that polygyny should be resorted to in order to insure the family succession. In the patriarchal family also a high valuation was necessarily set upon children, because the larger the family grew the stronger it was.

(5) Finally, religion came to sanction polygyny. The religious sanction of polygyny cannot be looked upon as one of its original causes, but when once established it reacted powerfully to reenforce and maintain the institution. How the religious sanction came about we can readily see when we remember that very commonly religions confuse the practice of the nobility with what is noble or commendable morally. The polygynous practices of the nobility, therefore, under certain conditions came to receive the sanction of religion. When this took place polygyny became firmly established as a social institution, very difficult to uproot, as all the experience of Christian missionaries among peoples practicing polygyny goes to show. We may note also the general truth, that while religion does

not originate human institutions or the forms of human association, it is preeminently that which gives fixity and stability to institutions through the supernatural sanction that it accords them.

Some judgment of the social value of polygyny may not be out of place in connection with this subject. Admitting, as all students of social history must, that in certain times and places the polygynous form of family has been advantageous, has served the interests of social survival and even of civilization, yet viewed from the standpoint of present society it seems that our judgment of polygyny must be wholly unfavorable. In the first place, as we have already seen, polygyny is essentially an institution of barbarism. It arose largely through the practice of wife capture and the keeping of female slaves. While often adjusted to the requirements of barbarous societies, it seems in no way adjusted to a high civilization. Polygyny, indeed, must necessarily rest upon the subjection and degradation of women. Necessarily the practice of polygyny must disregard the feelings of women, for women are jealous creatures as well as men. No high regard for the feelings of women, therefore, would be consistent with the practice of polygyny. Finally, all the evidence that we have goes to show that under polygyny children are neglected, and, at least from the standpoint of a high civilization, inadequately socialized. This must necessarily be so, because in the polygynous family the care of the children rests almost entirely with the mother. While we have no statistics of infant mortality from polygynous countries, it seems probable that infant mortality is high, and we know from experience with polygynous families in our own state of Utah, according to the testimony of those who have worked among them, that delinquent children are especially found in such households. Fatherhood, in the full sense of the word, can hardly be said to exist under polygyny.

Those philosophers, like Schopenhauer, who advocate the legalizing of polygyny in civilized countries, are hardly worth replying to. It is safe to say that any widespread practice of polygyny in civilized communities would lead to a reversion to the moral standards of barbarism in many if not in all matters. That polygyny is still a burning question in the United States of the twentieth century is merely good evidence that we are not very far removed yet from barbarism.

MONOGAMY, as we have already seen, has been the prevalent form of marriage in all ages and in all countries. Wherever other forms have existed monogamy has existed alongside of them as the dominant, even though perhaps not the socially honored, form. All other forms of the family must be regarded as sporadic variations, on the whole unsuited to long survival, because essentially inconsistent with the nature of human society. In civilized Europe monogamy has been the only form of the family sanctioned for ages by law, custom, and religion. The leading peoples of the world, therefore, practice monogamy, and it is safe to say that the connection between monogamy and progressive forms of civilization is not an accident.

What, then, are the social advantages of monogamy which favor the development of a higher type of culture? These advantages are numerous, but perhaps the most important of them can be grouped under six heads.

(1) The number of the two sexes, as we have already seen, is everywhere approximately equal. This means that monogamy is in harmony with the biological conditions that exist in the human species. The equal number of the two sexes has probably been brought about through natural selection. Why nature should favor this proportion of the sexes can perhaps be in part understood when we reflect that with such proportion there can be the largest number of family groups, and hence the best possible conditions for the rearing of offspring.

(2) Monogamy secures the superior care of children in at least two respects. First, it very greatly decreases mortality in children, because under monogamy both husband and wife unite in their care. Again, monogamy secures the superior upbringing and, therefore, the superior socialization of the child. In the monogamous family much greater attention can be given to the training of children by both parents. In other forms of the family not only is the death rate higher among children, but from the point of view of modern civilization, at least, they are inferiorly socialized.

(3) The monogamic family alone produces affections and emotions of the higher type. It is only in the monogamic family that the highest type of altruistic affection can be cultivated. It is difficult to understand, for example, how anything like unselfish affection between husband and wife can exist under polygyny. Under monogamy, husband and wife are called upon to sacrifice selfish desires in the mutual care of children. Monogamy is, therefore, fitted as a form of the family to foster altruism in the highest degree, and, as we have seen, the higher the type of altruism produced by the family life, the higher the type of the social life generally, other things being equal. It is especially to the credit of monogamy that it has created fatherhood in the fullest sense of the term, and therefore taught the male element in human society the value of service and self-sacrifice. Under polygynous conditions the father cannot devote himself to any extent to his children or to any one wife, since he is really the head of several households, and therefore, as we have already noted, fatherhood in the fullest sense scarcely exists under polygyny.

(4) Under monogamy, moreover, all family relationships are more definite and strong, and thus family bonds, and ultimately social bonds, are stronger. In the polygynous household the children of the different wives

are half brothers and half sisters, hence family affection has little chance to develop among them, and as a matter of fact between children of different wives there is constant pulling and hauling. Moreover, because the children in a polygynous family are only half brothers this immensely complicates relationships, and even the line of ancestors. Legal relations and all blood relationships are, therefore, more entangled. It is no inconsiderable social merit of monogamy that it makes blood relationships simple and usually perfectly definite. All of this has an effect upon society at large, because the cohesive power of blood relationship, even in modern societies, is something still worth taking into account. But of course the main influence of all this is to be found in the family group itself, because it is only under such simple and definite relations as we find in the monogamous family that there is ample stimulus to develop the higher family affections.

(5) From all this it follows that monogamy favors the development of high types of religion and morals, family affection being an indispensable root of any high type of ethical religion. That form of the family which favors the development of the highest type of this affection will, therefore, favor the development of the highest type of religion. We see this even more plainly, perhaps, in ancient times than in the present time, because it was monogamy that favored the development of ancestor worship through making the line of ancestors clear and definite, and thus monogamy helped to develop this type of religion, which became the basis of still higher types.

(6) Monogamy not only favors the preservation of the lives of the children, but also favors the preservation of the lives of the parents, because it is only under monogamy that we find aged parents cared for by their children to any extent. Under polygyny the wife who has grown old is discarded for a young wife, and usually ends her days in bitterness. The father, too, under polygyny is rarely cared for by the children, because the polygynous household has never given the opportunity for close affections between parents and children. That monogamy, therefore, helps to lengthen life through favoring care of parents by children in old age is an element in its favor, for it adds not a little to the happiness of life, and so to the strength of social bonds, that people do not have to look forward to a cheerless and friendless old age.

In brief, the monogamic family presents such superior unity and harmony from every point of view that it is much more fitted to produce a higher type of culture. From whatever point of view we may look at it, therefore, there are many reasons why civilized societies cannot afford to sanction any other form of the family than that of monogamy.

The Relation of the Form of the Family to the Form of Industry.—As we have already seen, the form of the family is undoubtedly greatly influenced by the form of industry. This is so markedly the case that some sociologists and economists have claimed that the form of the family life is but a reflection of the form of the industrial life; that the family in its changes and variations slavishly follows the changes in economic conditions. That such an extreme view as this is a mistake can readily be seen from a brief review of the causes which have produced certain types of family life in certain periods. Thus, the maternal type of the family cannot be said by any means to have been determined by economic conditions. On the contrary, primarily the maternal family, as we have seen, was determined by certain intellectual conceptions, namely, the absence of knowledge of the physiological connection between father and child, though the economic conditions of primitive life tended powerfully to continue the maternal family long after intellectual conditions had changed. Again, it has been said that the patriarchal family owed its existence entirely to a form of industry, namely, pastoral industry, but, as we have seen, other factors also operated to produce the patriarchal type of the family, such as war, religion, and perhaps man's inherent desire to dominate. Moreover, religion continued the patriarchal family in many cases long after pastoral industry had ceased to be the chief economic form.

So too with the forms of marriage. While polygyny has been claimed to be due entirely to economic causes, we have seen that these so-called economic causes have only been the opportunities for the polygynous instincts of man to assert themselves. These polygynous instincts of man have asserted themselves more or less under all conditions of society, but under certain conditions, when there was an accumulation of wealth, and especially with the institution of slavery, they had greater opportunity to assert themselves than elsewhere. Thus the basic cause of polygyny is not economic, but psychological; and given certain moral and economic conditions of society, these polygynous tendencies assert themselves. Monogamy, on the other hand, has in no sense been determined by economic conditions but is fundamentally determined by the biological fact of the numerical equality of the sexes. This is doubtless the main reason why monogamy has been the prevalent form of the family everywhere. Certain moral and psychological factors which go along with the development of higher types of culture have, however, powerfully reenforced monogamy. It is doubtful if economic conditions can to any extent be shown to have equally reenforced the monogamic life.

Our conclusion must be, then, that while the form of the family and the form of industry are closely related, so closely that the form of industry continually affects more or less the family life, yet there is no reason for concluding that the form of the family is wholly or even chiefly determined by the form of industry.

SELECT REFERENCES

For brief reading:

WESTERMARCK, *History of Human Marriage*, Chaps. XX-XXII.

For more extended reading:

MCLENNAN, *The Patriarchal Theory.*
MORGAN, *Ancient Society.*
PARSONS, *The Family.*
WAKE, *The Development of Marriage and Kinship.*

CHAPTER VI

THE HISTORICAL DEVELOPMENT OF THE FAMILY

While we cannot enter into the historical evolution of the family as an institution among the different civilized peoples, still it will be profitable for us to consider the history of the family among some single representative people in order that we may see the forces which have made and unmade the family life, and incidentally also to a great degree, the general social life of that people. We shall select the ancient Romans as the people among whom we can thus best study in outline the development of the family. While the family life of the ancient Hebrews is of particular interest to us because of the close connection of our religion and ethics with that of the Hebrews, yet in the family life of the ancient Romans constructive and destructive factors are more clearly marked and, therefore, the study of ancient Roman family life is best fitted to bring out those factors. The ancient Romans were among the earliest civilized of the Aryan peoples, and their institutions are, therefore, of peculiar interest to us as representing approximately the early Aryan type. What we shall say concerning Roman family life, moreover, will apply, with some modifications and qualifications, to the family life of other Aryan peoples, especially the Greeks. The Greeks and the Romans, indeed, were so closely related in their early culture that for the purpose of institutional history they may be considered practically one people. Without any attempt, then, to sketch the history of the family as an institution in general, let us note some of the salient features of the family life of the ancient Romans.

The Early Roman Family.—(1) *Ancestor Worship as the Basis of the Early Roman Family*. What we have said thus far indicates a close connection between the family life and religion among all peoples. This was especially true of the early Romans. It may be said, indeed, that ancestor worship was the constitutive principle of their family life. Among them the family seemed to have lost in part its character as a purely social institution and to have become specialized into a religious institution. At any rate, the early Roman family existed very largely for the sake of perpetuating the worship of ancestors. Of course, ancestor worship could have had nothing to do with the origin of the family life among the Romans. The type of their family life was patriarchal, and we have already noticed the causes which brought about the existence of the patriarchal family. But while ancestor worship had nothing to do with the origin of the family, once it was thoroughly established it became the basis of the family life and transformed the family as an institution.

The early Romans shared certain superstitions with many primitive peoples, which, if not the basis of ancestor worship, powerfully reinforced it. They believed, for example, that the soul continued in existence after death, and that persons would be unhappy unless buried in tombs with suitable offerings, and that if left unburied, or without suitable offerings, the souls of these persons would return to torment the living, Inasmuch as in the patriarchal family only sons could perform religious rites, that is, could make offerings to the departed spirits, these superstitions acted as a powerful stimulus to preserve the family in order that offerings might continue to be made at the graves of ancestors.

Thus, as we have already said, among the early Romans the family was practically a religious institution with ancestor worship as its constitutive principle. It is supposed by de Coulanges that in the earliest times the dead ancestors were buried beneath the hearth. At any rate, the hearth was the place where offerings were made to the departed ancestors, and the flame on the hearth was believed to represent the spirit of the departed. The house under such circumstances became a temple and the whole atmosphere of the family life was necessarily a religious one.

(2) *The Authority in the Early Roman Family* was vested, as in all patriarchal families, in the father or eldest living male of the family group. Under ancestor worship he became the living representative of the departed ancestors, the link between the living and the dead. Here we may note that the family was not considered as constituted simply of its living members, but that it included also all of its dead members. Inasmuch as the dead were more numerous and were thought to be more powerful than the living, they were by far the more important element in the life of the family. The position of the house father, as representative of the departed ancestors, and as the link between the living and the dead, naturally made his authority almost divine. Hence, the house father was himself, then, almost a deity, having absolute power over all persons within the group, even to the extent of life and death. This absolute power, which was known in the early Roman family as the "patria potestas," could not, however, be exercised arbitrarily. The house father, as representative of the departed ancestors, was necessarily controlled by religious scruples and traditions. It was impossible for him to act other than for what he believed to be the will of the ancestors. Disobedience to him was, therefore, disobedience to the divine ancestors, and hence was sacrilegious.

(3) *Relationship in the Early Roman Family* was determined by community of worship, inasmuch as only descendants upon the male side could perform religious rites, and inasmuch as married women worshiped the household gods of their husbands' ancestors; therefore, only descendants on the male side could worship the same ancestors and were relatives in the full

religious and legal sense. These were known as "agnates." Later, some relationship on the mother's side came to be recognized, but relatives on the mother's side were known as a "cognates," and for a long time property could not pass to them. Indeed, in the earliest times the property of the family, as we have already implied, was kept as a unit, held in trust by the eldest living member of the family group for the good of all the family. In other words, the house father in earliest times did not possess the right to make a will but the property of the family passed intact from him to his eldest male heir.

(4) *The Marriage Ceremony among the Early Romans* was necessarily of a religious character. It was constituted essentially of the induction of the bride into the worship of her husband's ancestors. But before this could be done the bride's father had first to free her from the worship of her household gods, in later times a certificate of manumission being given not unlike the manumission of the slave. After the bride had been released from the worship of her father's ancestors, the bridegroom and his friends brought her to his father's house, where a ceremony of adoption was practically gone through with, adopting the bride into the family of her husband. The essence of this ceremony, as we have already said, was the induction of the bride into the worship of her husband's ancestors through their both making an offering on the family hearth and eating a sacrificial meal together. After that the wife worshiped at her husband's altar and had no claim upon the household gods of her father.

Under such circumstances it is not surprising that marriage was practically indissoluble. A wife who was driven out of her husband's household or deserted was without family gods of any sort, having no claim upon those of her husband, and became, therefore, a social outcast. Under such circumstances it is not surprising that divorce was practically unknown. It is said, indeed, that for five hundred and twenty years after Rome was founded there was not a single divorce in Rome. While this may be an exaggeration, it is historically certain that divorce was so rare in early Rome as to be practically unknown.

In case of a failure of sons to be born there was no taking of a second wife, as among the Hebrews. Polygyny was unknown in early Rome. The Roman device to prevent the failure of the family succession in such cases was adoption. Younger sons of other families were adopted if no sons were born, and these adopted sons, taking the family name, became the same legally as sons by birth. Inasmuch as the position of younger sons in the patriarchal household was not an enviable one there was never lack of candidates for the position of eldest son in some family group in which no sons had been born.

Not only was the early Roman family life the most stable that the world has ever known, but it must also be considered to have been of a relatively pure type. Chastity was rigidly enforced among the women, but of course, as in all primitive peoples, was not enforced among the men. Still it was expected that the married men at least should remain relatively faithful to their wives. On the whole, therefore, the early Roman family life must be judged to have been of a singularly high and stable type. While the position of women and children in the early Roman family was one of subjection, the family itself was nevertheless of a high type. But it was inevitable that it should decay, and this decay began comparatively early. Inasmuch as the early Roman family was based upon ancestor worship, a religion which was fitted for relatively small isolated groups, it was inevitable that the family life should decay with this ancestor worship. How early the decay of ancestor worship began it is impossible to say. Perhaps the nature gods, Jupiter, Venus, and the rest, existed alongside of ancestor worship from the earliest times. At any rate, we find their worship growing rapidly within the period of authentic history and undermining the domestic worship, while at a still later period skeptical philosophy undermined both religions. Along with the decay of ancestor worship went many economic and political changes which marked the dissolution of the patriarchal family. Let us see what some of the steps in this decadence were.

(5) *The Decadence,* (a) One of the earliest steps toward the breaking down of the patriarchal family which we find is the limiting of the power of the house father. This took place very early—as soon as the Council of Elders, or Senate, was formed to look after matters of collective interest. Gradually the paternal power diminished, until it was confined to matters concerning the family group proper.

(b) A second step was when the right to make a will was conceded. This right, as we have seen, did not exist in the earliest Roman times, but with the development of property and of a more complex economic life the house father was given the right to divide his property among his children, at first only on the male side, but later among any of his children, and still later to bequeath it to whom he pleased.

(c) Thus women came to be given the right to hold property, a thing which was unknown in the earliest times; and becoming property holders, their other rights in many respects began to increase. Originally the wife had no right to divorce her husband, but in the second century B.C. women also gained the right of divorcing their husbands.

(d) The rights of children were increased along with the rights of women, particularly of younger children.

(e) The right of plebeians to intermarry with the noble families became recognized. All of these changes we should perhaps regard as good in themselves, but they nevertheless marked the disintegration of the patriarchal family. The decay of the family life did not stop with these changes, however, but went on to the decay of the family bonds themselves.

Later Roman Family Life.—By the beginning of the Christian era the relations between the sexes had become very loose. Men not only frequently divorced their wives, but women frequently divorced their husbands. Indeed, a complete revolution passed over the Roman family. Marriage became a private contract, whereas, as we have seen, in the beginning it was a religious bond. Many loose forms of marriage were developed, which amounted practically to temporary marriages. In all cases it was easy for a husband or wife to divorce each other for very trivial causes. Among certain classes of Roman society the instability of the family became so great that we find Seneca saying that there were women who reckoned their years by their husbands, and Juvenal recording one woman as having eight husbands in five years.

Women and children achieved their practical emancipation, as we would say. Women, especially, were free to do as they saw fit. Marriages were formed and dissolved at pleasure among certain classes, and among all classes the instability of the family life had become very great.

Along with all this, of course, went a growth of vice. It is not too much to say that the Romans of the first and second centuries A.D. approached as closely to a condition of promiscuity as any civilized people of which we have knowledge.

Causes of the Decadence. When we examine the causes of this great revolution in Roman family life from the austere morals and stable family of the early Romans to the laxity and promiscuity of the later Romans, we find that these causes can perhaps be grouped under four or five principal heads, (1) First among all the causes we must put the destruction of the domestic religion, namely, ancestor worship, through the growth of nature worship and skeptical philosophy. The destruction of the domestic religion necessarily shattered the foundations of the Roman family, since, as we have already seen, there was the closest connection between the family life of the early Romans and ancestor worship. But it is not probable that ancestor worship was destroyed merely through the growth of nature worship and of skeptical philosophy. As we have already seen, it was a religion which was mainly adapted to isolated groups. Changes in economic and political conditions, therefore, were to some extent prior to the decay of the domestic religion.

(2) Changes in economic conditions, that is, in the form of industry, were, then, among the more important causes of the decay of the early Roman family. The patriarchal family, as we have already seen, belonged essentially to the pastoral stage of industry, and as soon as settled agricultural life, commerce, and manufacturing industry developed, this destroyed the isolated patriarchal groups, and so also in time affected even the religion which was their basis. Again, the increase of population going along with the changes in the methods in obtaining a living destroyed the old conditions under which the family had been the political unit.

(3) We have therefore as a third cause the breaking up of old political conditions. Family groups were welded into small cities and the authority of the patriarch was destroyed. Legislation designed to meet the new social conditions often profoundly affected the whole family group, and weakened family bonds.

(4) The growth of divorce and of vice may be put down as a fourth cause of the decay of the Roman family. Some may say that this was an effect of the decay of the Roman family rather than a cause, but it was also a cause as well as an effect, for it is a peculiarity of social life that what is at one stage an effect reacts to become a cause at a later stage; and this was certainly the case with the growth of divorce and vice in Rome, in its effect upon the Roman family. Moreover, much of this came from Greece through imitation. The family life had decayed in Greece much earlier than it had in Rome, and when Rome conquered Greece it annexed its vices also. While the most radical social changes do not usually come about merely through imitation, yet the imitation of a foreign people is frequently, in the history of a particular nation, one of the most potent causes in bringing about social changes. It was certainly so in the case of the growth of divorce and vice in Rome.

To sum up and to generalize: we may say that the causes of the decay of the Roman family life were very complex, and that this is true of nearly all important social changes. It is impossible to reduce the causes of these changes to any single principle or set of causes. While we have seen that changes in economic conditions were undoubtedly very influential in bringing about the profound changes in the Roman family, still we have no ground for regarding the economic changes as determinative of all the rest. We know as yet little of the development of industry in antiquity. What little we do know, however, furnishes good ground for claiming that changes in the methods of getting a living are among the most influential causes of social change in general; but there is nothing which warrants the sweeping generalization of Karl Marx and his followers, "that the method of the production of the material life determines the social, political, and spiritual life process in general." On the contrary, the evolution of the

Roman family clearly shows moral and psychological factors at work quite independent of economic causes. The decay of ancestor worship, for example, cannot be wholly attributed to the change in the method of getting a living. The very growth of population and accompanying changes in political conditions probably had quite as much to do with the undermining of ancestor worship. Moreover, while religion may not be an original determining cause of social forms, it is, nevertheless, as we have already seen, especially that which gives them stability and permanency, so much so that the life history of a culture is frequently the life history of a religion. The decay of religious ideas and beliefs, therefore, from any cause, frequently proves the important element working for social change in all societies. So, too, changes in political conditions, especially changes in law through new legislation, frequently prove a profound modifying influence in societies. Lastly, there are certain moral causes inherent in the individual, oftentimes involving perverted expressions of instinct, which lead to profound social changes. Such was the vice which Rome copied very largely from Greece, but which proved the final solvent in its family life.

In general we may say, then, that there is no single principle which will explain the evolution of the family from the earliest times down to the present. Any attempt to reduce the evolution of the family to a single principle, or to show that it has been controlled by a single set of causes, must inevitably end in failure. The economic determinism of Marx and his followers, the ideological conceptions of Hegel, the geographical influences of Buckle and his school, and like explanations, are all found wanting when they are applied to the actual history of the family. It is not different with the theories of recent sociologists, who would strive to explain all social changes through a single principle. Professor Giddings' principle of "Consciousness of Kind" and Tarde's principle of "Imitation" will not go further in explaining the changes in the family life than some of the older principles that we have just mentioned. Human life is, indeed, too complex to be explained in terms of any single principle or any single set of causes. The family in particular is an organic structure which responds first to one set of stimuli and then to another. Now it is modified by economic conditions, now by religious ideas, now by legislation, now by imitation, and so on through the whole set of possible stimuli which may impinge upon and modify the activity of a living organism. So it is with all institutions.

The Influence of Christianity upon the Family.—While we cannot study further the evolution of the family in any detail, still it is necessary, in order to avoid too great discontinuity, to notice in a few sentences the influence of Christianity upon the family in Western civilization.

Early Christianity, as we have already seen, found the family life of the Greco-Roman world demoralized. The reconstruction of the family became, therefore, one of the first tasks of the new religion, and while other circumstances may have aided the church in this work, still on the whole it was mainly the influence of the early church that reconstituted the family life. From the first the church worked to abolish divorce, and fought as evil such vices as concubinage and prostitution, that came to flourish to such an extent in the Pagan world. Only very slowly did the early leaders of the church win the mass of the people to accepting their views as to the permanency of the marriage bond. In order to aid in making this bond more stable the early church recognized marriage as one of the sacraments, and, as implied, steadily opposed the idea of the later Roman Law that marriage was simply a private contract. The result was, eventually, that marriage came to be regarded again as a religious bond, and the family life took on once more the aspect of great stability. After the church had come fully into power in the Western world, legal divorce ceased to be recognized and legal separation was substituted in its stead. Thus the church succeeded in reconstituting the family life upon a stable basis, but the family after being reconstituted, was of a semipatriarchal type. Nothing was more natural than this, for the church had no model to go by except the paternal family of the Hebrew and Greek and Roman civilization. Nevertheless, the place of women and children in this semipatriarchal religious family established by the church was higher on the whole than in the ancient patriarchal family. The church put an end to the exposure of children, which had been common in Rome, and protected childhood in many ways. It also exalted the place of woman in the family, though leaving her subject to her husband. The veneration of the Virgin tended particularly to give women an honored place socially and religiously. Only by the advocacy and practice of ascetic doctrines may the early church be said to have detracted from the social valuation of the family. On the whole the reconstituting of the family by the church must be regarded as its most striking social work. But the thing for us to note particularly is that the type of the family life created by the church was what we might call a semipatriarchal type, in which the importance of husband and father was very much out of proportion to all the rest of the members of the family group. It was this semipatriarchal family which persisted down to the nineteenth century.

SELECT REFERENCES

For brief reading:

DE COULANGES, *The Ancient City*, Chaps. I-X.
LECKY, *History of European Morals*, Chap. V.
SCHMIDT, *Social Results of Early Christianity*, Chap. II.

For more extended reading:

HEARN, *The Aryan Household.*
HOWARD, *History of Matrimonial Institutions.*
GROTE, *History of Greece.*
MOMMSEN, *The History of Rome.*

On the early Hebrew family:

MCCURDY, *History, Prophecy, and the Monuments*, Vol. II.
ROBERTSON SMITH, *Kinship and Marriage in Early Arabia.*

On the early German family:

GUMMERE, *Germanic Origins.*

CHAPTER VII

THE PROBLEM OF THE MODERN FAMILY

Passing over the changes which affected the family during the Middle Ages and the still more striking changes which came through the Reformation, we must now devote ourselves to the study of the problems of the family as it exists at present. The religious theory of the family which prevailed during the Middle Ages, but which was more or less undermined by the Reformation, gave away entirely in those great social changes which ushered in the nineteenth century. Again, the view that marriage was a private contract came to prevail among the mass of the people, and even to be embodied in a great many of the constitutions and laws of the nineteenth century. At the same time profound economic changes tended largely to individualize society, and these were reflected in the democratic movement toward forms of popular government, which have tended on the whole to make the individual the political unit. The nineteenth century was, then, in all respects a period of great social change and unrest. Moreover, the growth of wealth has favored, in certain classes at least, lower moral standards and increasing laxity in family relationships. Thus it happens that we find the family life at the beginning of the twentieth century in a more unstable condition than it has been at any time since the beginning of the Christian era. The instability of the modern family is, indeed, so great that many have thought that the family, as an institution, in its present form at least, of permanent monogamy, will pass away. There can be no doubt, at any rate, that the whole problem of the modern family centers in the matter of its instability, that is, in divorce. The study of the divorce movement, then, will throw more light upon the condition of the modern family than the study of anything else. The instability of the modern family has been most evident in the United States. Hence, it is particularly American conditions that will concern us, although undoubtedly the disintegration of the family is not a peculiarly American phenomenon; rather it has characterized more or less all modern civilization, but is especially in evidence in America because American society has exaggerated the industrialism and individualism which are characteristic of Western civilization in general.

Without devoting too much time to the consideration of divorce statistics in their technical aspects, let us note, then, some of the main outlines of the modern divorce movement in this and other civilized countries.

Statistics of Divorce in the United States and Other Civilized Countries.—
For a long time the United States has led the world in the number of its
divorces. Already in 1885 this country had more divorces than all the rest of
the Christian civilized world put together. These statistics of the number of
divorces granted in different civilized countries in 1885 (taken from
Professor W. F. Willcox's monograph on *The Divorce Problem*) are of
sufficient interest to cite at length:

United States...................... 23,472
France............................. 6,245
Germany............................ 6,161
Russia............................. 1,789
Austria............................ 1,718
Switzerland........................ 920
Denmark............................ 635
Italy.............................. 556
Great Britain and Ireland.......... 508
Roumania........................... 541
Holland............................ 339
Belgium............................ 290
Sweden............................. 229
Australia.......................... 100
Norway............................. 68
Canada............................. 12

It will be noted that in this particular year (1885), when the United States
had 23,472 divorces, all the other countries mentioned together had only
20,131. For 1905, twenty years later, the following statistics are available:

United States...................... 67,976
Germany............................ 11,147
France............................. 10,860
Austria-Hungary.................... 5,785
Switzerland........................ 1,206
Belgium............................ 901
Holland............................ 900
Italy (1904)....................... 859
Great Britain and Ireland.......... 821
Denmark............................ 549
Sweden............................. 448
Norway............................. 408
Australia.......................... 339
New Zealand........................ 126
Canada............................. 33

It is evident from the above figures that the United States has more than kept its lead over the rest of the world in this matter of dissolving family ties, for it would seem probable from these figures that in 1905, when the United States had nearly 68,000 divorces, all the rest of the Christian civilized world put together had less than 40,000. Moreover, the divorce rates of the different countries tell the same story. In 1905 in France, there was only one divorce to every thirty marriages; in Germany, but one to every forty-four marriages; in England, but one to every four hundred marriages. Even in Switzerland, which has the highest divorce rate of any country of Europe, there was only one divorce in 1905 to every twenty-two marriages. Let us compare these rates with that of the United States, and particularly with the rates of several of the states that lead in the matter of divorces. In 1905 there was in the United States about one divorce to every twelve marriages, but the State of Washington had one divorce to every four marriages; Montana, one divorce to every five marriages; Colorado, Texas, Arkansas, and Indiana all had one divorce to every six marriages; California and Maine had one divorce to every seven marriages; New Hampshire, Missouri, and Kansas, one divorce to every eight marriages. While these rates are those of the states in which divorces are most numerous, yet, nevertheless, the number of states in which the divorce rates range from one to every six marriages to one to ten marriages are so numerous that they may be said to be fairly representative of American conditions generally. Some cities and localities have, of course, even higher divorce rates than any of the states that have been named. According to the United States Census Bulletin No. 20, there was in 1903 one divorce in Kansas City, Missouri, to every four marriages, and one divorce in the city of San Francisco to every three marriages.

Increase of Divorces in the United States. Not only does the United States lead the world in the number of its divorces, but apparently divorces are increasing in this country much more rapidly than the population. In 1867, the first year for which statistics for the country as a whole were gathered, there were 9937 divorces in the United States, but by 1906, the last year for which we have statistics, the total number of divorces granted in this country, yearly, had reached 72,062. Again, from 1867 to 1886 there were 328,716 divorces granted in the United States, but during the next twenty years, from 1887 to 1906, the number reached 945,625, or almost a total of 1,000,000 divorces granted in twenty years. Again, from 1867 to 1886 the number of divorces increased 157 per cent, while the population increased only about 60 per cent; from 1887 to 1906 the number of divorces increased over 160 per cent, while the population increased only slightly over 50 per cent. Thus it is evident that divorces are increasing in the United States three times as fast as the increase of population. It becomes, therefore, a matter of some curious interest to speculate upon what will be the end of this movement. If divorces should continue to increase as they have during the past forty years, it is evident that it would not be long before all marriages would be terminated by divorce instead of by death. In 1870, 3.5 per cent of all marriages were terminated by divorce; in 1880, 4.8 per cent were terminated by divorce, and in 1900, about 8 per cent. Professor Willcox has estimated that if this increasing divorce rate continues, by 1950 one fourth of all marriages in the United States will be terminated by divorce, and in 1990 one half of all marriages. Thus we are apparently within measurable distance of a time when, if present tendencies continue, the family, as a permanent union between husband and wife, lasting until death, shall cease to be. At least, it is safe to say that in a population where one half of all marriages will be terminated by divorce the social conditions would be no better than those in the Rome of the decadence. We cannot imagine such a state of affairs without the existence alongside of it of widespread promiscuity, neglect of childhood, and general social demoralization. Without, however, stopping at this point to discuss the results or the effects of the divorce movement upon society, let us now consider for a moment how these divorces are distributed among the various elements and classes of our population.

Distribution of Divorces. It is usually thought by those who have observed the matter most carefully that divorce especially characterizes the wealthy classes and the laboring classes, but is least common among the middle classes. We have no statistics to bear out this belief, but it seems probable that it is substantially correct. The divorce statistics which we have, however, indicate certain striking differences in the distribution of divorces by classes and communities.

(1) The divorce rate is higher in the cities than in their surrounding country districts. We have just noted, for example, that the divorce rate in Kansas City, Missouri, is one divorce to every four marriages, while in the state as a whole it is one to every eight marriages. There are, however, certain exceptions to this generalization.

(2) A curious fact that the census statistics show is that apparently the divorce rate is about four times as high among childless couples as among couples that have children. This doubtless does not mean that domestic unhappiness is four times more common in families where there are no children than in families that have children, but it does show, nevertheless, that the parental instinct, is now, as in primitive times, a powerful force to bind husband and wife together.

(3) While we have no statistics from this country telling us exactly what the distribution of divorces is among the various religious denominations, still we know that because the Roman Catholic Church is strongly against

divorce, divorces are very rare in that denomination. In Switzerland, where the number of divorces among Protestants and Catholics has been noted, it is found that divorces are four times as common among Protestants as among Catholics. Some observers in this country have claimed that divorces are most common among those of no religious profession, next most common among Protestants, next among Jews, and least common among Roman Catholics.

(4) From this we might expect, as our statistics indicate, that the divorce rate is much higher among the native whites in this country than it is among the foreign born, for many of the foreign born are Roman Catholics, and, in any case, they come from countries where divorce is less common than in the United States.

(5) For the last forty years two thirds of all divorces have been granted on demand of the wife. This may indicate, on the one hand, that the increase of divorces is a movement connected with the emancipation of woman, and on the other hand it may indicate that it is the husband who usually gives the ground for divorce.

(6) The census statistics show three great centers of divorce in the United States. One is the New England States, one the states of the Central West, and one the Rocky Mountain and Pacific Coast states. These three centers are also typical centers of American institutions and ideas. The individualism of the New England, the Central West, and the Rocky Mountain and Pacific Coast regions has always been marked in comparison with some other sections of the country. But during the last twenty years divorce has also been increasing rapidly in the Southern states, and we now find such states as Texas, Arkansas, and Oklahoma well up toward the front among the states with a high divorce rate.

This distribution of divorces among the various elements and classes of the country suggests something as to the causes of divorce, and this will come out fully later in a discussion of the causes of the increase of divorce.

The Grounds for Granting Divorce.—There are no less than thirty-six distinct grounds for absolute divorce recognized by the laws of the several states, ranging from only one ground recognized in New York to fourteen grounds recognized in New Hampshire. For this reason some have supposed that many of the divorces in this country are granted on comparatively trivial grounds. Several states have, for example, what is known as an "Omnibus Clause," granting divorce for mere incompatibility and the like. But the examination of divorce statistics shows that very few divorces are granted on trivial grounds. On the contrary, most divorces seem to be granted for grave reasons, such as adultery, desertion, cruelty, imprisonment for crime, habitual drunkenness, and neglect on the part of the husband to provide for his family. These are usually recognized as grave reasons for the dissolution of the marriage tie. None of them at least could be said to be trivial. Professor Willcox showed that for the twenty year period, 1867 to 1886, over ninety-seven per cent of all divorces were granted for these six principal causes. Moreover, he also showed that over sixty per cent were granted for the two most serious causes of all,—adultery and desertion. Again, of the one million divorces granted from 1887 to 1906 over ninety-four per cent were granted for the six principal causes and over fifty-five per cent for adultery and desertion, while in still other cases adultery and desertion figured in combination with other causes (a total of over sixty-two per cent in all). Therefore, it seems probable that in nearly two thirds of the cases the marriage bond had already practically been dissolved before the courts stepped in to make the dissolution formal. We must conclude, therefore, that divorce is prevalent not because of the laxity of our laws, but rather because of the decay of our family life; that divorce is but a symptom of the disintegration of the modern family, particularly the American family.

In other words, divorce is but a symptom of more serious evils, and these evils have in certain classes of American society apparently undermined the very virtues upon which the family life subsists. This is not saying that vice is more prevalent to-day than it was fifty years ago. We have no means of knowing whether it is or not, and there may well be a difference of opinion upon such a subject. It is the opinion of some eminent authorities that there has been no growth of vice in the United States along with the growth of divorce, but this would seem to be doubtful. The very causes for which divorce is granted suggest a demoralization of certain classes. While there may not have been, therefore, any general growth of vice in the United States along with the growth of divorce, it is conceivable that it may have increased greatly in certain classes of American society. Be this as it may, it is not necessary to assume that there has been any growth of vice in the American population, for if actual moral practices are no higher than they were fifty years ago that alone would be a sufficient reason to explain considerable disintegration of our family life. It is an important truth in sociology that the morality which suffices for a relatively simple social life, largely rural, such as existed in this country fifty years ago, is not sufficient for a more complex society which is largely urban, such as exists at the present time. Moreover, recognized moral standards within the past fifty years have largely been raised through the growth of general intelligence. It follows that immoral acts, which were condoned fifty years ago and which produced but slight social effect, to-day meet with great reprobation and have far greater social consequences than a generation ago. This is particularly true of the standards which the wife imposes upon the husband. For centuries, as we have already seen, the husband has secured divorce for adultery of the wife, but for centuries no divorce was given to the wife for the adultery of the husband; and this is even true to-day in modern England, unless the adultery of the husband be accompanied by other flagrant violations of morality. Conduct on the part of the husband, which the wife overlooked, therefore, a generation ago, is to-day sufficient to disrupt the family bonds and become a ground for the granting of a divorce. Even if vice, then, has not increased in our population, if moral practices are no higher to-day than fifty years ago, we should expect that this alone would have far different consequences now than then. The growth of intelligence and of higher and more complex forms of social organization necessitates realization of higher standards of conduct if the institutions of society are to retain their stability.

But there are grave reasons for believing that there has been in certain classes of society a decay of the very virtues upon which the family rests, for the family life requires not only chastity, but even more the virtues of self-sacrifice, loyalty, obedience, and self-subordination. Now there is abundant evidence to show that these particular virtues which belong to a self-subordinating life are those which have suffered most in the changes and new adjustments of modern society. We have replaced these virtues largely by those of self-interest, self-direction, and self-assertiveness.

Causes of the Increase of Divorce in the United States.—Let us note somewhat more in detail the causes of the increased instability of the American family during the past four or five decades. We have already in a rough way indicated some of these causes in studying the distribution of divorce and the grounds upon which it is granted. But the causes of the instability of the family so affect our whole social life and all of our institutions that they are well worth somewhat more detailed study.

(1) As the first of these causes of the increase of divorce in the United States we should put the decay of religion, particularly of the religious theory of marriage and the family. As we have already seen, no stable family life has existed anywhere in history without a religious basis, but within the last few decades religious sentiments, beliefs, and ideals have become largely dissociated from marriage and the family, and the result is that many people regard the institutions of marriage and the family as a matter of personal convenience. This decay of the religious view of the marriage bond has, however, had other antecedent causes, partially in the moral and intellectual spirit of our civilization, partially in our industrial conditions.

(2) We should put, therefore, as a second cause of the increase of divorces in this country the growing spirit of individualism. By individualism we mean here the spirit of self-assertion and self-interest, the spirit which leads a man to find his law in his own wishes, or even in his whims and caprices.

Now, this growing spirit of individualism is undoubtedly more destructive of the social life than anything else. It makes unstable all institutions, and especially the family, because the family must rest upon very opposite characteristics. Our democratic government, the development of our industry, and our education have all been responsible to some extent for making the individual take his own interests and wishes as his law.

(3) Moreover, this individualism has spread within the last fifty years especially among the women of the population, and a great movement has sprung up which is known as the "Woman's Rights Movement," or simply the "Woman's Movement." Now this woman's movement has accompanied and in part effected the emancipation of women legally, mentally, and economically. The result is that women, as a class, have become as much individualized as the men, and oftentimes are as great practical individualists.

No one would claim that the emancipation of woman, in the sense of freeing her from those things which have prevented the highest and best development of her personality, is not desirable. But this emancipation of woman has brought with it certain opportunities for going down as well as for going up. Woman's emancipation has not, in other words, meant to all classes of women, woman's elevation. On the contrary, it has been to some, if not an opportunity for license, at least an opportunity for self-assertion and selfishness not consistent with the welfare of society and particularly with the stability of the family. We may remind ourselves once more that the Roman women achieved complete emancipation, but they did not thereby better their social position. On the contrary, the emancipation of woman in Rome meant woman's degradation, and ultimately the demoralization of Roman family life. While this is not necessarily an accompaniment of woman's emancipation, still it is a real danger which threatens, and of which we can already see many evidences in modern society. As in all other emancipatory movements, the dangers of freedom are found for some individuals at least to be quite as great as the dangers of subjection.

That the woman's movement has had much to do with the growth of divorce in this country gains substantiation from the fact that many of the leaders of that movement, like Miss Susan B. Anthony and Mrs. Elizabeth Cady Stanton, advocated free divorce, and their inculcation of this doctrine certainly could not have been without some effect.

But the woman's movement would have perhaps failed to develop, or at least failed of widespread support, if it had not been for the economic emancipation of woman through the opening to her of many new industrial callings and the securing for her a certain measure of economic independence. This, again, while perhaps a good thing in itself, has, nevertheless, facilitated the growing tendency to form unstable family relations. But this economic independence of woman, we need hardly remark, is the necessary and, indeed, inevitable outcome of modern industrial development.

(4) The growth of modern industrialism must, then, be regarded as one of the fundamental factors which has brought about the increase of divorce in the United States. By industrialism we mean manufacturing industry. As we have already noticed, the growth of manufacturing industry has opened a large number of new economic callings to woman and has rendered her largely economically independent of family relations. Moreover, the labor of women in factories has tended to disrupt the home, particularly in the case of married women, as we have already seen. For the laboring classes it has tended to make the home only a lodging place, with little or no development of a true family life. Again, such labor has set the sexes in competition with each other, has tended to reduce their sexual differences and to stimulate immensely their individualism. Finally, inasmuch as modern industrialism has tended to destroy the home, the result has been the production of unsocialized children, and especially of those that had no tradition of a family life. Girls, for example, through industrialism, have failed to learn the domestic arts, failed to have any training in homemaking, and therefore when they came to the position of wife and mother, they were frequently not fitted for such a life, and through their lack of adjustment rendered the homes which they formed unstable.

(5) Closely connected with the growth of modern industrialism is the growth of modern cities, and, as we have already seen, divorce is usually much more common in the cities than in the rural districts. The growth of the cities, in other words, has been a cause of the increase of divorce. City populations, on account of the economic conditions under which they live, are peculiarly homeless. A normal home can scarcely exist in the slums and in some of the tenement districts of our cities. Again, in the city there is perhaps more vice and other immorality, less control of the individual by public opinion, and more opportunity, on account of close living together and high standards of living, for friction, both within and without the domestic circle.

(6) The higher standards of living and comfort which have come with the growth of our industrial civilization, especially of our cities, must also be set down as a cause of increasing instability of the family. High standards of living are, of course, desirable if they can be realized, that is, if they are reasonable. But many elements of our population have standards of living and comfort which they find are practically impossible to realize with the income which they have. Many classes, in other words, are unable to meet

the social demands which they suppose they must meet in order to maintain a home. To found and maintain a home, therefore, with these rising standards of living, and also within the last decade or two with the rising cost of living, requires such a large income that an increasingly smaller proportion of the population are able to do this satisfactorily. From this cause, undoubtedly, a great deal of domestic misery and unhappiness results, which finally shows itself in desertion or in the divorce court.

It is evident that higher standards of taste and higher standards of morality may also operate under certain circumstances to render the family life unstable in a similar way.

(7) Directly connected with these last mentioned causes is another cause,— the higher age of marriage. Some have thought that a low age of marriage was more prolific in divorces than a relatively high age of marriage. But a low age of marriage cannot be a cause of the increase of divorce in the United States, because the proportion of immature marriages in this country is steadily lessening, that is, the age of marriage is steadily increasing, and all must admit that along with the higher age of marriage has gone increasing divorce; and there may possibly be some connection between the two facts. As we have already seen, the higher standards of living make later marriage necessary. Men in the professions do not think of marriage nowadays until thirty, or until they have an independent income. Now, how may the higher age of marriage possibly increase the instability of the family? It may do so in this way. After thirty, psychologists tell us, one's habits are relatively fixed and hard to change. People who marry after thirty, therefore, usually find greater difficulty in adjusting themselves to each other than people who marry somewhat younger; and every marriage necessarily involves an adjustment of individuals to each other. This being so, we can readily understand that late marriages are more apt to result in faulty adjustments in the family relation than marriages that take place in early maturity.

(8) Another cause of the increase of divorce in the United States that has been given is the popularization of law which has accompanied the growth of democratic institutions. Law was once the prerogative of special classes, and courts were rarely appealed to except by the noble or wealthy classes; but with the growth of democratic institutions there has been a great spread of legal education, especially through the modern newspaper, and consequently a greater participation in the remedies offered by the courts for all sorts of wrongs, real or imagined. Many people, for example, who would not have thought of divorce a generation ago, now know how divorce may be secured and are ready to secure it. However, it would seem as though this cause of the increase of divorce might have operated to a greater extent twenty-five or thirty years ago than it has during the last two

decades, for it cannot be said that since the nineties there has been much increase of legal education among the masses, or much greater popularization of the law.

(9) Increasing laxity of the laws regarding divorce and increasing laxity in the administration of the laws has certainly been a cause of increasing divorce in the United States, though back of these causes doubtless lie all the other causes just mentioned, and also increasing laxity in public opinion regarding marriage and divorce. To assume that laxity of the laws and of legal administration has no influence upon the increase of divorce in a population is to go contrary to all human experience. The people of Canada and of England, for example, are not very different from ourselves in culture and in institutions, yet there is almost no divorce in England and in Canada as compared with the United States. Canada has a few dozen divorces annually, while we have over seventy thousand. Unquestionably the main cause of this great difference between Canada and the United States is to be found in the difference of their laws. This is not saying, however, that instability of the family does not characterize Canada and England as well as the United States, even though such instability does not express itself in the divorce courts.

Interesting statistics have been collected in numerous places in the country to show the laxity of the administration of the divorce laws. In many of the divorce courts of our large cities, for example, it has repeatedly been shown that the average time occupied by the court in granting a divorce is not more than fifteen minutes. In other words, divorce cases are frequently rushed through our divorce courts without solemnity, without adequate investigation, with every opportunity for collusion between the parties, so as to favor a very free granting of divorces. On the other hand, about one fourth of all the applications for divorce which come to trial are refused by the courts, showing that the courts are not so lax in all cases as they are sometimes pictured to be.

Moreover, the divorce courts have two excuses for their laxity. First, the divorce courts are always greatly overburdened with the number of cases before them; and, secondly, public opinion, which the courts as well as other phases of our government largely reflect, favors this laxity. This is shown by the fact that public opinion stands back of the lax divorce statutes of many states, all efforts to radically change these statutes having failed of recent years.

(10) Our study of the family has accustomed us to the thought that the family is an institution which, like all other human institutions, undergoes constant changes. Now at periods of change in any institution, periods of transition from one type to another, there is apt to be a period of

confusion. The old type of institution is never replaced at once by a new type of institution ready-made and adjusted to the social life, but only gradually does the new institution emerge from the elements of the old. In the meantime, however, there may be a considerable period of confusion and anarchy. This social principle, we may note, rests upon a deeper psychological principle, that old habits are usually not replaced by new habits without an intervening period of confusion and uncertainty. In other words, in the transition from the old habit to the new habit there is much opportunity for disorganization and disintegration. It is exactly so in human society, because social institutions are but expressions of habit.

Now, the old semipatriarchal type of the family, which prevailed down to the beginning of the nineteenth century, the type of the family which we might perhaps properly call the monarchical type, has been disappearing for the past one hundred years,—is in fact already practically extinct, at least in America, but we have not yet built up a new type of the family to take its place. The old semipatriarchal family of our forefathers has gone, but no new type of the family has yet become general. A democratic type of the family in harmony with our democratic civilization must be evolved. But such a democratic type of the family can be stable only upon the condition that its stability is within itself and not without. Authority in various coercive forms made the old type of the family stable, but a stable basis for a new type of the family has not yet been found, or rather it has not been found by large elements of our population. Unquestionably a democratic ethical type of the family in which the rights of every one are respected and all members are bound together, not through fear or through force of authority, but through love and affection, is being evolved in certain classes of our society. The problem before our civilization is whether such a democratic ethical type of the family can become generalized and offer a stable family life to our whole population. It is evident that in order to do this there must be a considerable development, not only of the spirit of equality, but even more, a considerable development of social intelligence and ethical character in the minds of the people. To construct a stable family life of this character, however, which is apparently the only type which will meet the demands of modern civilization,—is not an impossibility, but is a delicate and difficult task which will require all the resources of the state, the school, and the church. There is, however, no ground as yet for pessimism regarding the future of our family life; rather all its instability and demoralization of the present are simply incident, we must believe, to the achievement of a higher type of the family than the world has yet seen. Such a higher type, however, will not come about without effort and forethought on the part of society's leaders.

Remedies for the Divorce Evil.—That the instability of the family and divorce, so far as it is an expression of that instability, is an evil in society is implied in all that has thus far been said concerning the origin, development, and functions of the family as an institution. We shall not stop, therefore, to argue this point since all preceding chapters amount to an argument upon this question. It may be added, however, that in so far as observations have been made of the results of divorce upon children, that the argument has been substantiated, for apparently the children of separated or divorced parents are much more apt to drift into poverty, vice, or crime, that is, into the unsocialized classes, than children who do not come from such disrupted homes. Assuming, then, without further argument that divorce, or rather the instability of the family, is an evil in modern society, the question arises, how can it be remedied?

If, as has already been implied, the real evil is not so much divorce as the decay of the family life, then it at once becomes evident that legislation can do little to correct the real evil. That it can do nothing, and that an attitude of *laissez-faire* is justified upon this question, is, of course, not implied. As we have already noted, the difference between the few divorces of the Dominion of Canada and the many divorces of the United States is largely due to a difference of laws; nevertheless, we cannot assume from this that there is a like difference in the state of the family life of the two countries. Unquestionably, however, legislation can do something even in the way of setting moral ideals before a people. Divorce laws should not be too lax if we do not wish a state to set low moral standards for its citizens. It is not too much to say, therefore, that the lax divorce laws of many of our states are a crime against civilization, even though making these laws much stricter might not of itself greatly check the decay of the family. Again, reasonable restrictions upon the remarriage of divorced parties might very well be insisted upon by law for the sake of public decency if nothing more. Present laws in many states permit the remarriage of divorced parties immediately upon granting of divorce. It would seem that a law requiring the innocent party to wait at least six months, and the guilty party to wait from two to five years and then give evidence of good conduct before being permitted to remarry, would work a hardship upon no one. Again, a uniform federal divorce and marriage law might have some good effects upon the family life of the nation. Divorce and marriage are of such general importance that they should be controlled by federal statutes rather than by state laws. If such an amendment to our present federal constitution were enacted, it might not result in greatly decreasing the number of divorces in this country, but it would result in bringing about uniformity in the different states in the matter of marriage as well as in the matter of divorce, which, from many points of view, is desirable. Moreover, if divorce were under federal control this would throw all divorce cases into the federal courts, and would, perhaps, secure a stricter administration of divorce laws.

But it is evident that the main reliance in combating the evils which have given rise to the present instability of our family life must be placed upon education rather than upon legislation. Legislation, we may here note, has many shortcomings as an instrument of social reconstruction or reform. Legislation is necessarily external and coercive. It fails oftentimes to change the habits of individuals, and very generally fails to change their opinion. Education, on the other hand, alters human nature directly, changing both the opinions and habits of the individual. Neither education nor legislation can be neglected in social reconstruction. Both are necessary, but supplement each other. But from the time of Plato down all social thinkers have perceived the fact that education is a surer and safer means of reorganizing society than legislation. While, therefore, I would not oppose education to legislation, I would say that emphasis in all social reform should be laid upon education rather than coercive legislative action, and especially in this case of relaying the foundations for a stable family life in our country. The main reliance, then, in this matter must be placed upon the education which the school, the church, and the home can give to the rising generation. Until children are taught to look upon the family as a socially necessary and therefore sacred institution, until they are taught to look upon marriage as something other than an act to suit their own convenience and pleasure, we must expect that our family life will be unstable. The reconstruction of our family life, indeed, practically involves the reconstruction of our whole social life. Things in industry, in business, in politics, in the conventions and ideals and general spirit of our people, that are opposed to stability in family relations, must be remedied before we can strike at the root of the evil. All of this may be taken for granted; but it would seem that the moral education of the young is the key to the situation in any event. The importance of a pure and wholesome family life in society should, therefore, be emphasized by our whole system of public education, while the responsibility which rests upon the church in this connection is especially obvious; but the home itself must, it may be admitted, be the chief means of inculcating in the young the sacredness of the family. Inasmuch as this cannot be done in homes that are already demoralized, the main hope must be that such education will be given to children in homes that are as yet relatively pure and stable. Movements toward such education already exist in society, and, as we have already said, there is no reason for pessimism, if we take a long view of the situation. But it is nevertheless evident that the instability of the family must be regarded as the greatest of our social problems to-day.

Summary Regarding the Influence of Industrial Conditions upon the Present Instability of the Family.—As we have already seen, the development of modern industry is one of the chief causes of the decay of modern family life. Certain aspects of our industrialism, such as the labor of women and children in factories, the growth of cities, and the loss of the home through the slum and the tenement, the higher standards of living and comfort, and the resulting higher age of marriage,—all of these have had, to a certain extent at least, a disastrous effect upon the family. Some of these things, like the growth of cities, seem inseparable from modern industrial development. The problem must be, therefore, how to overcome the evil effect of these tendencies in industry upon the home. There is no reason for believing that such evil effects cannot be overcome, although the problem is a difficult one. Our aim should be, not to stop industrial development, but to guide it and control it in the interest of the higher development of the family. That this is entirely feasible may already be seen from what has been accomplished in the way of regulating the labor of women and children and in the way of providing better conditions in the homes of the working population.

There is, however, nothing in evidence in the causes of increasing divorce in the United States which warrants the belief that American industrial development is alone responsible for the increasing instability of our family life. The industrial development of America is less peculiar in many ways than its political and social development. Divorce and instability of the family, as we have seen, characterize the American people more than any other civilized population. This fact, then, cannot be explained entirely in terms of American industrial development, but we must look also, as has already been emphasized, to certain peculiarities in American character, American institutions, and American ideas and ideals. The divorce movement in the United States affords no proof of the theory of economic determinism.

SELECT REFERENCES

For brief reading:

WILLCOX, *The Divorce Problem: A Study in Statistics.*
ADLER, *Marriage and Divorce*, Lecture II.
Special Report on *Marriage and Divorce*, 1867-1906, Bureau of the Census.

For more extended reading:

HOWARD, *History of Matrimonial Institutions.*
LICHTENBERGER, *Divorce: A Study in Social Causation.*
WOLSEY, *Divorce and Divorce Legislation.*
WRIGHT, *First Special Report of United States Commissioner of Labor:
    Marriage and Divorce*, 1891.

CHAPTER VIII

THE GROWTH OF POPULATION

Mass is a factor in the survival of a social group. Other things being equal, that society will stand the best chance of surviving which has the largest population. Moreover, the larger the mass of a given group the greater can be the industrial and cultural division of labor in that group. Hence, other things being equal, a large population favors the growth not only of a higher type of industry, but also of a higher type of culture or civilization in a given society. The questions which center around the growth of population, therefore, are among the most important questions which sociology has to deal with.

The growth of population is, of course, more or less indirectly connected with the family life, since the growth of population in the world as a whole is dependent upon the surplus of births over deaths. But population has so long been looked at as a national question that perhaps it will be best to study it from the standpoint of the national group. The population of modern national groups, the influences which augment and deter the growth of the population of these groups, and the laws of population in general, will be what will concern us in this chapter.

Population Statistics of Some Modern Nations.—The following table of statistics will show the status of the populations of the largest nations of Europe and America in the nineteenth century:

	Population, 1801.	Population, 1901.	Increase per Year, per cent.
Russia (in Europe) ...	40,000,000	106,159,000	1.36
Germany	24,000,000	56,367,000	1.39
France	26,800,000	38,961,000	0.12
Great Britain and Ireland	16,300,000	41,605,000	1.21
Austria	25,000,000	45,310,000	0.91
Italy	17,500,000	32,449,000	0.73
Spain	10,500,000	18,000,000	0.32
United States	5,308,000	76,303,000	2.09

This table shows, that while the population of nearly all of these nations has increased rapidly within the nineteenth century, that the increase is relatively unequal in some cases. If we project Russia's increase of population to the year 2000 A.D., we shall find that its probable population will be in the neighborhood of 300,000,000; Germany's probable population, say 167,000,000; Great Britain and Ireland's probable population, 135,000,000; while France's probable population in the year two thousand, if it continues to increase only at its present slow rate, will be but 45,000,000. While these forecasts of population cannot be considered certain in any sense, still they are sufficient to show that the growth of modern nations in population is relatively unequal. Inasmuch as the mere element of numbers is one of the greatest factors for the future greatness of any nation, this is a highly important matter. A nation of only 40,000,000 a century hence, it is safe to say, will be no more important than Holland and Belgium are now. On the other hand, it is very probable that a century hence the civilized nations that lead in population will also lead in industrial and cultural development. Many other factors, of course, enter into the situation, but the factor of mere numbers should not be neglected, as all practical statesmen recognize.

A century hence it is probable that the population of continental United States will be about 300,000,000. It would be considerably more than this if the present annual rate of increase were to continue, but inasmuch as that is not likely, an estimate of 300,000,000 is sufficiently high. [Footnote: The official estimate by the Census Bureau is 200,000,000; but this for many reasons seems too low.] We have already seen that it is probable that Russia's population may equal 300,000,000 by the year 2000. It seems probable, therefore, that the United States and Russia may be the two great world powers a century hence, particularly if Russia emerges from its present social and political troubles and takes on fully Western civilization, while the other nations may tend to ally themselves with the one or the other of these great world powers. Of course, China is the X—the unknown quantity—in the world's future. Should its immense population become civilized and absorb Western ideas, this would certainly bring into the theater of the world's political evolution a new and important factor.

The population and vital statistics of the various civilized countries show:—

(1) The population of all civilized countries, with one or two exceptions, has been increasing rapidly since the beginning of the nineteenth century. Previous to that time we have no statistics that are reliable, but it seems probable that the population of Europe stood practically stationary during the Middle Ages and increased only slowly down to the nineteenth century; but during the nineteenth century the population of the leading industrial nations has increased very rapidly. This is due primarily, without doubt, to improved economic conditions, which has made it possible for a larger population to subsist within a given area. Back of these improved economic conditions, however, has been increased scientific knowledge in ways of mastering physical nature, and accompanying them has been a very greatly decreased death rate, due in part at least to the advance of medical science.

(2) This increase in population has been due, not to an increase in birth rate, but to a decreased death rate. During the nineteenth century the death rate decreased markedly in practically all civilized countries. As we have already noted, this is due primarily to improved living conditions, particularly in the food, clothing, and shelter for the masses, but it has also been due in no small part to the advance in medical science, and especially that branch of it which we know as "public sanitation." Because the death rate decreases with improved material, and probably also with improved moral conditions, it is a relatively good measure, at least of the material civilization or progress of a people. We may note that the death rate is measured by the number of deaths that occur annually per thousand in a given population. The death rate of the countries most advanced in sanitary science and in industrial improvement apparently tends to go down to about fifteen or sixteen per thousand annually.

(3) The birth rate of civilized countries has also fallen markedly during the nineteenth century, especially during the latter half. On the whole, this is a good thing. The birth rate should decrease with the death rate. This leaves more energy to be used in other things; but when the birth rate falls more rapidly than the death rate or falls beyond a certain point, it is evident that the normal growth of a nation is hindered, and even its extinction may be threatened. While an excessively high birth rate is a sign of low culture on the whole, on the other hand an excessively low birth rate is a sign of physical and probably moral degeneracy in the population. When the birth rate is lower than the death rate in a given population, it is evident that the population is on the way to extinction. In order that a birth rate be normal, therefore, it must be sufficiently above the death rate to provide for the normal growth of the population. On the whole, it seems safe to conclude that we have no better index of the vitality of a people, that is, of their capacity to survive, than the surplus of births over deaths. Such a surplus of births over deaths is also a fairly trustworthy index of the living conditions of a population, because if the living conditions are poor, no matter how high the birth rate may be, the death rate will be correspondingly high, and the surplus of births over deaths, therefore, relatively low.

Vital statistics are, therefore, an indication of more than the mere health or even the material condition of a given population. Probably there are no social facts from which we may gather a clearer insight into the social conditions of a given population than vital statistics.

Without going into the vital statistics of modern nations in any detail, the following table of birth rates and death rates will serve to illustrate the decrease in the death rates and the birth rates of the three leading European nations, the birth rate being computed the same as the death rate, that is, the number of births per thousand annually of the population:

DEATH RATE

1871-1890 1893-1902 1904

England 20.3 17.6 16.2
Germany 26.0 21.5 19.6
France 22.8 20.8 19.4

BIRTH RATE

1871-1890 1893-1902 1904

England 34.0 29.3 28.0
Germany 38.1 35.9 35.2
France 24.6 22.8 20.9

From the above table it is evident that while birth rates and death rates have been declining in all civilized peoples, the decline has been unequal in different peoples. Both England and Germany in the above table show still a good surplus of births over deaths; in the case of England in 1904 this surplus being 11.8 per thousand of the population annually, while in the case of Germany it was 15.6. In the case of France, however, the surplus of births over deaths for a number of years has been very insignificant, and in the year 1907 there were actually about 20,000 more deaths than births in all France (773,969 births against 793,889 deaths). France's population has, therefore, been practically stationary for a number of years, while within the last year or two it seems to be actually declining.

The causes of the stationary population of France are probably mainly economic, although all the factors which influence the family life in any degree must also influence birth rate. For a number of years the economic conditions of France have not been favorable to the growth of a large population, and at the same time the law necessitating the equal division of the family's property among children has tended to encourage small families. Unquestionably, however, other factors of a more general social or moral nature are also at work in France as well as in all other populations that are decreasing in numbers.

The Decrease in the Native White Stock in the United States. Certain classes in the United States also show a very slight surplus of births over deaths and in some cases absolutely declining numbers. In general the United States Census statistics seem to indicate that the native white stock in the Northern states is not keeping up its numbers. This is suggested by the decreasing size of the average family in the United States. The average size of the family in the United States in 1850 was 5.6 persons; in 1860, 5.3; in 1870, 5.1; in 1880, 5.0; in 1890, 4.9; and in 1900, 4.7. Moreover, if we include only private families in 1900, the average size of the family was only

4.6. Thus, between 1850 and 1900 the size of the average family in the United States decreased by nearly one full person. This decrease is most evident in the North Atlantic and North Central states. In Maine, Vermont, and New Hampshire, for example, the average size of the family in 1900 was 4.1 persons.

Moreover, the vital statistics kept by the state of Massachusetts for a number of years show conclusively that the native white stock in that state is tending to die out. In 1896, for example, in Massachusetts the native born had a birth rate of only 16.58, while the foreign born had a birth rate of 50.40. Again, the following table of birth rates and death rates for 1890 in the city of Boston [Footnote: Taken from Bushee's *Ethnic Factors in the Population of Boston*, Publications American Economic Association, Vol. IV., No, 2, 1903.] for the native born and sections of the foreign born shows conclusively that the native-born element is not keeping up its numbers:

Birth Rate Death Rate

	Birth Rate	Death Rate
Native born	16.40	17.20
Irish	45.60	25.20
Germans	48.00	15.00
Russian Jews	94.60	15.90
Italians	104.60	25.30

It is evident from this table that the foreign born are increasing in Boston very rapidly in numbers through birth, while the native born are apparently not even holding their own. The high birth rate of the foreign born is, of course, in part to be explained through the fact that the foreign-born population is made up for the most part of individuals in the prime of life, that is, in the reproductive age. Nevertheless, while this explains the excessively high birth rate of some of these foreign elements, it does not explain the great discrepancy between their birth rate and that of the native born. If the present tendencies continue, it is apparently not difficult to foresee a time in the not very distant future when the old Puritan New England families will be replaced in the population of Boston entirely by the descendants of recent immigrants.

Moreover, so far as vital statistics concerning different classes can be gathered in the northern tier of the states, practically everywhere the same tendencies are manifest, that is, everywhere we find the native-born white population failing to hold its own alongside of the more recent immigrants. Apparently, therefore, we must conclude that the birth rate in the native whites in the United States is declining to such an extent that that element in our population threatens to become extinct if present tendencies continue. Only the Southern whites present an exception to this generalization. The Southern white people, from various causes not well understood,—partially, perhaps, from family pride, partially, perhaps, from racial instinct, but even more probably on account of certain economic conditions,—keep up their numbers, increasing more rapidly even than the negro population which exists alongside of them.

Causes of the Decrease in Birth Rate in the Native White Stock in the United States. What, then, are the causes of this decrease in the birth rate of the native white stock in the United States? It is worth our while to inquire briefly into these causes, for they illustrate the factors which are at work in favoring or deterring the growth of population.

(1) Economic conditions are without doubt mainly at the bottom of the decreasing birth rate in the native white American population. Certain unfavorable economic conditions have developed in this country of recent years for this particular element; especially have higher standards of living increased among the native white population in the United States more rapidly than their income. This has led to later marriages and smaller families. Again, more intense competition along all lines has forced certain elements of the native stock into occupations where wages are low in comparison with the standard of living. This has, perhaps, especially come about through the increased competition which the foreign born have offered to the native white element. The foreign born have taken rapidly all the places which might be filled by unskilled labor and many of the places filled by skilled labor. The native born have shrunk from this competition and have retired for the most part to the more socially honorable occupations, such as clerkships in business, the professions, and the like. In many of these occupations, however, as we have already said, the wages are low as compared with the standards of living maintained by that particular occupational class; hence, as we have already said, later marriages and fewer children. Rising standards of living and rising costs of living have, therefore, impinged more heavily upon the native born than upon the foreign born. It is difficult to suggest a remedy for this condition of affairs. No legislator can devise means of encouraging a class to have large families when by so doing that class would necessarily have to sacrifice some of its standards of living. However, it may be that the native born can be protected to some extent from the competition of the foreign born through reasonable restrictions upon immigration, and it may also be that unreasonable advances in standards of living may be checked, but both of these propositions seem to be of somewhat doubtful nature.

(2) No doubt the pressure of economic conditions is not responsible for small families in some elements of the native white population in the United States, for oftentimes the smallest families are found among the wealthy, among whom there could be no danger of a large family lowering the standards of living or pressing upon other economic needs. We must

accept as a second factor in the situation, therefore, the inherent selfishness in human nature which is not willing to be burdened with the care of children. In other countries, and apparently in all ages, the wealthy have been characterized by smaller families than the poor. The following table from Bertillon, [Footnote: Quoted by Newsholme, Vital Statistics, p. 75.] showing the number of births per thousand women between fifteen and fifty years of age in Paris, Berlin, and London among the various economic classes, shows conclusively that it is not altogether the pressure of economic wants which leads to the limiting of a population:

BIRTHS PER THOUSAND WOMEN PER ANNUM

Paris Berlin London.

	Paris	Berlin	London
Very poor	108	157	147
Poor	95	129	140
Comfortable	72	114	107
Rich	53	63	87
Very rich	34	47	63

(3) Besides economic conditions and individual selfishness we must unfortunately add another cause of decreasing birth rate in our population which has been definitely ascertained, and that is vice. Vice cuts the birth rate chiefly through the diseases which accompany it. About 20 per cent of American marriages are childless, and medical authorities state that in one half of these childless marriages the barrenness is due to venereal diseases. According to Dr. Prince A. Morrow, in his *Social Diseases and Marriage*, 75 per cent of the young men in the United States become impure before marriage. This serves to disseminate venereal diseases among the general population, especially among innocent women and children. The consequence is, on the one hand, a considerable number of sterile marriages and on the other hand a high infant mortality. It need not be assumed, as we have already said, that vice is more prevalent to-day than in previous generations, but on account of the conditions of our social life diseases which accompany vice are now more widely disseminated than they have been at any time in our previous history; therefore, even the physical results of vice are different to-day than they were a generation or more ago.

(4) Education has been alleged as a cause of decreasing birth rate in the native white American stock. This, however, is true only in a very qualified sense. While it is a fact, as collected statistics have shown, that if Harvard and other universities depended on children of their alumni for students their attendance would actually decrease in numbers, it is not true that college graduates have had a lower birth rate than the economic and social

classes to which they belong. So far as statistics have been collected, indeed, they seem to indicate that the wealthy uneducated are producing fewer children than the educated classes who associate with them. The influence decreasing the birth rate among the educated is, therefore, not education itself, but the high standards of living and the luxury of the classes with whom they associate.

On the other hand, the higher education of women seems to be, down to the present time, operating as a distinct influence to lessen the birth rate among the educated classes for the reason that apparently a majority of educated women do not marry. The higher education has not yet gone far enough, however, to give us any definite facts with which to judge what the ultimate effect of woman's higher education will be. If the higher education of woman is going to lead to a large per cent of the best and most intellectual women in society leading lives of celibacy, then, of course, ultimately the higher education of woman will be disastrous to the race. But probably the relative infrequency of marriage among women who are college graduates is a transitory phenomenon due to the fact that neither women nor men are as yet adjusted to the higher education of women.

(5) Some phases of the "woman's movement" have without doubt tended to lessen the birth rate in certain sections of American society. Some of the leaders of the woman's movement have advocated, for example, that women should choose a single life, while others have advocated that families should not have more than two children. Mrs. Ida Husted Harper, indeed, has gone so far as to claim that if families would have but two children this would be a cure-all for many social troubles. Indeed, this ideal of two children in the family has been so widely disseminated in this country that it is often spoken of as the "American Idea." Of course, such teachings could not be without some effect. Without attempting to reply to the advocates of this theory of but two children to a family, it will be sufficient to remark that for a population simply to remain stationary three children at least must be born to each family on the average; otherwise, if only two children are born, as one of the children is apt to die or fail to marry, the population will actually decrease in numbers. Under the best modern conditions one out of three children now born either fails to live to maturity or fails to reproduce. There must be, therefore, more than three children born to the average family for a population to grow. From the sociological point of view the ideal family would seem to be one in which from three to six children are born.

(6) Finally, not all of the childless and small families in the native American stock are due by any means to voluntary causes, or even involuntary causes of the kind that we have mentioned. There are also certain other obscure physiological causes at work producing sterility in American women. The

sterility of American women is greater than that of any other civilized population, even apart from the causes which have just been mentioned. Some say this is due to physical deterioration in the native white American stock, and there are other things which seem to point in that direction. It may be, however, that this deterioration is in no sense racial, but only individual, affecting certain individuals who lead a relatively unnatural life. Our American civilization puts a great strain upon certain elements of our population, and this strain in many cases falls even more upon the women than upon the men. The social life of the American people, in other words, is oftentimes such as to produce exhaustion and physical degeneracy, and this shows itself in the women of a population first of all in sterility. It is evident that the remedy for this cause is a more natural and more simple life on the part of all, if it is possible to bring this about.

Thus, the causes which influence birth rate are evidently very complex. In the main they are doubtless economic causes among all peoples, but there is no reason to believe that these economic causes act alone in determining birth rate, nor is there any reason to believe that the other psychological and biological causes may be in any way derived from the economic. So far as we can see, then, industrial conditions are mainly responsible for the lessened birth rate in the native white American stock. But mingled with these industrial conditions, operating as causes, are certain psychological (or moral) and biological factors that have to be considered as in the main independent. It is furthermore evident that the causes which lead to the decline and extinction of any population, whether civilized or uncivilized, are complex. All efforts to explain the extinction of peoples of antiquity, or modern nature peoples, such as the North American Indians and the Polynesians, through any single set of causes, must be looked at as unscientific. It can readily be shown that in all these cases the causes of the decline of the birth rate and the ultimate extinction of the stock are numerous and are not reducible to any single set of causes.

Causes which Influence the Death Rate. Before we can fully understand the causes of the growth of a population, that is, of the surplus of births over deaths, we must understand something also about the things which influence the death rate as well as the things which influence the birth rate, because, let it be borne in mind, the growth of a given population (excluding immigration always) is due to the combined working of these two factors.

Within certain limits the death rate is more easily controlled than the birth rate. It is very difficult for society deliberately to set about to increase the birth rate, but it is comparatively easy for it to take deliberate measures to decrease the death rate, because all individuals have a selfish interest in decreasing the death rate; but the increase of the birth rate does not appeal to the self-interest of individuals. Modern medical science, as we have seen, has done much to decrease the death rate in civilized countries, and it promises to do even more. Fifty years ago a death rate of fifty or sixty per thousand population in urban centers was not unusual, but now a death rate of thirty to forty in a thousand in the same communities is considered an intolerable disgrace, and the time will shortly come, no doubt, when even a death rate of twenty per thousand of the population will be considered disgraceful to any community. As we have already seen, the normal death rate of the most enlightened European and American communities tends to establish itself around fifteen or sixteen.

Of course the sanitary and hygienic conditions which influence the death rate are so numerous that we cannot enter into and discuss them. We can only mention some of the more general social influences which are often overlooked and are of particular interest to the sociologist.

(1) The effect of war upon the death rate, particularly of the victorious, is not so great as many people suppose. Considerable wars are apparently often waged without very greatly increasing the number of deaths in a given population. This is, however, only true, as has already been said, of the victorious side. With the defeated it is far different. The death rate among the defeated in a modern war is oftentimes very greatly raised, but this is due not so much to the large number killed in battle as to the fact that the defeated have their territory invaded, their industries disturbed, and their general industrial and living conditions depressed. The vital statistics of France and Germany in the Franco-Prussian War of 1870-1871 illustrate this point. In Germany the death rate in 1869, the year before the war, was 28.5; in 1870, the first year of the war, 29; and in 1871, the culminating year of the war, 31. These figures include the armies in the field. For France, however, the defeated party, the figures were far different. In 1869 the death rate in France was 23.4; in 1870, 28.3; in 1871, 34.8. Thus, while Germany had its death rate increased by the Franco-Prussian War merely 2.5 per thousand of the population, France had its death rate increased 11.4. From this it is plain that it is the economic disturbances which accompany war, and particularly those which are manifest among the defeated, which cause a very large part of the higher death rate.

(2) As already implied, then, economic depression exercises a very considerable influence upon death rate, particularly when economic depression causes very high prices for the necessities of life and even widespread scarcity of food. This cause produces far more deaths in modern nations than war. The doubling of the price of bread in any civilized country would be a far greater calamity than a great war. While modern civilized peoples fear famine but little, there are many classes in the great industrial nations that live upon such a narrow margin of existence

that the slightest increase in the cost of the necessities of life means practically the same as a famine to these classes. Statistics, therefore, of all modern countries, and particularly of all great cities, show an enormous increase in sickness and death among the poorer classes in times of economic depression.

(3) Climate and season are rather constant factors in the death rate of all communities. The rule here is that in northern countries the death rate is higher in winter, while in southern countries and in great cities the death rate is higher in summer. Taking 100 as an arbitrary standard, in Sweden in February deaths rise to 113, in August they go down to 79; while in Italy in February deaths are at 106 as compared with the standard, and in August at 111,—the period of minimum death rate in Italy being in the spring and autumn. In a great city like Berlin, if 100 be taken as the standard, deaths are 88 in February and 144 in August, owing very largely to the higher death rate of children in the summer months in great cities.

(4) The biological fact of sex also influences death rate. Males in general are shorter-lived than females. This is in part due to the fact that in human populations men are more exposed to the dangers of industry in earning a livelihood, while women are more secluded in the home. But this does not explain entirely the discrepancy in the death rate of the two sexes, for boy babies under the same conditions die more frequently than girl babies. As we have already seen, the female organism is the more stable, biologically, and hence females, while having less physical strength, have more vitality than males. In Great Britain the death rate (1872-1880) for the males was 22.7 per thousand of the male population annually, while the death rate for the females was 20.2 per thousand of their population annually.

(5) Conjugal condition is also a factor which affects death rate. The differences between the death rates of the married and unmarried have long been noted. The following table of the death rates of males and females of different conjugal classes between the ages of forty and fifty years (in Germany, 1876-1880), taken from Professor Mayo-Smith's *Statistics and Sociology*, illustrates this:

Single males .... 26.5 per thousand
Married males .... 14.2 " "
Widowed males .... 29.9 " "

Single females .... 15.4 " "
Married females .... 11.4 " "
Widows .... 13.4 " "

It will be seen from these figures that the death rate among the single is in all the more advanced years of life higher than among the married. The probable explanation of this, however, is not that the married state is better physiologically, as has been so often claimed, but that it is better socially. These figures are a testimony, in other words, to the social advantages of the home. Single persons, particularly in the more advanced years of life, who are without homes, are more liable to fall sick, and when sick are less liable to receive proper care. That these figures show the great social advantage of the home in preserving life is evident from the fact that among the widowed males, whose homes have been broken up, the death rate is higher even than among the single males. Moreover, in interpreting such statistics we must bear in mind that the unmarried in the higher ages of life are made up very often of those who are relatively abnormal, either physically or mentally, that is, of the biologically unfit. Inasmuch as the single persons include many of this class, and also lack the comforts of home, it is not surprising that the death rate is much higher among them.

(6) Infantile mortality is one of the most interesting phases of vital statistics. We have already said that the death rate is a good rough measure of a people's civilization. Even more can we say that the death rate among children, particularly those under one year of age, is an index to a people's sanitary and moral condition. Taking the world as a whole, it is still estimated that one half of all who are born die before the age of five years. This represents an enormous waste of energy. Even in many of the most civilized countries the death rate among children, and especially among infants under one year of age, is still comparatively high. Most of this death rate is unnecessary, could be avoided, and, as we have already said, represents a waste of life. Dr. Newman [Footnote: In his work on *Infant Mortality*.] gives the following statistics for different civilized countries for the ten-year period of 1894-1903. These statistics, we may note, are based on the percentage of deaths among children under one year of age and not upon the one thousand of their population. In Russia, 27 per cent of all children born during the ten-year period of 1894-1903 died the first year; in Germany, 19.5 per cent; in Italy, 17 per cent; in France, 15.5 per cent; in England, 15 per cent; in Ireland, 10 per cent; in Norway, 9.4 per cent; in New Zealand, 9.7 per cent; while in the United States in 1900, according to the census, 16.2 per cent of all children born in the registration area died the first year.

The Laws of the Growth of Population.—Can the growth of population be reduced to any principle or law? This is a problem which has puzzled social thinkers for a long time. Many have thought that the growth of population can be reduced to one or more relatively simple laws, but we have seen from analyzing the statistics of birth rate and death rate that this is hardly probable. A formula that would cover the growth of population would have to cover all of the variable causes influencing birth rate and death rate and so entering into the surplus of births over deaths. It is evident that these causes are too complex to be reduced to any such formula among modern civilized peoples. In the animal world and among uncivilized peoples, however, conditions are quite different, and the growth of population is regulated by certain very simple principles or laws. Thus it is probable that for centuries before the whites came, the Indians of North America were stationary in their population, for the reason that under their stationary condition of culture a given area could support only so many people. In conditions of savagery, and even of barbarism, therefore, we can lay down the principle that population will increase up to the limit of food supply, will stop there and remain stationary until food supply increases. This is the condition which governs the growth of the population of all animal species, and, as we have already said, of the savages and barbarians among the human species. But among civilized men who have attempted the control of physical nature, and to some extent even the control of human nature, many other factors enter in to influence both birth rate and death rate, and so the growth of the population.

Nevertheless, many social thinkers of the past have conceived, as has already been said, that the growth of population might be reduced to very simple and definite laws. Among the first who proposed laws governing population was an English economist, Thomas Robert Malthus, whose active career coincides with the first quarter of the nineteenth century. In 1798 Malthus put forth a little book which he entitled *An Essay on the Principle of Population as it affects the future improvement of society*. This essay went through numerous editions and revisions, and in it Malthus elaborated his famous economic theory of the growth of population. Inasmuch as this theory of Malthus has been the storm center of sociological and economic writers for the past one hundred years, it is worth our while to note very briefly what Malthus's theory was, and why it is inadequate as a scientific statement of the laws governing the growth of population.

Malthus's Theory of Population. In the first edition of his essay Malthus contended that population tends to increase in geometric ratio, while food at best will increase only in arithmetical ratio; and that this means that constant discrepancies between population and food supply would appear, with the result that population would have to be cut down to food supply. Later Malthus saw how crude this statement of his theory was and abandoned any attempt at mathematical statement, presenting substantially the following theory: (1) Population is necessarily limited by food; (2) Population always increases where food increases and tends to increase faster than food; (3) The checks that keep population down to food supply may be classified as positive and preventive. Positive checks are those which increase the death rate, such as famine, poverty, vice, disease, and the like. Preventive checks are those that decrease the birth rate, such as late marriage and prudence in the birth of children. Inasmuch as Malthus believed that the positive checks must always operate where the preventive checks did not, he advocated the use of the preventive checks as the best means to remedy human misery. The inherent tendency of population to outstrip food supply, Malthus believed to be the main source of human misery in all of its forms.

Criticisms of Malthus's Theory. (1) It is evident that Malthus's theory applies only to a stationary society, that is, a non-progressive society, because in a progressive society human invention and, therefore, food supply, may far outstrip any increase of population. This has been the case in practically all civilized countries during the nineteenth century, where improvements in machinery and agriculture have greatly increased the food supply. If it be replied that this increase of food is but temporary, and that sooner or later Malthus's theory must operate, then it may be said, on the other hand, that as yet we see no limit of man's mastery over nature, and that apparently we are just entering upon the stage of material progress. Moreover, so far as any given country is concerned, wealth is potential food supply, and in the United States during the last fifty years wealth has increased four times as fast as the population. Malthus, of course, did not foresee the inventions and agricultural progress of the nineteenth century. Still, it is evident that his theory is a static one and cannot be made to apply to any progressive society.

(2) Similarly, the theory makes no allowance for the increased efficiency which may come with increased population, because increase of population makes possible better coöperation. As we have already seen, coöperation and division of labor in a society depend upon the size of the group to a certain extent, that is, the larger the group there is for organization the better can be the organization and division of labor in that group. Every increase of population, therefore, opens up new and superior ways of applying labor; and coöperation and the division of labor make it possible for men to do more as a group than they could possibly accomplish working as individuals. Improved means of coöperation, therefore, operate very much the same way in human society in controlling nature as new inventions.

(3) The theory of Malthus makes no allowance for the general law of animal fertility, which is that as the rate of individual evolution increases the rate of reproduction decreases. Of course, Malthus's theory antedates this law of animal fertility, which was first stated by Herbert Spencer. Some scientists declare that this law does not apply within the human species, and it must be admitted that it is not yet certain that it does. As we have already seen, however, the lower and less individualized classes in human society

reproduce much more rapidly than the upper or more individualized classes. Increase of food supply, of wealth, and so on, does not necessarily mean increase of population, and the fatal error in Malthus's theory is that he assumes that wherever food increases population always increases also.

(4) The overpopulation which Malthus feared, so far from being an evil, has been shown by the labors of Darwin to be the condition essential to the working of the process of natural selection in the human species. Overpopulation, at least until artificial selection arrives, is not an evil, but a good in human society. Without it there would not be sufficient elimination of the unfit in human society to prevent wholesale social degeneration. Even with artificial selection, however, some overpopulation would be necessary for the working of any scheme of selection. We must conclude, then, that Malthus's theory, either as an explanation of the growth of modern populations or as an implied practical ethical doctrine, is of no value whatever.

This is not saying, of course, that Malthus's theory may not have some elements of truth in it. Undoubtedly Malthus's theory does apply to stationary, non-progressive peoples, like savages and barbarians in certain stages of culture, and also perhaps to certain classes in modern society who fail to participate in modern social progress. But these lower classes or elements in human society are constantly decreasing, especially in America, where the tendency to individual improvement is so marked. Again, Malthus's theory, so far as it depends upon the economic law of diminishing returns in agriculture, has also certain elements of truth in it, and in so far as it merely asserts that the struggle for existence in human society is, in the last analysis, a struggle for food. Finally, Malthus meant his theory chiefly as a criticism of socialistic and communistic schemes, which would equalize wealth and do away with competition in society. Unquestionably any such scheme to equalize wealth and do away with competition in society would result in the enormous increase of the lower and more brutal element of society—those that have not yet participated in modern culture. Malthus's theory as a criticism of socialistic schemes that would do away with competition (this, however, does not apply to modern scientific socialism) is unquestionably as good to-day as when it was written.

Most modern economists and sociologists recognize the failure of Malthus to formulate a successful theory of population, and so many have attempted to form theories independent of Malthus; but it must be said regarding most of these attempts that they have succeeded no better than Malthus. For example, a French economist and sociologist, Arsène Dumont, has formulated the theory that society is like a sponge so far as population is concerned,—that it will take up just as many new individuals as it has industrial room for, and that population will in all cases expand to meet these increased economic opportunities. Dumont's theory is that population will increase so far as what he calls the power of social capilarity extends. The law of population is, then, the capilarity of society. Where there are new economic opportunities population will increase; where there are no new economic opportunities there will be no increase. France has no new economic opportunities, so the population will not increase. The same is true of certain classes in the United States. This theory tries to make population depend even more entirely upon economic conditions than Malthus's theory. At first it appears more plausible than Malthus's theory, but this is probably because it is more vague. Economic influences are powerful influences, as we have already seen, in determining the growth of a population, but they are not the only ones. The factors which make up the surplus of births over deaths are so complex that they cannot possibly be lumped together and called collectively economic conditions. Dumont's theory of the growth of population has no more scientific value than Malthus's theory.

In conclusion, we may say that we are unable to formulate any laws of population which are worthy of the name of laws as yet, and it seems probable that, while we may understand clearly enough the factors which enter into the growth of population, we shall never be able to reduce these factors to a single formula or law. Social phenomena are too complex, we may here note, to reduce to simple formulas or laws as physical phenomena are reduced. Indeed, it is doubtful whether laws exist among social phenomena in the same sense in which they exist among physical phenomena, that is, as fixed relations among variable forces. Human society has in it another element than mechanical causation or physical necessity, namely, the psychic factor, and this so increases the complexity of social phenomena that it is doubtful if we can formulate any such hard and fixed laws of social phenomena as of physical phenomena. This is not saying, however, that social phenomena cannot be understood and that there are not principles which are at work with relative uniformity among them. It is only saying that the social sciences, even in their most biological or physical aspects, cannot be reduced to the same exactness as the physical sciences, though the knowledge which they offer may be in practice just as trustworthy.

SELECT REFERENCES

For brief reading:

MAYO-SMITH, *Statistics and Sociology*, Chaps. IV-VIII.
BAILEY, *Modern Social Conditions*, Chaps. III-VI.

For more extended reading:

BONAR, *Malthus and his Work.*
BOWLEY, *Elements of Statistics.*
MALTHUS, *Essay on the Principle of Population.*
NEWSHOLME, *Vital Statistics.*

CHAPTER IX

THE IMMIGRATION PROBLEM

In new countries population may increase by immigration as well as by the surplus of births over deaths. Immigration is, therefore, a secondary means of increasing the population of a country, and in new countries is often of great importance.

Immigration, or the migration of a people into a country, along with its correlative emigration, or the migration of a people out of a country, constitutes a most important social phenomenon. All peoples seem more or less migratory in their habits. Man has been a wanderer upon the face of the earth since the earliest times. According to modern anthropology the human species probably evolved in a relatively narrow area and peopled the earth by successive migrations to distant lands. In all ages, therefore, we find more or less migratory movements of populations. But the movements in modern times, particularly in the nineteenth century, probably exceed, in the number of individuals concerned, any other migratory movements of which we have knowledge in history. Ancient migrations were, moreover, somewhat different from modern immigration and emigration. Ancient migrations were largely those of peoples or tribes, while in modern times migration is more of an individual matter. The Huns, for example, came into Europe as a nation, but the immigration into the United States at the present time is wholly an individual movement. The causes of migration are more or less universal, but corresponding to the difference in ancient and modern migrations we find the causes varying somewhat in ancient and modern times. The causes of ancient migrations and the primary causes of all migrations seem to be: (1) lack of food; (2) lack of territory for an expanding population; (3) war. In modern times we find other causes operating, like, (4) the labor market; men now migrate chiefly to get better economic opportunities; (5) government; in modern times the oppression of unjust governments has often caused extensive migration; (6) religion; religious persecution and intolerance have in modern times been important among the causes of migration.

History of Immigration into the United States.—The great economic opportunities offered by the settlement of the vast territory of the United States, together with a combination of causes in Europe, partly political, partly religious, and partly economic, have caused, during the last century, a flood of immigrants from practically all European countries, to invade the United States, greater in number of individuals than any recorded migration in history. Between 1820, the first year for which we have immigration statistics, and 1907, 25,318,000 immigrants sought homes, temporarily or permanently, in this country,—more than one half of them coming since 1880. Before 1820 it is improbable that immigration into the United States assumed any large proportions. Even up to 1840 the number of immigrants was comparatively insignificant. Thus in 1839 the number was only 68,000, and not until 1842 did the number of immigrants first cross the 100,000 mark. Owing to the potato famine in Ireland in the forties, however, and to the unsuccessful revolution in Germany in 1848, the number of immigrants from Europe began greatly to increase. From 1851 to 1860 inclusive no less than 2,598,000 immigrants sought homes in this country. The number fell off greatly during the Civil War, and did not reach the same proportions again until the eighties, when from 1881 to 1890 the volume of immigration rose to 5,246,000. The number of immigrants again declined during the nineties, owing largely to the financial depression in the United States, to 3,800,000; but during the decade, 1901-1910, it surpassed all former records, and amounted to nearly 9,000,000.

It is curious to note how the maximum periods of immigration have hitherto been about ten or twenty years apart. Thus the first noteworthy maximum of 427,000, in 1854, was not surpassed again until 1873, when another maximum of 459,000 was recorded; in 1882 another maximum was reached of 788,000, and in 1903 another maximum of 857,000. After 1903, however, immigration went on increasing until 1907. These fluctuations in immigration correspond to the economic prosperity of the country, and, as Professor Commons has shown, are almost identical with the fluctuations in foreign imports. This shows very conclusively the prevailing economic character of modern migration.

During 1905, 1906, and 1907, indeed, the United States received more immigrants than its total population at the time of the Declaration of Independence. In 1905 the number was 1,027,000; in 1906, 1,100,000; in 1907, 1,285,000. It seems probable, however, that about twenty-five per cent will have to be deducted from these immigration statistics in prosperous years to allow for emigrants returning to their home countries. In a year of economic depression like 1908 when only 782,000 immigrants entered the country, the number of emigrants returning was over one half of the total number who entered.

Previous to 1890, nearly all of the immigrants who came to us came from the countries of Northern Europe. It has been claimed that as high as ninety per cent came from Teutonic and Celtic countries, and were, accordingly, almost of the same blood as the early settlers; but since 1890 the character of our immigration has changed so that since that time nearly seventy per cent have come from non-Teutonic countries, such as Russia,

Austria-Hungary, Italy, and Greece. The period of maximum immigration for the Irish to this country was the forties and fifties; the period of maximum immigration for the Germans was the fifties and eighties; and for the English, the seventies and eighties. But the period of maximum immigration for the Italians can scarcely as yet be reckoned by decades at all. The Italians first began coming in numbers exceeding 100,000 only in 1900, but in 1906, 273,000 of our immigrants were Italians, and in 1907, 285,000. This latter number is larger than any single European nationality ever sent to us in a single year, unless we except the 338,000 people of various nationalities sent to us by Austria-Hungary in the same year. The immigration from Austria-Hungary, also, to the United States did not exceed 100,000 until the year 1900, but by 1905 it had reached 275,000, and, as has been said, in 1907 reached 338,000. The immigration from Russia, consisting largely of Russian Jews and Poles began to be considerable, if we include Poland in Russia, by 1892, when it reached 122,000. In 1903, after falling off, it reached 136,000; in 1906, 215,000; and in 1907, 258,000.

Present Sources of our Immigration. These statistics have been cited to show the change in the sources from which we are receiving immigrants. This can be brought out still more clearly by contrasting a typical year previous to 1890 with one of the latest years. The year 1882 was the year, previous to 1890, of maximum immigration into this country. During that year we received 788,000 immigrants. Nearly all, as the table which we are about to give will show, came from countries of Northern Europe. In order to contrast the sources of our immigration a quarter of a century ago with the present sources, we will compare the year 1882 with the year 1907, which thus far has been the year of maximum immigration into the United States,—the total number of immigrants for 1907 being 1,285,000:

IMMIGRATION, 1882.

Per cent.

Great Britain and Ireland 179,423 22.8
Germany 250,630 31.7
Scandinavia 105,326 13.3
Netherlands, France, Switzerland, etc. 27,795 3.5

Total Western Europe 71.3

Italy 32,159 4.1
Austria-Hungary 29,150 3.7
Russia, etc. 22,010 2.7

Total Southern and Eastern Europe 10.5

All other countries .... 18.2 [Footnote: 1. Of the immigration from "other countries" 98,295 was from British North America, or 12.4 per cent of the total. This,added to the 71.3 per cent from Western Europe, makes a total of 83.7 of the immigrants in 1882 of West European stock.]

100.0

IMMIGRATION,   1907.

Per cent.

Great Britain and Ireland 113,567 8.8
Scandinavia 49,965 3.9
Germany 37,807 2.9
Netherlands, France, Switzerland, etc. 26,512 2.1

Total Western Europe 17.7

Austria-Hungary 338,452 26.3
Italy 285,731 22.2
Russia 258,943 20.1
Greece, Servia, Roumania, etc. 88,482 6.9

Total Southern and Eastern Europe 75.5

All other countries 6.8

100.0

It will be noted that while in 1882, 71.3 per cent of our immigrants came from the countries of Western Europe, only 10.5 per cent came from the countries of Southern and Eastern Europe. In 1907 the situation was very nearly reversed. In 1907 Great Britain and Ireland, and Scandinavia, Germany, The Netherlands, Belgium, France, and Switzerland—the countries which had furnished 71.3 per cent of our immigrants in 1882— furnished only 17.7 per cent, while Austria-Hungary, Italy, Russia, Greece, Servia, Roumania, and Turkey in Europe—the countries which had furnished but 10.5 per cent in 1882—furnished 75.5 per cent. This matter of changed sources from which we receive our immigrants evidently is one of first importance in any consideration of the present immigration problem of the United States.

The Distribution of Immigrants. If immigrants would distribute themselves evenly over the United States, the immigration problem would be quite different from what it is. Instead of this, there is a massing of immigrants in some states and communities, and very little evidence to show that these immigrants ever distribute themselves normally over the whole country. In 1906, for example, the Commissioner of Immigration reported that 68.3

per cent of the 1,100,000 immigrants who came that year went to the North Atlantic states; 22.1 per cent to the North Central states; 4.4 per cent to the Western states; and 4.2 per cent to the Southern states. If these figures are at all trustworthy, they indicate a congestion of our recent immigrants in the North Atlantic states and in certain states of the Central West. So far as the census is concerned, it tends to confirm these statistics of the Commissioner of Immigration. Our last census returns, being for 1900, can show little, of course, of the distribution of the great number of recent immigrants that have come from Southern and Eastern Europe. Still the 1900 census contains some interesting facts regarding the distribution of foreign born, or immigrants, that have been received previous to 1900. According to the census of 1900 the number of foreign born in the United States was 10,460,000, or 13.7 per cent of the total population. But these foreign born were confined almost entirely to the Northern states, that is, the North Atlantic states and North Central states. In 1900 the Southern states (South Atlantic and South Central) contained but 4.6 per cent of the total foreign born of the country. The reason why so few of our immigrants have thus far settled in the South is perhaps chiefly because of the competition which the cheap negro labor of the South would offer to them, and also because the South is still largely agricultural, offering few opportunities for the industrial employments, into which a majority of our immigrants go. In the North Atlantic states in 1900 nearly one fourth of the population was foreign born, and 20.7 per cent in the Western states. The following statistics will show the percentage of foreign born in typical states: North Dakota, 35.4 per cent; Rhode Island, 31.4 per cent; Massachusetts, 30 per cent; Minnesota, 28.9 per cent; New York, 26 per cent; Wisconsin, 24.9 per cent; California, 24.7 per cent; Montana, 27.6 per cent; Indiana, 8.5 per cent; Maryland, 7.9 per cent; Missouri, 7 per cent; North Carolina, 0.2 per cent; and Mississippi, 0.5 per cent. The influence of the foreign born in a community, however, is better shown, perhaps, if we consider the number of those of foreign parentage, that is, the foreign born and their children, than if we consider the number of foreign born alone. In a large number of states more than one half of the population is of foreign parentage. Thus North Dakota had in 1900, 77.5 per cent of its population of foreign parentage; Minnesota, 74.9 per cent; Wisconsin, 71.2 per cent; Rhode Island, 64.2 per cent; Massachusetts, 62.3 per cent; South Dakota, 61.1 per cent; Utah, 61.2 per cent; New York, 59.4 per cent. Connecticut, New Jersey, Illinois, Michigan, Montana, Nevada, and California all also had more than one half of their population of foreign parentage in 1900. For the United States as a whole the number of foreign parentage in 1900 amounted to 34.3 per cent, or 26,000,000 out of a total population of 76,000,000. Many of our large cities also have a high percentage of foreign born and of foreign parentage in their population. The percentage of foreign born in some of our largest cities in 1900 was as follows:

Per cent.

New York.. 37
Chicago... 34.6
Philadelphia.. 22.8
Saint Louis... 19.4
Boston.. 35.1
Baltimore... 13.5
San Francisco....................................... 34.1
Cleveland... 32.6

These same cities had the following percentage of foreign parentage in their population:

Per cent.

New York.. 76.9
Chicago... 77.4
Philadelphia.. 54.9
St. Louis... 61.0
Boston.. 72.2
Baltimore... 38.2
San Francisco....................................... 75.2
Cleveland... 75.6

These figures show the tendency of our immigrants to mass together in certain states and also in our great cities; so that it has come about that it is said that New York is the largest German city in the world except Berlin; the largest Italian city except Rome; the largest Polish city except Warsaw, and by far the largest Jewish city in the world.

Only one nationality distributes itself relatively evenly over the country, and that is the British. All other nationalities have certain favorite sections in which they settle. Thus, the Irish settle mainly in the North Atlantic states; the Germans have two favorite settlements in the United States, one of them consisting of New York and Pennsylvania, and the other of Wisconsin and Illinois, though Michigan, Iowa, and Missouri also contain a large number of Germans. The Scandinavians locate chiefly in the Northwest, especially in Minnesota, North and South Dakota; and the large number of foreign parentage in those states is due to Scandinavian immigration. All these nationalities, however, readily assimilate with our population, as they have very largely the same social and political standards and ideals. But this is not true regarding some of the more recent immigrants from Southern and Eastern Europe, whose massing in large communities of their own must be regarded as a more serious matter. The census does not help us to find out how far these recent immigrants have massed in certain localities, but the Commissioner of Immigration has kept statistics of the destination of these recent immigrants, and they show the following results: In 1907, of the 294,000 Italian speaking immigrants who came to us in that year, 120,000 settled in the state of New York; 53,000 in Pennsylvania; 19,000 in Massachusetts; and 17,000 in New Jersey. Three fourths of the Italian immigrants, in other words, apparently go to these four states. Of the 138,000 Poles who came in 1907, 33,000 were bound to Pennsylvania, 31,000 to New York, 12,000 to New Jersey, and 17,000 to Illinois. These four states seem to constitute the favorite places of settlement for the Slavs. Of the 149,000 Russian and Polish Hebrews who came in 1907, 93,000 settled in New York state, 15,000 in Pennsylvania, and 9000 in Massachusetts, these three states being the favorite places of settlement for recent Jewish immigrants.

It seems clear from these figures that the congestion of recent immigrants is serious, and it is a question whether with such congestion it will be possible to assimilate these recent comers, so unlike ourselves in social traditions and ideals, to the American type. It is claimed by some that there is no serious congestion of immigrants in this country, and that the immigrants distribute themselves through the operation of normal economic influences in the places where they are most needed, and that we need not, therefore, be concerned about the congestion of foreign born in certain communities. This view, however, that economic laws or forces will sufficiently attend to this matter of the distribution of our immigrants, is not borne out by the facts of ordinary observation and experience.

The Distribution of Immigrants in Industry. It is probably safe to say that four fifths of our recent immigrants belong to the unskilled class of laborers, though the percentage of unskilled fluctuates greatly from year to year and from nationality to nationality. Out of the total of 1,285,000 immigrants in 1907 only 12,600 were recorded by the Commissioner of Immigration as belonging to the professional classes; 190,000, or about 15 per cent, were skilled laborers, including all who had any trade; while 760,000 were unskilled laborers, including farm and day laborers, 304,000 being persons of no occupation, including women and children. When we consider the matter by races, the contrast is even more striking. Of the 242,000 South Italian immigrants in 1907 only 701 were professional men; 26,000, or 11 per cent, were skilled laborers; while the number of unskilled amounted to 161,000, or 66 per cent. Of the 138,000 Poles who came in 1907, only 273 were professional men; 8000, or 6 per cent, were skilled laborers; and 107,000, or 77 per cent, were unskilled. In the case of the Hebrews, however, there is a much higher percentage of skilled laborers and professional men. It is claimed by those who favor the policy of unrestricted immigration that what this country needs at present is a large supply of unskilled laborers, and so the fact that the mass of immigrants belong to the unskilled class of laborers, it is said, is no objection to them.

Again, the census of 1900 shows a very uneven distribution of the foreign born among the different classes of occupations. Thus, while the foreign born constituted about one seventh of the population, over one third of those engaged in manufacturing were foreign born; one half of those engaged in mining were foreign born; one fourth of those engaged in transportation were foreign born; one fourth of those engaged in domestic service were also foreign born, while only one eighth of those engaged in agriculture were foreign born. This shows that the tendency of the foreign born is to mass in such industries as mining, manufacturing, and transportation. It is undoubtedly in these industries that there is the greatest demand for cheap labor, and the presence of a large number of unskilled foreign laborers has made it possible for the American capitalists to develop these industries under such conditions probably faster than they would otherwise have been developed. At the same time, however, all of this has been a hardship to the native-born American laborer, and the tendency has been to eliminate the native born from these occupations to which the immigrants have flocked.

Some Other Social Effects of Immigration.—(1) The influence on the proportion of the sexes of immigration into this country has without doubt been considerable. In 1907, out of a total of 1,285,349 immigrants, 929,976 were males and 355,373 were females. For a long period of years about two thirds of all the immigrants into the United States have been males. This has considerably affected the proportion of the sexes in the United States, making the males about 1,000,000 in excess in our population. The influence of such a discrepancy in the proportion of the sexes is difficult to state, but it is obvious, from all that has previously been said about the importance of the numerical equality of the sexes in society, that the influence must be a considerable one, and that not for good.

(2) The following table shows how far the increase of population in the United States in the decennial periods since 1800 has been due to immigration and to reproduction. Until 1840 the increase by immigration was so small as to be hardly noticeable, and therefore no account of it is taken.

Total Increase By Immigration By Birth
Year Per cent. Per cent. Per cent.

1800 35.70 1810 36.38 1820 34.07 1830 33.55 1840 32.67 4.66 28.01 1850
35.87 10.04 25.83 1860 35.58 11.12 24.46 1870 22.63 7.25 15.38 1880 30.08
7.29 22.79 1890 24.86 10.40 15.40 1900 20.73 5.86 14.87

This table shows that it is not certain that immigration has increased the total population of the United States, as a decrease of the natural birth rate seems to have accompanied increasing immigration. For this reason Professor Francis A. Walker held that it was doubtful that immigration had added anything to the population of the United States. At any rate, the population of the country was increasing just as rapidly before the large volume of immigration was received as it increased at any later time. Again, the Southern states, which have received practically no immigrants since the Civil War, have increased their population as rapidly as the Northern states, that is, the increase of population among the Southern whites has been equal to that of the Northern assisted by immigration. These two facts suggest that the immigrants have simply displaced an equal number of native born who would have been furnished by birth rate if the immigrants had never come.

(3) Immigration has very largely aided in maintaining a considerable amount of illiteracy in the United States in spite of the effects of the propaganda for popular education which has been carried on now for the last fifty years or more. In 1900 there were still 6,246,000 illiterates above the age of ten years in the United States, which was 10.7 per cent of the population above that age. Of these, about 3,200,000 were whites, and of this number, again, 1,293,000 were foreign born. Nearly all of the native white illiterates in the United States are found in the Southern states, the white illiteracy in the Northern states being practically confined to the foreign born. Thus, in the state of New York 5.5 per cent are illiterate, but of the native whites only 1.2 per cent are illiterate, while 14 per cent of the foreign population can neither read nor write. Again, in Massachusetts 5 per cent of the population are illiterate, but of the native whites only 0.8 per cent are illiterate, while 14.6 per cent of the foreign born are illiterate. Statistics of illiteracy for our cities show the same results. Thus, in the city of New York 6.8 per cent of the population are illiterate, but only 0.4 per cent of the native whites are illiterate, while 13.9 per cent of the foreign born are illiterate. Boston has 5.1 per cent of its total population illiterate, but only 0.2 per cent of its native white population are illiterate, while 11.3 per cent of its foreign-born population are illiterate. Of the total immigration in 1907, 30 per cent were illiterate. The number of illiterates from different countries varies greatly. In 1907, 53 per cent of the immigrants from Southern Italy were illiterate. In the same year 40 per cent of the Poles were illiterate, 25 per cent of the Slovaks from Austria, 56 per cent of the Ruthenians from Austria, 29 per cent of the Russian Jews, and 54 per cent of the Syrians. The bulk of our

immigration is now made up of these people from Southern and Eastern Europe, among whom the illiteracy is high. It is interesting to contrast the condition of these people with the immigrants from Northern and Western Europe, whence our immigration was mainly received a few years ago. The percentage of illiteracy among the immigrants from Western Europe is very low. Thus, in 1907 among the French it was only 4 per cent; among the Germans, 4 per cent; Irish, 3 per cent; English, 2 per cent; and Scandinavians, less than 1 per cent. Connected more or less with this fact of illiteracy is the number in our population who cannot speak English. In 1900 the number of persons in the United States above the age of ten years who could not speak English was reported by the census to be 1,463,000, but it is probable, owing to the recent large immigration, that the number is at least twice that at the present time.

(4) Crime and Poverty. It is said that crime is apt to accompany migration. However, down to 1904 our immigrants have not shown any exaggerated tendency to crime. The special prison census of 1904 showed that 23.7 per cent of the male white prisoners were foreign born, while 23 per cent of the general male white population above the age of fifteen years were foreign born. This shows a tendency to crime among the foreign born not greatly out of proportion to their numbers in the population. The same census, however, showed that 29.8 per cent of all white male prisoners committed during 1904 were born of foreign parents, while this element constituted only 18.8 per cent of the general white male population. Thus, among the children of the foreign born there appears to be an exaggerated tendency to crime, while not among the foreign born themselves. The probable explanation of this is that the children of the foreign born are often reared in our large cities, and particularly in the slum districts of those cities. Thus the high criminality of the children of the foreign born is perhaps largely a product of urban life, but it may be suggested also that the children of the foreign born lack adequate parental control in their new American environment. Certain elements among our immigrants, however, seem strongly predisposed to crime. This is especially true of the Southern Italian. For example, the census of 1904 showed that 6.1 per cent of the foreign-born prisoners committed during 1904 were Italian, while Italians constituted but 4.7 per cent of the total foreign-born population. Moreover, if we consider simply serious offenses, the evidence of the criminality of the Italian immigrant is even still more striking, for 14.4 per cent of the foreign-born major offenders committed during 1904 were Italians, while, as was just said, Italians constituted only 4.7 per cent of the total foreign-born population.

In the matter of poverty and dependence the foreign born make a more unfavorable showing. In the special census report on paupers for 1904 the proportion of foreign born among almshouse paupers was about twice as great as among the native born. Again, in a special investigation conducted by the Commissioner of Immigration in the year 1907-1908, out of 288,395 inmates of charitable institutions there were 60,025 who were foreign born, or about 21 per cent, and out of 172,185 inmates of insane hospitals, 50,734, or about 29 per cent, were foreign born. Inasmuch as the foreign born probably did not constitute in 1907-1908 more than 15 or 16 per cent of the total population of both sexes, it is seen that the foreign born contribute out of their proportion both to inmates of charitable institutions and to the number of the insane. The experience of Charity Organization Societies in our large cities, especially New York, confirms these findings. It is not surprising, indeed, that many of our immigrants should soon need assistance after landing in this country, inasmuch as a very large proportion of them come to the United States bringing little or no money with them. Thus, for a number of years the amount of money brought by immigrants from Russia has varied from nine to fifteen dollars per head. On account of the difficulties of economic adjustment in a new country it is not surprising, then, that many of the immigrants become more or less dependent, some temporarily and some permanently.

Immigration into Other Countries.—It has been suggested that with the opening up of other new countries the immigration problem of the United States would solve itself, and that so many emigrants from Europe will soon be going to South America, South Africa, and Australia that this country will be in no danger of receiving more than its share. Down to recent years, however, there have been little or no signs of such a diversion of the stream of immigration from Europe into those countries. The principal countries which receive immigrants other than the United States are Brazil, Argentina, Canada, and Australia. While Brazil has received between 1855 and 1904 a total of 2,096,000 immigrants, the present number of immigrants into Brazil seems to be comparatively small, for in 1904 it was only 12,400. Argentina, next to the United States, receives the most considerable immigration from Europe. From 1857 to 1906 Argentina received 3,639,000 immigrants. In 1906 the number was 252,000, of whom 127,000 were Italian, 17,000 Russian Hebrews, and the remainder from various European nationalities. The foreign immigration into other South American countries is comparatively insignificant. In 1906 Australia received 148,000 immigrants, most of whom were British, but the emigration from Australia almost equaled the immigration into Australia in that year. Again, in 1906 the Dominion of Canada received 189,000 immigrants, chiefly from Great Britain and the United States. An unknown number, however, of Canadians migrated across the border into the United States,—no record being kept of Canadian immigration into the United States since 1885, except of those who come by way of seaports. Thus it is certain that the United States receives more immigration at the present time than all the other countries of the world combined, and, as we have said, there is as yet little or no evidence that the stream of European emigration will be diverted for some years to come to these other countries. The problem of immigration in the United States is not, therefore, a problem of the past, but is still a problem of the future. Therefore, the question of reasonable restrictions upon immigration into this country and of the improvement of the immigrants that we admit is still a pressing problem of the day.

Proposed Immigration Restrictions.—There are no good moral or political grounds to exclude all immigrants from this country. The question is not one of the prohibition of immigration, but one of reasonable restrictions upon immigration, or, as Professor Commons has said, of the *improvement* of immigration.

There can be no question as to the moral right of the United States to restrict immigration. If it is our duty to develop our institutions and our national life in such a way that they will make the largest possible contribution to the good of humanity, then it is manifestly our duty to exclude from membership in American society elements which might prevent our institutions from reaching their highest and best development. All restrictions to immigration, it must be admitted, must be based, not upon national selfishness, but upon the principle of the good of humanity; and there can be no doubt that the good of humanity demands that every nation protect its people and its institutions from elements which may seriously threaten their stability and survival. The arguments in favor of further restrictions upon the immigration into this country may be summed up along four lines:

(1) *The Industrial Argument.* Many of the immigrants work for low wages, and, as we have already seen, offer such competition that the native born, in certain lines of industry, are almost entirely eliminated. This has been, no doubt, a hardship to the native-born American workingman. While we have been zealous to protect the American workingman from the unfair competition of European labor by high protective tariffs, yet inconsistently we have permitted great numbers of European laborers to compete with the American workingman upon his own soil. On the other hand, this large supply of cheap labor, as we have already seen, has enabled American capitalists to develop American industries very rapidly, to dominate in many cases the markets of the world, and to add greatly to the wealth of the country. It has been chiefly the large employers of labor in the United States, together with the steamship companies, who have opposed any considerable restrictions upon immigration, and thus far their power with Congress has successfully prevented the passing of stringent immigration

laws. On the whole, it is probably true that if industrial arguments alone are to be taken into consideration upon the immigration problem, the weight of the argument would be on the side of unrestricted immigration. But industrial arguments are not the only ones to be taken into consideration in considering the immigration problem, and this has been hitherto one of the great mistakes of many in discussing the problem.

(2) *The Social Argument.* Many of our recent immigrants are at least very difficult of social assimilation. They are clannish, tend to form colonies of their own race in which their language, customs, and ideals are preserved. This is especially true of the illiterate immigrants from Southern and Eastern Europe. As we have already seen, the rate of illiteracy among certain of our recent immigrants is so high that they can scarcely be expected to participate in our social life. Just the social effect of such colonies of different peoples and nationalities upon our own social life and institutions cannot well be foreseen, but it can scarcely be a good effect. The public school, it is true, does much to assimilate to American ideals and standards the children of even the most unassimilable immigrants. The public school is not as yet, however, a perfect agency of socialization, and even when attended by the children of these immigrants they fail to receive from it, in many cases, the higher elements of our culture and still continue to remain essentially foreign in their thought and actions.

(3) *The Political Argument.* Many of these immigrants are, therefore, incapable of understanding and appreciating our free institutions. They are not fit to vote intelligently, but are nevertheless quickly naturalized and form a very large per cent of our voting population, especially in our large cities. As a rule, they do not sell their votes, but their votes are often under the control of a few leaders, and thus they are able to hold, oftentimes, the balance of power between parties and factions. It is questionable whether free institutions can work successfully under such conditions.

(4) *The Racial or Biological Argument.* Undoubtedly the strongest arguments in favor of further restriction upon immigration into the United States are of a biological nature. The peoples that are coming to us at present belong to a different race from ours. They belong to the Slavic and Mediterranean subraces of the white race. Now, the Slavic and Mediterranean races have never shown the capacity for self-government and free institutions which the peoples of Northern and Western Europe have shown. It is doubtful if they have the same capacity for self-government. Moreover, the whole history of the social life and social ideals of these people shows them to have been in their past development very different from ourselves. Of course, if heredity counts for nothing it will only be a few generations before the descendants of these people will be as good Americans as any. But this is the question, Does heredity count for nothing? or does blood

tell? Are habits of acting and, therefore, social and institutional life, dependent, more or less, on the biological heredity of peoples, or are they entirely independent of such biological influence? There is much diversity of opinion upon this question, but perhaps the most trustworthy opinion inclines to the view that racial heredity, even between subraces of the white race, is a factor of great moment and must be taken into account. It is scarcely probable that a people of so different racial heredity from ourselves as the Southern Italians, for example, will develop our institutions and social life exactly as those of the same blood as ourselves. It is impossible to think that the Latin temperament would express itself socially in the same ways as the Teutonic temperament. Certainly the coming to us of the vast numbers of peoples from Southern and Eastern Europe is destined to change our physical type, and it seems also probable that if permitted to go on it will change our mental and social type also. Whether this is desirable or not must be left for each individual to decide for himself.

Another phase of this biological argument is the necessity of selection, if we are to avoid introducing into our national blood the degenerate strains of the oppressed peoples of Southern and Eastern Europe. If selection counts in the life of a people, as practically all biologists agree, then the American people certainly have a great opportunity to exercise selection on a large scale to determine who shall be the parents of the future Americans. While it is undesirable, perhaps, to discriminate among immigrants on the ground of race, it would certainly be desirable to select from all peoples those elements that we could most advantageously incorporate into our own life. The biological argument alone, therefore, seems to necessitate the admission of the importance of rigid selection in the matter of whom we shall admit into this country. At present, however, almost nothing is being accomplished in the way of insuring such a selection of the most fit. All that is attempted at the present time is to eliminate the very least fit, and the elimination amounts to only about one per cent of all who come to us.

Our present immigration laws debar a number of classes, chiefly, however, persons suffering from loathsome or dangerous diseases, persons who are paupers or likely to become public charges, and contract laborers, besides Chinese laborers. Practically all who are debarred at the present time come under these heads. Other classes who are debarred, however, are idiots, imbeciles, epileptics, insane, criminals, assisted immigrants, polygamists, anarchists, prostitutes, and procurers. Only an insignificant number, however, of immigrants are debarred upon these latter grounds. In 1907, with a total immigration of 1,285,000, only 13,064 were debarred as coming under these excluded classes, or a trifle over one per cent. For a number of years, indeed, since we have had any restriction laws at all, the number debarred has been a trifle over one per cent. Of course, this constitutes no adequate selection of immigrants which would satisfy biological or even high social requirements. It would seem, therefore, that our immigration laws, from a biological and sociological standpoint, are extremely deficient and that some means of more adequate selection among immigrants should speedily be found.

It has been suggested that a better selection of immigrants may be secured by imposing an illiteracy test upon all male immigrants between the ages of sixteen and fifty years coming to us, excluding those male immigrants between these ages who cannot read or write in some language. It is not proposed that this test should take the place of the present restrictions, but should be in addition to the present restrictions. It is argued by those who favor this test: (1) that it would exclude those elements that we desire to exclude, namely, the illiterates from Southern and Eastern Europe; (2) that it is easy to apply this test; (3) that immigrants would know before leaving European ports whether they would be admitted or not; (4) that such a test would have a favorable educational and, therefore, social effect upon the countries from which we now draw our largest proportion of illiterate immigrants.

It would seem, however, that the more important tests should be certain tests as to biological, social, and economic fitness. It would be no hardship upon any one for this country to require that all immigrants come up to a certain biological standard and that this standard should be a very strict one, say, the same as that required for admission to the United States army; and that furthermore they should possess enough money to insure the probability of their economic adjustment in this country. Such tests, moreover, might be enforced by our government practically without cost, as the burden of making such tests could be placed entirely upon the steamship companies that bring immigrants to the United States. It has been shown that a heavy fine of from one hundred to five hundred dollars for every person that is brought to the United States that does not conform to the requirements of our immigration laws is sufficient to make the steamship companies exercise a very stringent selection upon all whom they bring to us as immigrants.

Finally, something may probably be done to secure a better distribution of our immigrants through the coöperation of the federal government with state immigration societies, and with various private employment and philanthropic agencies. In any case the requirement that the immigrant shall possess beyond his ticket a certain amount of money, say $25.00, would help to secure a wider distribution of our immigrants.

Asiatic Immigration.—What has been said regarding there being no good social or political argument for the prohibition of immigrants does not apply to Asiatic immigration. Here the importance of the racial factor becomes so pronounced that it may well be doubted if a policy of exclusion toward Asiatic immigration would not be the wisest in the long run for the people of this country.

It is true that but few Asiatic immigrants have as yet come to this country, but there are grave reasons for believing that if the policy of exclusion had not been adopted a quarter of a century ago, Asiatic immigration would now constitute a very considerable proportion of our total immigration. It is chiefly the Chinese who are the main element in Asiatic immigration, and between 1851 and 1900 the Chinese sent us a total of only 310,000 immigrants; but in 1882, the year before the first Chinese Exclusion Law was put into effect, 39,000 Chinese immigrants entered the United States, and if their rate of increase had been kept up the Chinese would now be sending us from 100,000 to 300,000 immigrants annually. The Chinese Exclusion Act of 1882, reenacted and strengthened again in 1892 and in 1902, excluded all Chinese laborers from the United States. Consequently in 1890 the census showed only a total of 107,000 Chinese in this country, and in 1900 only 93,283, exclusive of Hawaii. In Hawaii, however, there were 25,767 Chinese in 1900, most of whom were residents of the islands previous to the annexation. The Chinese in continental United States were, moreover, massed in 1900 chiefly in the Pacific Coast states, there being 67,729 Chinese in the Rocky Mountain and Pacific Coast states, of which number 45,753 were in California alone.

In judging this question of Asiatic immigration we should accept to a certain extent the opinion of the people of the Pacific Coast regarding the problems which these Asiatic immigrants create. At any rate, the opinion of any group of people who are closest to a social problem should not be disregarded, as there are probabilities of error on the part of the distant observer of conditions as well as on the part of those who stand very close to a social problem. Just as we should accept the opinion of the Southern people in regard to the negro problem as worth something, so we should accept the judgment of the people of our Western states in regard to the Chinese and Japanese also as worth something. Now, as regards the Chinese, the people of the Pacific Coast say they would rather have the negro among them than the Chinese. They have numerous objections to the Chinese, similar to the various lines of argument which have already been given in favor of the restriction of immigration. They say, namely, (1) that the Chinese work for wages below the minimum necessary to maintain life for the white man, and so reduce the standard of living and crowd out the white working-man. There can scarcely be any question that the white laboring man is not able to compete economically with the Chinese laborer.

(2) Again, they claim that the Chinese make no contribution to the welfare of the country; that they come here to remain several years, to attain a competence, and then return to China.

(3) It is claimed that the Chinese are grossly immoral, that they are addicted to the opium habit and other vices, and that so few women come among the Chinese immigrants that Chinese men menace the virtue of white women.

(4) The Chinese do not readily assimilate. They keep their language, religion, and customs. They live largely by themselves, and are even more completely isolated from American social life than the negro. In comparison with them, indeed, one is struck with the fact that the negro has our customs, our religion, our language, and, in so far as he has been able to attain them, our moral standards, but this is not the case with the Chinese. It is, moreover, impossible for the Chinese to assume the white man's standards without losing his own social position among members of his own race.

(5) The last and strongest argument in favor of the general exclusion of Chinese laborers from this country, however, is the racial argument. The Chinese are just as different in race from us as the negro, and if racial heredity counts for anything it is fatuous to hope to assimilate them to the social type of the whites. Moreover, if we should open our doors to the mass of Chinese laborers China would be able to swamp us with Chinese immigrants. With its hundreds of millions of population China could spare to us several hundred thousand immigrants each year without feeling the loss. If we wish to keep the western third of our country, therefore, a white man's country it would be well not to open the doors to Chinese immigrants. It is certain that if we open our doors to the mass of Chinese immigrants we shall have another racial problem in the West such as we now have in the South with the negro. Those who claim upon the basis of sentiment or humanity that we should open our doors and attempt to civilize and christianize the flood of Chinese who would come to us, probably do not appreciate fully the social status of the Chinese or the social status of the American people. The truth is we are not yet ourselves enough civilized to undertake the work of civilizing and christianizing a very considerable number of people alien to ourselves in race, religion and social ideals. Again, those who advocate the free admission of the Chinese probably do not appreciate the importance of the element of racial heredity in social problems. The negro problem should have taught us by this time that this factor of racial heredity is not to be discounted altogether.

All that has been said regarding Chinese immigration applies to Asiatic immigration in general. It is not surprising, therefore, that since the

Japanese laborers have begun to come to us in large numbers the people of the Pacific Coast should demand the exclusion of the Japanese immigrants. While Japan has not the immense population of China and while the Japanese are perhaps a more adaptable people than the Chinese, still it would seem that in the main the people of the Pacific Coast are justified in their fears of the results of a large Japanese immigration. For the peace of both countries and of the world, therefore, it is to be hoped that the flow of Japanese laborers into the Western states will be checked without any disruption of the friendship of the United States and Japan. The same thing can be said regarding the Hindoo immigrants who are just beginning to come to us. It would appear that the wisest policy, therefore, regarding, all Asiatic immigration is the exclusion of Asiatic laborers, and as these would constitute over nine tenths of all Asiatic immigrants who might come to us, this would assure a practical solution of the problem.

SELECT REFERENCES

For brief reading:

COMMONS, *Races and Immigrants in America.*
HALL, *Immigration and Its Effect upon the United States.*
MAYO-SMITH, *Emigration and Immigration.*

For more extended reading:

GROSE, *The Incoming Millions.*
STEINER, *On the Trail of the Immigrant.*
WHELPLEY, *The Problem of the Immigrant.*
Reports of the United States Commissioner-General of Immigration.

On Chinese Immigration:

COOLIDGE, *Chinese Immigration.*

CHAPTER X

THE NEGRO PROBLEM

Already we have been brought in our study of the immigration problem to race problems—problems of the relations of races to one another and of their mutual adjustment. The negro problem is one of many race problems which the United States has, but because it is the most pressing of all of our race problems it is frequently spoken of as *the race problem*. An unsolved factor in all race problems is the biological influence of racial heredity, and this factor we must seek to understand and estimate at the very outset of any scientific study of the negro problem.

Racial Heredity as a Factor in Social Evolution.—We have already seen that racial heredity is the most important and at the same time the least known factor in the problem of immigration. While there is still much disagreement among scientific men as to the importance of racial heredity in social problems, it can be said that the weight of opinion inclines to the view that racial heredity is a very real factor, and one which cannot be left altogether out of account in studying social problems. The view of Buckle that racial heredity counted for nothing in explaining the social life of various peoples is not upheld by modern biologists. On the contrary the biological view would emphasize the importance of species and racial heredity in all problems connected with life; thus no one denies that between different species of animals heredity counts for everything in explaining their life activities, and, as between the different breeds or races of a single species, no other position is possible from the biological point of view. Nevertheless it may be admitted that man no longer lives a purely animal life and that racial heredity as a factor in his social life may be easily exaggerated. On the whole, it is a safe rule to follow that racial heredity should not be invoked to explain the social condition of a people until practically all other factors have been exhausted. Nevertheless as between the different races or great varieties of mankind there must be a great difference in racial heredity. It could not, indeed, be otherwise, since these different races were developed in different geographical environments or "areas of characterization." Natural selection has developed in each race of mankind an innate character fitted to cope with the environment in which it was evolved. This is clearly perceptible in regard to their bodily traits, and all modern research seems to show that their native reactions to different stimuli also vary greatly, that is, heredity affects their thoughts, feelings and mode of conduct as well as the color of skin, texture of hair, and shape of head. In other words, the instincts or native reactions of the different races of man vary considerably in degree if not in quality, and from this it follows that their feelings, ideas, and modes of conduct must also vary considerably.

It may be noted, however, that taking racial heredity into full account by no means leads to an attitude of fatalism as regards racial problems. On the contrary modern biology clearly teaches that racial heredity is modifiable both in the individual and in the race. It is modifiable in the individual through education or training; it is modifiable in the race through selection. Therefore racial heredity does not foredoom any people to remain in a low status of culture; only it must be taken into account in explaining the cultural conditions of all peoples, and especially in planning for a people's social amelioration.

The Racial Heredity of the Negro.—It is generally agreed by anthropologists and biologists that mankind constitutes but a single species, developed from a single pre-human anthropoid stock. The various races of mankind have had, therefore, a common origin, but having developed in different geographical areas they each present certain peculiar racial traits adapting each to the environment in which it was developed. Now, the negro race is that part of mankind which was developed in the tropics. In all the negro's physical and mental make-up he shows complete adaptation to a tropical environment. The dark color of his skin, for example, was developed by natural selection to exclude the injurious actinic rays of the sun. The various ways in which the negro's tropical environment influenced the development of his mind, particularly of his instincts, cannot be here entered into in detail. Suffice to say that the African environment of the ancestors of the present negroes in the United States deeply stamped itself upon the mental traits and tendencies of the race. For example, the tropical environment is generally unfavorable to severe bodily labor. Persons who work hard in the tropics are, in other words, apt to be eliminated by natural selection. On the other hand, nature furnishes a bountiful supply of food without much labor. Hence, the tropical environment of the negro failed to develop in him any instinct to work, but favored the survival of those naturally shiftless and lazy. Again, the extremely high death rate in Africa necessitated a correspondingly high birth rate in order that any race living there might survive; hence, nature fixed in the negro strong sexual propensities in order to secure such a high birth rate.

It is not claimed that the shiftlessness and sensuality of the masses of the American negroes to-day can be wholly attributed to hereditary influences, but it would be a great mistake to suppose that the African environment did not have something to do with these two dominant characteristics of the present American negro. So we might go through the whole list of the conspicuous traits and tendencies of the American negro, and in practically every case we would find good reason for believing that these racial traits and tendencies are at least in part instinctive, that is, due to the influence of racial heredity.

The question is frequently raised whether the negro is inferior by nature to the white man or not. It is obvious from what has been said that the negro may, on the side of his instinctive or hereditary equipment, be inferior to the white man in his natural adaptiveness to a complex civilization existing under very different climatic conditions from those in which he was evolved. This does not mean, however, that the negro is in any sense a degenerate. On the contrary, from the point of view of a tropical environment, as we have already made plain, the negro may be regarded as the white man's superior. It is only in countries out of his own natural environment, under strange conditions of life to which he has not yet become biologically adapted, that the negro is inferior to the white man. In Africa he is the white man's superior if we adopt survival as the test of superiority.

Influence of Slavery on the Negro.—There is no longer any doubt that the influence of slavery on the negro, as a form of industry, was both beneficent and maleficent. The negroes brought to America by the slave traders were subject to a very severe artificial selection, which, perhaps, secured a better type of negro physically on the whole, and a more docile type mentally; but the chief beneficent influence of slavery on the negro was that it taught him to work, to some extent at least. Moreover, it gave the negro the Anglo-Saxon tongue and the rudiments of our morality, religion, and civilization.

On the other hand, slavery did not fit the individual or the race for a life of freedom, and did not raise moral standards much above those of Africa. The monogamic form of the family was, to be sure, enforced upon the slaves, but the family life was often broken up; for even when the owner of the slaves was kind-hearted and humane, on his death his property would be sold and the families of his slaves scattered. Under such conditions it is not surprising that the negro learned little of family morality. Again, being property himself, the negro could not be taught properly to appreciate the rights of property. Finally slavery failed to develop in the slave that self-mastery and self-control which are necessary for free social life. Admirable as slavery was in some ways as a school for an uncultivated people, it failed utterly in other ways; and it surely should not be difficult to devise methods of training at the present time which are superior to anything that slavery as a school for the industrial training of the negro could possibly have accomplished.

Statistics of the Negro Problem in the United States. The following table will show the percentage of negroes in the population of the United States at different decades (Negro, in census terminology, includes all persons of negro descent):

Per cent.

1790 .... 19.37 1800
.... 18.88 1810 ....
19.03 1830 .... 18.10 1840
.... 16.84 1850 ....
15.69 1860 .... 14.13 1870
.... 12.60 1880 ....
13.12 1890 .... 11.93 1900
.... 11.63

In 1860 the total number of negroes in the population of the United States was 4,441,000. Forty years later, in 1900, the number had just doubled, having reached 8,840,000. Nevertheless, it will be seen from the above table that the percentage of negroes in the total population has steadily diminished, although the negro population doubled between 1860 and 1900. Between 1890 and 1900 the comparative rates of increase for the whites and negroes were: whites, 21.49 Per cent; negroes, 18.10 per cent.

Geographical Distribution of the Negroes. The negro problem would not be so acute in certain sections of the country if negroes were distributed evenly over the country instead of being massed as they are in certain sections. Ninety per cent of the total number of negroes in the country live in the South Atlantic and South Central states. Moreover, over eighty per cent live in the so-called "Black Belt" states,—the "Black Belt" being a chain of counties stretching from Virginia to Texas in which over half of the population are negroes. The following table shows the percentage of negro population in these states of the "Black Belt":

Per cent.

Alabama... 45.2
Arkansas... 28.0
Florida.. 43.6
Georgia... 46.7
Louisiana.. 47.1
Mississippi.. 58.5
North Carolina..................................... 33.0
South Carolina..................................... 58.4
Tennessee.. 23.8
Texas.. 20.4
Virginia... 35.7

While in only two of these states there is an absolute preponderance of negroes, yet these statistics give no idea of the massing of negroes in certain localities. In Washington County, Mississippi, for example, the negroes number 44,143, the whites 5002; in Beaufort County, South Carolina, the negroes number 32,137, the whites 3349. In many counties in the "Black Belt" more than three fourths of the population are negroes. It is in these states that the negro population is rapidly increasing.

Increase of Negro in States since 1860. The following table will show the percentage of negroes in the population in former slave-holding states in 1860 and in 1900:

States	1860	1900
	Per cent	Per cent
Alabama	45.4	45.2
Arkansas	25.6	28
Florida	44.6	43.6
Georgia	44	40.7
Kentucky	20.4	13.3
Louisiana	49.5	47.1
Maryland	24.9	19.8
Mississippi	55.3	58.5
Missouri	10	5.2
North Carolina	30.4	33
South Carolina	58.6	58.4
Tennessee	25.5	23.8
Texas	30.3	20.4
Virginia	42	35.7

It will be noted that the states whose relative negro population has increased since the war are Arkansas, Mississippi, and Georgia, while in South Carolina and Alabama, the relative proportion of negroes has stood stationary.

In the decade from 1890 to 1900, Florida, Alabama, Mississippi, and Arkansas of the above states showed a more rapid increase of their negro population than of their white population. In other Southern states, however, the white population increased more rapidly than the negro population, although in Georgia both races increased about equally.

In certain Northern states the census of 1900 shows the negro population to be increasing much more rapidly than the white population. In New York, Pennsylvania, Illinois, Indiana, and Massachusetts, for example, the negro population increased about twice as fast as the white population, but the number of negroes in these states was still in 1900 comparatively small,

New York having 99,000; Pennsylvania, 156,000, Illinois, 85,000, Indiana, 57,000; and Massachusetts, 31,000. This increase of negro population in certain Northern states is, of course, due to the immigration of the negro into those states, and may be regarded on the whole as a fortunate movement, serving to distribute the negro population more evenly over the whole country, were it not that the negro death rate in these Northern states is so very high that the negroes who go to these states do not as a rule maintain their numbers.

The Urban Negro Population.—Seventeen per cent of the total negro population in 1900 lived in cities of over 8000 population while the remainder lived in small towns and country districts. The following great cities had a high percentage of negroes:

Per cent.

Memphis 48.8
Washington 31.1
New Orleans 27.1
Louisville 19.1
St. Louis 6.2
Philadelphia 4.8
Baltimore 15.6

Some smaller Southern cities have, of course, a much higher percentage of negroes in their population, such as Jacksonville, Florida, 57.1 per cent; Charleston, South Carolina, 56.5 per cent; Savannah, Georgia, 51.8 per cent. On the whole, however, it will be seen that the mass of the negroes in the United States still live in rural districts, although directly after the Civil War and again within recent years there has been a considerable movement of the negroes to the cities. This is extremely significant for the social conditions of the race, because the negro, while not adapted in general to the environment of civilization, is still less adapted to the environment which the modern city affords him.

The Social Condition of the Negroes in the United States.—(1) *Intermixture of Races.* Ever since the negro came to this country he has been having his racial characteristics modified by the infusion of white blood. The census of 1890 attempted to make an estimate of the number of negroes of mixed blood in the United States. The number returned as being of mixed blood was 1,132,000, but all authorities agree that this number understates the actual number. The census officials themselves repudiated these figures as being entirely misleading. Experts in ethnology have estimated that from one third to one half of the negroes in the United States show traces of white intermixture. The lower estimate, that one third of the negroes of the United States have more or less white blood, is quite generally accepted by those who have carefully investigated the matter. Of course the proportion of negroes of mixed blood varies greatly in different localities. In communities in the border states frequently more than one half of the negroes show marked traces of white intermixture. But in the isolated rural regions of the South, where the negroes predominate, the full-blood negro is by far the more common type.

This infusion of white blood into a portion of the negro population is significant sociologically. It is the negroes of mixed blood who are ambitious socially and who present some of the most acute phases of the negro problem. It is from the mixed bloods that the leaders of the race in this country have come. The pure negro without intermixture has hitherto seemed incapable of leadership. Such men as Booker T. Washington, Professor Du Bois, and most other negro leaders have a considerable mixture of white blood. A list of 2200 negro authors was once compiled by the Librarian of Congress, and investigation showed that with very few exceptions these negro authors came from the mixed stock. Indeed, practically all of the negroes who have been eminent in literature, science, art, or statesmanship have come from this class of mixed bloods.

But the infusion of white blood has also in some ways been a detriment to the negro. The illegitimate offspring resulting from the unions of white fathers and negro mothers are frequently the product of conditions of vice. The consequence is that the child of mixed origin frequently has a degenerate heredity and, coming into the world as a bastard, is more or less in disfavor with both races; hence the social environment of the mulatto as well as his heredity is oftentimes peculiarly unfavorable. It is not surprising, therefore, to find among the mulattoes a great amount of constitutional diseases and a great tendency to crime and immorality. Again mulatto women are more frequently debauched by white men than the pure blood negro women, and for this reason negro women of mixed blood are more apt to be immoral. So we see that while the mixed bloods have furnished the leaders of their race, they have also furnished an undue proportion of its vice and crime. This is exactly what we should expect when we understand the social conditions existing between the races and the origin and social environment of the mulatto.

The crime and vice and constitutional diseases of the mulatto do not prove that degeneracy results from the intermixture of the two races, as was once supposed. On the contrary, as we have already seen, all of these things result from the fact that the crossing of the races takes place under socially abnormal conditions, that is, under conditions of vice. This is not, however, true in all cases and particularly it was not true of all intermixture that took place under the regime of slavery. Rather intermixture under such circumstances approached not vice, as we understand the word, but polygyny. Consequently some of the best blood of the South runs in the veins of some of the mulattoes. Again, we have examples from other countries of the crossing of the two races, negro and white, without physical degeneracy. In the West Indies and in Brazil this crossing is frequently taking place, and many of the best families of those countries have a slight amount of negro blood in their veins. From instances like this, gathered from all over the world, it has generally been concluded by anthropologists that no evil physiological results necessarily follow the intermixture of races, even the most diverse, but that all supposed physiological evils coming from the intermixture of races really come from social rather than from physiological causes.

From the point of view of the white race and from the point of view of the negro race such racial intermixture, outside of the bounds of law, may be for many reasons undesirable. But we are here concerned with noting only the social effect of the intermixture that has gone on in the past; and we see that on the one hand it has resulted in creating a class of so-called negroes in whom white blood and the ambitions and energy of the white race predominate, and on the other hand it has also resulted in creating a degenerate mixed stock who furnish the majority of criminals and vicious persons belonging to the so-called negro race.

(2) *Criminality of the Negro.* One of the most important features of the negro problem in the United States is the strong tendency among the negroes toward crime; and this, as we have just seen, is especially manifest in those of mixed origin. Professor Willcox has shown that in 1890 there were in the South six white prisoners to every ten thousand whites, but twenty-nine negro prisoners to every ten thousand negroes, while in the North there were twelve white prisoners to every ten thousand whites, but sixty-nine negro prisoners to every ten thousand negroes. These statistics show that the negro is everywhere more criminal than the white, and that his tendency toward crime increases as we go North, doubtless largely because in the North he is in a strange and more complex environment and finds greater difficulty in making social adjustments. Moreover, negro crime is increasing. From 1880 to 1890 the negro prisoners of the United States increased 29 per cent, while the white prisoners only increased 8 per cent. Later statistics show the same result. As yet there has been no check to the steady increase of negro crime in this country since the Civil War. In some Northern cities, like Chicago, in some years the number of arrests of negroes has equaled one third of the total negro population of those cities. The criminality of the negro is doubtless in part a matter of social environment, because we see that negro crime increases in cities and in the more complex Northern communities; but it is also to some extent a matter of the negro's heredity.

Of course vice accompanies crime among the American negroes. The statistics of illegitimacy in Washington cited by Hoffman in his *Race Traits and Tendencies of the American Negro* show that in fifteen years in Washington, from 1879 to 1894, the percentage of illegitimate births among the whites was 2.9 per cent, while the percentage among the negroes was 22.5. In other words, from one fifth to one fourth of all the negro births in Washington during that fifteen-year period were illegitimate. Statistics collected in other cities show approximately the same result. Of course statistics of illegitimacy are not exactly the same thing as statistics of vice, but they, at any rate, throw a light upon the moral condition of the negro in this regard, and particularly show the demoralization of his family life.

(3) *Negro Pauperism.* We have no good statistics on negro pauperism, but such as we have seem to indicate that the state of dependence of the negro is very great. In the city of Washington, where 30 per cent of the population is made up of negroes, 84 per cent of the pauper burials are those of negroes; and in Charleston, where 57 per cent of the population are negroes, 96.7 per cent of the pauper burials are those of negroes. In nearly all communities where organized charities exist the negroes contribute to the dependent population far out of proportion to their numbers. It is safe to say that from 50 to 75 per cent of the total negro population of the United States live in poverty as distinguished from pauperism, that is, live under such conditions that physical and mental efficiency cannot be maintained.

(4) *Negro Vital Statistics.* The negro death and birth rates are both very high. No definite statistics of negro death and birth rates have been kept except in cities and in a few rural districts. In Alabama in a few registered districts the negro birth rate has been found to be equal to about twice the death rate. On the other hand it is a curious fact that in the North the negro fails to reproduce sufficiently to keep up his numbers, consequently the negro population in Northern states would die out if it were not for immigration. In Massachusetts in 1888, for example, there were 511 negro births and 579 negro deaths. Statistics from other Northern communities tell the same story.

The vital statistics of Southern cities show that the negro death rate is very much higher than the white death rate. In ten Southern cities, for example, Hoffman gives the average death rate for the whites as 20 per thousand for the white population, and for the negroes as 32.6 per thousand of the negro population. These same cities in 1901-1905 showed an annual average death rate for the whites of 17.5 and for the negroes of 28.4. In several cities the negro death rate is nearly twice that of the whites. When these mortality statistics are analyzed, moreover, while they show that negro mortality at all ages is greater than white mortality, it is greatest among negro children under fifteen years of age. This is of course largely because of the ignorant manner in which negroes care for their children, but it also indicates that natural selection is at work among the American negroes rapidly eliminating the biologically unfit.

Conclusions from Negro Vital Statistics. Three important conclusions may be drawn from the negro vital and population statistics which are well worth emphasizing. (1) The negro population is not increasing so fast as the white, owing largely to its high death rate, yet it is increasing, and there is no indication as yet that the negro population will decrease. It is probable, indeed, that at the end of the twentieth century the negro population of the United States will be between twenty and thirty millions. The view of some students of the negro problem that the negro is destined to an early extinction in this country is merely a speculative hypothesis, and as yet is not substantiated by any statistical facts.

(2) While the negro is destined to be with us always, so far as we can see, yet owing to the fact of intermixture of races he will be less and less a pure negro, so that at the end of the twentieth century the negroes in the United States will be much nearer the white type than at the present time.

(3) The high death rate among the negroes indicates that a rapid process of natural selection is going on among them. Now, natural selection means the elimination of the unfit,—the dying out of those who cannot adapt themselves to their environment. This selective process will tend toward the survival of the more fit elements among the negroes, and, therefore, towards bringing the negro up to the standard of the whites. The misery and vice which we see among the present American negroes are simply in a large degree the expression of the working of a process of natural selection among them. It would be preferable, however, if the white race could by education and other means substitute to some degree at least artificial selection for the miseries and brutality of the natural process of eliminating the unfit. This the superior race should do to protect itself as well as to raise the negro.

Industrial Conditions Among the Negroes.—Recently a committee of the American Economic Association estimated that all of the taxable property in the United States owned by negroes amounted to $300,000,000, or about $33.00 per head,—this estimate being based upon the 1900 census returns. Thirty-three dollars per head of the negro population seems of course very small when compared to the $1,000.00 per capita owned by the whites; but we must remember that the negro at his emancipation was in no way equipped to acquire property, and, with the exception of a few freedmen, the negro at the close of the war had no property whatsoever. In a few cases their old masters set up the emancipated negroes with small farms. In

1900 there were 746,715 farms occupied by negroes either as tenants or owners. Twenty-five per cent of these farms were owned by negroes and about ten per cent were owned unencumbered.

There are, of course, two ways of looking at these statistics. They are discouraging if we care to look at them in that way, but on the other hand, if we consider the disadvantageous position in which the negro was placed at the close of the Civil War, the statistics may be taken as showing a marked advance.

It must be said here that, as Booker Washington has urged, the negro problem is largely of an industrial nature. It is the unsatisfactoriness of the negro as a worker, as a producing agent, that gives rise largely to the friction between the two races. The negro has not yet become adapted to a system of free contract and is frequently unreliable as a laborer. This breeds continued antagonism between the races. It is only necessary here to remark that when the negro becomes an efficient producer and a property owner the negro problem will be practically solved.

Educational Progress Among the Negroes.—The educational progress among the negroes has been more satisfactory than their industrial progress. At the time of the emancipation 95 per cent of all the negroes in the United States were illiterate, since nearly all the slave states had laws forbidding the education of negroes. Since the emancipation there has been a rapid decrease of illiteracy. In 1880 seventy per cent of the negroes above the age of ten years were still reported as illiterate. In 1890, 56.8 per cent; and in 1900, 44.6 per cent. The number of illiterate negro voters in the United States in 1900 was 47.3 per cent of the total number of negro males above the age of twenty-one. The per cent of illiterate negro voters ranged all the way in former slave-holding states from 61.3 per cent in Louisiana to 31.9 per cent in Missouri, while in Massachusetts the percentage of negro illiteracy was only 10 per cent.

In the school year 1907-08, in the sixteen Southern states there were 1,665,000 negro children enrolled in the public schools, this number being 54.36 per cent of the negro population of the school age (five to eighteen). The number of white children enrolled was 4,692,000, or 70.34 per cent of the white population of school age. But these statistics fail to indicate the utter inadequacy of many provisions for the education of the negro children. In many districts of the South the negro schools are open only from three to five months in a year,—the equipment of the school being very inadequate and the teacher poorly trained. Nevertheless the sixteen Southern states have spent, since the emancipation, over $175,000,000 to maintain separate schools for negroes, a much larger sum than all that has been given by Northern philanthropy. In addition to the common schools for negroes there were in 1907-08 one hundred and thirty-five institutions for the higher education of the negro with an annual income of over $2,800,000. In these there were 4185 negro students receiving collegiate or professional training, 17,279 were receiving a high school course, and 23,160 industrial training. The latter figure is important because it indicates that in 1907-08 a little more than one per cent of the total number of negro children in school were receiving industrial training. The percentage is increasing, through the fact that industrial training is being introduced into a number of the city schools for negroes, both North and South; but at present not much over one per cent of the negro children are receiving industrial training.

Political Conditions.—Not much need be said concerning the political condition of the negro. The movement to disfranchise the negro by legal means came in 1890 when the new Mississippi constitution adopted in that year provided that every voter should be able to read or interpret a clause in the constitution of the United States. Since then a majority of the Southern states and practically all of the states of the "Black Belt" have embodied either in their constitutions or laws provisions for disfranchising the negro voter. Louisiana made the provision that a person must be able to read and write or be a lineal descendant of some person who voted prior to 1860. This is the famous "Grandfather Clause," which has since proved popular in a number of Southern states. While these laws and constitutional provisions have evidently been designed to disfranchise the negro voter, the Federal Supreme Court has upheld them in spite of the Fourteenth Amendment to the Federal Constitution.

Regarding all of this legislation it may be said that it has had perhaps both good and bad effects. In so far as it has tended to eliminate the negro from politics this has been a good effect, but it has oftentimes rather succeeded in keeping the negro question in politics; and the evident injustice and inequality of some of the laws must, it would seem, react to lower the whole tone of political morality in the South. Again, the very provision of these laws to insure the disfranchisement of the illiterate negro has tended in some instances, at least, to discourage negro education, because the promoters of these laws in most cases did not aim to exclude simply the illiterate negro vote, but practically the entire negro vote. It is evident that a party designing to disfranchise the negro through this means would not be very zealous for the negro's education.

Proposed Solutions of the Negro Problem.—Among the various solutions proposed from time to time for the negro problem, more or less seriously, are: (1) admission at once of the negroes to full social equality with the whites; (2) deportation to Africa or South America; (3) colonization in some state or in territory adjacent to the United States; (4) extinction by natural selection; (5) popular education. Regarding all these solutions it must be said at once that they are either impossible or fatuous. They may be dismissed, then, without further discussion. Mr. Booker T. Washington has said that the negro is bound to become adjusted to our civilization because he is surrounded by the white man's civilization on every hand. This optimistic view, which seems to dismiss the negro problem as requiring no solution, is, however, not well supported by many facts, as we have just seen. Everywhere we have evidence that the negro when left to himself, reverts to a condition approximating his African barbarism, and the statistics of increasing vice and crime which we have just given show quite conclusively that the negro is not becoming adjusted to the white man's civilization in many cases in spite of considerable efforts which are being put forth in his behalf. While we are very far from taking a pessimistic view toward this or any other social problem, we believe that most of the solutions that have thus far been tried or urged are failures, and that more radical methods need to be adopted if the negro becomes a useful social and industrial element in our society.

As we have already seen, the negro is still essentially unadjusted to our civilization, and it would not be too much to say that the masses of negroes in this country are still not far removed from barbarism, though living in the midst of civilization. Slavery failed, as we have already seen, to render the mass of negroes capable of participating in our culture, and all that has been done for the negro since emancipation has likewise failed to adjust the mass of the race to the social conditions in which they find themselves. We may say, then, roughly, without any injustice to the negro, that the negro masses of this country are still essentially an uncultivated or a "nature" people living in the midst of civilization. The negro problem, in other words, is not greatly different from what it would be if the present negroes were descendants of savage aborigines that had peopled this country before the white man came. The problem of the negro and of the Indian, and of all the uncivilized races, is essentially the same. The problem is, how a relatively large mass of people, inferior in culture and perhaps also inferior in nature, can be adjusted relatively to the civilization of a people much their superior in culture; how the industrially inefficient nature man can be made over into the industrially efficient civilized man.

Undoubtedly the primary adjustment to be made by the American negro is the adjustment on the economic side. Only when the negro becomes adjusted to the economic side of his life will there be a solid foundation for the development of something higher. People must be taught how to be efficient, self-sustaining, productive members of society economically before they can be taught to be good citizens. The American negro in other words must be taught to be "good for something" as well as to be good.

The failure of common-school education with the negro has been largely for the reason that it has failed to help him in any efficient way to adjust himself industrially. Oftentimes indeed it has had the contrary effect and the slightly educated negro has been the one who has been least valuable as a producer. The common-school education has not been such a failure with the white child, for the reason that the white child has been taught industry and morality at home, but these the negro frequently fails to get in his home life. Moreover, the common-school education of the white child has usually been simply the foundation upon which after school days he, as a citizen, has built up a wider culture. But the negro, on account of his environment, if not naturally, has proved incapable of going on with his education and building on it after getting out of school. Moreover, as we have already noted, under the present complex conditions of our social life the common school is no longer an efficient socializing agent, even for the white children. The present school system is a failure, not only for the negro race, but also, though not in the same degree, for the white race. Popular education on the old lines can never do very much to solve the negro problem.

This does not lead, however, to the conclusion that all training and education for the negro race is foredoomed to failure. On the contrary all the experiments of missionaries in dealing with uncivilized races has led to the conclusion that an all-round education in which industrial and moral training are made prominent can relatively adjust to our civilization even the most backward of human races. Wherever the missionaries have introduced industrial education and adjusted their converts to what is perhaps the fundamental side of our civilization, the economic, they have met with the largest degree of success. This success of missionary endeavors along this line has led to the establishment of similar industrial training schools for the negro in this country, and it must be said regarding such schools for the negro as Hampton and Tuskegee that they have proved an even more unqualified success than their predecessors originated by the missionaries. But these schools are as yet very far from solving the negro problem in this country, for the reason, as we have already seen, that they affect such a relatively small proportion of the negro population. Only about one per cent of negro children at the present time are probably receiving industrial training.

It should be remarked that this industrial training in no way precludes an all-round education. It is not meant that industrial education shall replace all other forms of education, but rather that it shall be added to literary education in order to enrich the educational process; and it may be remarked also that industrial training, while of itself having a strong uplifting moral influence, is not sufficient to socialize without explicit moral teaching being also added thereto. Schools that attempted to give such an all-round education to negro children would, of course, in no way cut off the possibility of higher and professional education for the small number who are especially fitted, and who should be encouraged to go on with such studies.

Accepting, then, without qualification the now widespread view that industrial training coupled with an all-round education is the best possible solution of the negro problem, let us look into the practical difficulties which confront any attempt to apply such a solution at the present time. These difficulties may be summed up under three heads: (1) The difficulty of securing adequately equipped schools to give such training; (2) the difficulty of obtaining teachers who are qualified to give this training, and who have the right spirit; (3) the present lack of intelligent coöperation by the members of both races.

As regards the first of these difficulties, it must be said that it is under our present system of school administration practically insuperable. Adequately equipped schools for industrial education will cost a great deal of money,— money which the whites of the South will probably not be willing to give for many years to come, and which we think they should not be asked to give. As we have already seen, there are more illiterate native whites in the South than in any other section of the Union. This is due in part to the effects of the war which left a majority of the Southern communities poverty-stricken, and in many communities there is still not yet sufficient money to maintain proper school facilities, even on the old lines; much less can it be expected that such communities can start at once industrial schools for the training of negro children.

As regards the difficulty of obtaining properly trained teachers with a proper spirit to do this work, it must be said that as yet these teachers could not be found, and certainly they could not within the negro race. The mass of negro teachers are still so far below even the low standards of the white schools that not one half of them would be licensed to teach if the same standards were applied to them as to the whites. Moreover, through the increase of race friction white teachers have gradually, since the Civil War, been excluded from negro schools. This has been brought about largely also by the negroes demanding these positions for themselves. But it is an old adage that "if the blind lead the blind both will fall into the ditch," and it would seem that a majority of negro teachers are unqualified for their task of civilizing and socializing their race; hence one reason for the failure of the negro common school. It would seem also that, while competent negro teachers should be encouraged in every way, white teachers should not be absolutely excluded from negro schools; and particularly that white teachers would be necessary if industrial and moral training were to be emphasized in the education of the negro. This brings us to the third difficulty,—the lack of intelligent coöperation by the members of both races. Unfortunately the negroes do not care for the newer education, the education which emphasizes industrial training. Most of them, misled by unwise leaders, prefer the education of the older type and think that industrial training will only fit them to be "hewers of wood and drawers of water" to the whites. On the other hand, the masses of uneducated Southern people also do not wish the new education for the negro, because they believe that it will give him superior advantages over the white children. They fail to see that anything that is done for a depressed element in society, like the negro, will ultimately benefit all society. They are, therefore, not willing to tax themselves to bring about, even gradually, the new education for the negro. While educated Southern people have supported Booker T. Washington in his propaganda for the industrial training of the negro, it is notorious that Washington's ideas have met with as much opposition from the uneducated whites as from the negroes themselves.

On the whole, however, while the situation is a difficult one, it is not, as we have already seen, one which justifies pessimism. Time is the great element in the solution of all problems, and it must be especially an element in the solution of this negro problem. A beginning has been made toward the training and the education of the negro in the right way, and it may be hoped that from centers like Hampton and Tuskegee the influence will gradually radiate which will in time bring about the popularization of industrial education. What is needed, perhaps, most of all is sufficient funds to carry on wider and wider experiments along these lines. The Southern states should not be expected to furnish these funds. They have already done their full share in attempting to educate the negro. The negro problem is a national problem, and as a national problem it should be dealt with by the Federal Government. The burden of educating the negro for citizenship should rest primarily upon the whole nation and not upon any section or community, since the whole nation is responsible for the negro's present condition. The trouble is, however, again, that the mass of the Southern people would at the present time undoubtedly resent any attempt on the part of the Federal Government to aid in the education of the negro. The question, therefore, ultimately becomes a question of educating the whites and forming a proper public sentiment regarding the education of the negro. When the leaders of both races once become united on a plan of training the negro for efficient citizenship, undoubtedly the funds will be forthcoming. While the negro question is, therefore, from one point of view primarily a question of the industrial training and adjustment of the negro, from another point of view it is a moral question which can never be solved until the superior race comes to take a right attitude toward the inferior race, namely, the attitude of service.

SELECT REFERENCES

For brief reading:

HOFFMAN, *Race Traits and Tendencies of the American Negro*, Vol. XI of Pub. of Am. Economic Ass'n.
STONE, *Studies in the American Race Problem.*
BAKER, *Following the Color Line.*

For more extended reading:

DOWD, *The Negro Races.*
DU BOIS, *The Negroes of Philadelphia.*
DU BOIS, editor, *The Atlanta University Publications.*
KEANE, *Ethnology.*
KEANE, *Man, Past and Present.*
MERRIAM, *The Negro and the Nation.*
PAGE, *The Negro: the Southerner's Problem.*
SMITH, *The Color Line.*
TILLINGHAST, *The Negro in Africa and America*, Pub. Am. Economic Ass'n, 3d series, Vol. III.
WASHINGTON, *The Future of the American Negro.*

CHAPTER XI

THE PROBLEM OF THE CITY

Professor J.S. McKenzie says "The growth of large cities constitutes perhaps the greatest of all the problems of modern civilization." While the city is a problem in itself, creating certain biological and psychological conditions which are new to the race, the city is perhaps even more an intensification of all our other social problems, such as crime, vice, poverty, and degeneracy.

The city is in a certain sense a relatively modern problem, due to modern industrial development. While great cities were known in ancient times, the number was so few that the total population affected by city living conditions was comparatively small. Moreover, the populations of ancient cities have often been exaggerated. Probably at the height of its power, the population of Athens did not exceed 100,000; Carthage, 700,000; Rome, 500,000; Alexandria, 500,000; Nineveh and Babylon, 1,000,000. All the great cities of the ancient world practically disappeared with the fall of Rome. After Rome's fall, Constantinople was the only large city with over 100,000 population in all Europe for centuries. Down to 1600 A.D., indeed, there were only fourteen cities in all Europe with a population of over 100,000; and even in 1800, at the beginning of the nineteenth century, there were only twenty-two such cities. But at the end of the nineteenth century, in 1900, there were one hundred and thirty-six such cities in Europe, representing twelve per cent of the entire population. Moreover, while in 1800 less than three per cent of the total population of Europe lived in cities, in 1900 the total urban population was twenty-five per cent. Again, all of the great European capitals developed their present enormous population almost wholly within the nineteenth century. Thus, the population of London in 1800 was 864,000, while in 1901 it had reached 4,536,000, or in the total area policed, 6,581,000; the population of Paris in 1800 was 547,000, in 1901 it was 2,714,000; the population of Berlin in 1800 was only 172,000, in 1901 it was 1,888,000; the population of Vienna in 1800 was 232,000, in 1901 it was 1,674,000. These figures are cited to show that from four fifths to nine tenths of the growth of the greatest cities of the world has taken place within the nineteenth century.

Dr. Weber in his *Growth of Cities in the Nineteenth Century* illustrates the striking difference between the urban development of the nineteenth century and that of the eighteenth century by comparing the population of Australia in 1890 with the population of the United States in 1790. Australia in 1890, out of a population of 3,809,000 had 1,264,000, or 33.2 per cent, living in cities of 10,000 or over; while the United States in 1790, out of a population of 3,929,000 had only 123,000, or 3.14 per cent living in cities. Both countries, it will be noticed, had about the same total population at the two periods and the same area, but Australia in 1890 represented in its population the industrial development of the nineteenth century with its tendency toward urbanization, while the United States in 1790 represented the civilization of the eighteenth century with its predominating rural life.

The Growth of Cities in the United States.—A word about census terminology will be helpful before discussing the growth of cities in the United States. According to the United States census, a city is a place with a population of 8000 or over; a *small* city is a place with a population of 8000 to 25,000; a *large* city is a place with a population of from 25,000 to 100,000, and a *great* city is a place with a population above 100,000. These distinctions are necessary in discussing the problems of the city, because the problems of cities change rapidly when the population goes above 100,000. It is mainly the problem of the great city which we shall discuss in this chapter.

In 1800 there were only six cities in the United States with over 8000 population. Philadelphia was the largest of these, with 69,000, and New York second with 60,000. These cities contained a fraction less than four per cent of the population of the United States. In 1900, on the other hand, there were 546 cities in the United States with a population of over 8000. Moreover, over thirty-three per cent of the total population of the United States lived in cities of 8000 and over, while nearly one fifth of the total population lived in the thirty-eight great cities. Between 1890 and 1900 the gain in the urban population of the country was sixty per cent, while the gain in the rural population was only fifteen per cent. During that decade, in other words, the cities grew four times as fast as the country districts in population. Moreover, for that particular decade, the great cities grew faster than the smaller ones, but since 1900 certain state census statistics seem to show that the cities from 25,000 to 100,000 population are growing faster than those above 100,000.

Distribution of the Urban Population of the United States. If the urban population of the United States were distributed relatively uniformly among the several States, perhaps the problem of the city would not be so pressing as it is, but the urban population is largely concentrated in a very few states. Over fifty per cent of the urban population is found in the North Atlantic states alone. The five states of New York, Pennsylvania, Massachusetts, Illinois, and Ohio contain also more than half of the urban population of the whole country. If we add to these five states New Jersey and Missouri, then these seven states contain nearly two thirds of the urban population of the United States.

It will be noticed that these states with a large urban population are the great manufacturing states of the Union. The proportion of urban to rural population indeed is a good index to industrial progress. The states with over half their population urban in 1900 were, Rhode Island, 81 per cent; Massachusetts, 76 per cent; New York, 68.5 per cent; New Jersey, 61.2 per cent; Connecticut, 53.2 per cent. States with more than one fourth of their population urban were, Illinois, 47.1 per cent; Maryland, 46.9 per cent; Pennsylvania, 45.5 per cent; California, 43.7 per cent; Delaware, 41.4 per cent; New Hampshire, 38.6 per cent; Ohio, 38.5 per cent; Colorado, 38.1 per cent; Washington, 31.9 per cent; Michigan, 30.9 per cent; Missouri, 30.8 per cent; Wisconsin, 30.7 per cent; Louisiana, 29.3 per cent; Montana, 27 per cent; Minnesota, 26.8 per cent; Utah, 25.2 per cent. It will be noticed that only one of these states with the population more than one fourth urban is distinctively southern, namely, Louisiana. This is due to the fact that heretofore the South has been largely agricultural in its industries, consequently only a few of the great cities of the country are found within its borders.

There are but few countries in Europe that come up with the most urban of our American states. Certain countries of Western Europe, however, equal the most urban of our states, and the following countries have at least one quarter of their population urban: England and Wales, Scotland, Belgium, Saxony, Holland, Prussia, and France. The most urban of our states, however, such as Massachusetts, Rhode Island, and New York, surpass all European countries in the number of their population living in cities, with the exception of England and Wales. This again is due to the fact that certain of our states have specialized in manufacturing industries more than any European country, with the exception of England and Wales.

Before leaving the statistics of the growth of cities, it is worth our while to note that certain great urban centers are developing in this country which promise to show, even in the near future, the most extensive urbanization of population known to the world; for example, a line of cities and suburban communities is now developing which will in the near future connect New York and Boston on the one hand and New York, Philadelphia, and Washington on the other hand. Thus in a few years, stretching from Washington to Boston, a distance of five hundred miles, there promises to be a continuous chain of urban communities with practically no rural districts between them. In a sense, this will constitute one great city with a population of twenty millions or upwards. Other urban centers, though not so extensive, are also developing at other points in the United States. At the end of the twentieth century it is safe to say that this country will have at least a dozen cities with a population of over one million. Moreover, so far as we can see at the present time, there is no end in the near future to this growth of the urbanization of our population; for the causes of this great growth of cities seem inherent in our civilization. Let us see what these causes are.

Causes of the Growth of Great Cities.—There may be distinguished two classes of causes of the growth of cities: (1) general or social causes, and (2) minor or individual causes. It is the social causes, the causes inherent in our civilization, which are of particular interest to us. Among these social causes we shall place:

1. *The Diminishing Importance of Agriculture in the Life of Man.* Once agriculture was the all-embracing occupation. Practically all goods were produced upon the farm. Now, however, man's wants have so greatly increased that the primitive industries of the farm can no longer satisfy these wants, and in order to satisfy them men have developed large manufacturing industries. Moreover, fewer men are needed on the farms to produce the same amount of raw material as was produced formerly by the labor of many. This has come about mostly through labor-saving machines. The invention and application of labor-saving machines to the industries of the farm has made it possible to dispense with a great number of men. It is estimated that fifty men with modern farm machinery can do the work of five hundred European peasants without such machinery. Consequently, the four hundred and fifty who have been displaced by farm machinery must find other work, and they find it mainly in manufacturing industries. Again, the scientific and capitalistic agriculture of the present has much the same effect as labor-saving machines. They have greatly increased agricultural production and at the same time lessened the amount of labor. The opening up also of new and fertile regions which were very productive in the nineteenth century had a similar effect.

Every improvement in agricultural industry instead of keeping men on the farm has tended to drive them from it. Scientific agriculture carried on with modern machinery necessarily lessens the need of a great proportion of the population being employed to produce the foodstuff and other raw materials which the world needs. Hence it has tended to free men from the soil and to make it possible for a larger and larger number to go to the city. Therefore the relatively diminishing importance of agriculture has been one of the prime causes of the growth of the cities in the nineteenth century; and so far as we can see this cause will continue to operate for some time to come.

2. *The Growth and Centralization of Manufacturing Industries.* This is perhaps the most vital cause of the growth of cities. The great city, as we have already

said, is very largely the product of modern industrialism. Improved machinery, improved transportation, and enlarged markets, together with the increased wants of men, not only have made possible a great growth of manufacturing industries, but also these same factors have tended to centralize manufacturing industries in the cities. Let us note briefly why it is that manufacturing industries are grouped together in great cities rather than scattered throughout the rural communities. In centralizing manufacturing plants in cities, certain industrial economies are secured, such as: (1) economy in motor power, whether it be water or coal; (2) economy in machinery—it is not necessary to duplicate machines; (3) economy in wages—one superintendent, for example, can oversee a large plant; (4) utilization of by-products—when many factories are grouped together by-products, which are sometimes more valuable than the main products, can be better utilized. (5) There is economy in buying raw material and in selling finished products when many factories are grouped together. For all these reasons, along with the further reason that those who labor in factories must live close to them, manufacturing has been a prime cause of the modern city, and, so far as we can see, will continue to further urbanize our population in the future.

3. *The Increase of Trade and Commerce.* Between different communities there developed during the nineteenth century, upon the growth of better transportation, a great increase of trade and commerce, for along with the better transportation went a specialization in industry, on the part of both communities and classes. The modern city is often largely a product of modern transportation. We find all the great cities located at natural breaks in transportation. The cities of the Middle Ages were largely centers of trade and commerce where goods were distributed to various minor centers. The modern city has not lost this characteristic through developing into an industrial center. On the contrary, the status of the city in trade and commerce makes it at the same time a valuable center for the development of manufacturing industries. The break between land and water transportation is particularly favorable to the development of large cities. Thus, we find New York located where goods shipped to Europe must be transferred from land to water transportation; Chicago, located at the head of the water transportation of the Great Lakes; St. Louis, at the head of the navigation of the Mississippi River. Only Denver and Indianapolis among the great cities of the United States in 1910 are not located on a river or some other navigable water.

Minor Causes. These are the chief social causes of the growth of cities, and, as we have seen, they are wholly industrial in their nature. Undoubtedly the modern city is a product of modern industry. Certain non-economic factors may also enter into the growth of cities, but these are of but slight importance; such are the greater intellectual and educational advantages which the city offers, the great opportunities for pleasure and amusement in the city and the like. Such minor and individual causes have had but little part in the growth of the great cities of the present.

Social And Moral Conditions Of City Life.—Certain social conditions in our cities are worthy of attention in order that we may understand the effect of the city upon social and racial evolution.

1. *City Populations have a Larger per Cent of Females than Rural Populations.* All of our fifteen largest cities, except three, contain a larger per cent of females than the states in which they are located. Thus New York state has 50.37 per cent of its population female; New York city, 50.56 per cent; Pennsylvania, 49.29 per cent of its population female; Philadelphia, 51.18 per cent; Missouri, 48.38 per cent of its population female; St. Louis, 49.51 per cent. In towns of the United States of more than 2500 population the per cent of females is 50.03, while the rural districts of the United States have only 48.08 per cent of their population female. The cause of this is perhaps to be found in the fact that in cities there is always a larger infantile mortality among males than among females, and that in towns there is a larger proportion of female children born than in the rural districts.

2. *People in the Active Period of Life, from Fifteen to Sixty-five Years of Age, predominate in the City.* According to Dr. Weber, out of every 1000 individuals in the United States as a whole there are 355 under fifteen years of age, 603 between fifteen and sixty-five, and 29 above sixty-five years of age. But in the great cities there are only 299 under fifteen years of age, and only 29 above sixty-five years of age, while 668 are of the age between fifteen and sixty-five years. (In both cases the age of three in a thousand was unknown.) The cause of the predominance of those in the active period of life is undoubtedly due to the immigration into the cities from the country districts. This makes the life of cities more energetic and active, more strenuous than it would otherwise be.

3. *The Great Cities in the United States have over twice as many Foreign-born in their Population as the United States as a whole.* This has been sufficiently discussed under the head of immigration.

4. *The Birth Rate is higher in the Cities than in the Rural Districts.* This is primarily due to there being more women of child-bearing age in the cities. In the United States it is also due to the presence of so many foreign-born in the cities. The marriage rate is also higher in the cities than in the rural districts. The following statistics based on a thousand population show the relative difference between the cities and the rural districts of the New England States in marriage rate, birth rate, and death rate for 1894-95:

	Marriage Rate	Birth Rate	Death Rate
Boston......................	23.10	31.24	23.23
Cities over 50,000............	18.89	29.72	19.49
Rural Districts..............	13.77	21.76	17.38

5. *The Death Rate in Cities is also higher than in the Rural Districts*, as the above table has just shown. This is undoubtedly due to the poor sanitary and living conditions of large cities.

6. *The Physical Condition of City Populations.* Measurements by Dr. Beddoe and others show that the stature and other measurements of men of the great cities of Great Britain are far below those of the rural population. The latest English commission to investigate the conditions of city life also reports that the population of the British cities at least shows marked signs of physical deterioration.

7. *Mental and Moral Degeneracy in our Cities.* (1) A larger number of insane are found in our cities than in the rural districts. In the United States as a whole there were in 1890 seventeen hundred insane per million of population, while in the cities of over 50,000 there were 2429 insane per million.

(2) The suicide rate is much higher in the cities than in other districts. In general the suicide rate in the United States seems to be two or three times as high in our large cities as in the rest of the country.

(3) Poverty and pauperism are much more common in our cities than in rural districts. About one third of the population of great cities may safely be said to live below the poverty line, while in such cities as New York and Boston from ten to twenty per cent of the population require more or less charitable assistance during the year.

(4) The amount of crime in the cities is about twice as great as in the rural districts.

(5) Illegitimacy in the cities is from two to three times as great as in rural districts, and it is well known that vice centers very largely in our cities.

All these facts show that mental and moral degeneracy is much more common in our urban population than in our rural populations, and that the biological and moral aspects of our city life present pressing problems.

8. *Educational and Religious Conditions in Cities.* We have already seen that illiteracy for the native white population is much less in our cities than in the rural districts. This is undoubtedly due in the main to the better facilities for education in our cities, and it is here chiefly that we find the bright side of city life; for the cities are not only centers of the evil tendencies of our civilization but are also the centers of all that is best and uplifting. The

urban schools in general are open much longer than the rural school, the attendance in them is better, and the teaching is much more efficient. In 1890 the urban schools held 190 days in the year, while the rural schools held only 115 days. The attendance in the urban schools was seventy per cent of the enrollment, while in the rural schools it was only sixty-two per cent. Besides the schools, of course, must be mentioned many other educational facilities to be found in our cities, such as in connection with social settlements, lecture and concert halls, theaters, libraries, art galleries, and museums,—all of which the city has practically exclusively.

The census of 1890 included a religious census, and it seemed to show that on the whole religious conditions were better in our cities than in the country districts. In cities above 25,000 the church membership was 37.9 per cent of the population, while it was only 32.85 per cent of the total population. Again, in cities above 100,000 it was 39.1 per cent of their total population, although in the four largest cities—New York, Chicago, Philadelphia, and St. Louis—it was only 35.6 per cent of the total population. [Footnote: The special religious census of 1906, the results of which are not yet fully published, shows an even greater preponderance of church membership in cities.] Some recent studies, however, while not extensive enough to justify a conclusion, seem to indicate that in some of the largest cities the church is losing its hold, and that more and more the population of our largest urban centers is becoming churchless, if not without religion. Even if this is so, however, it also remains a fact that the various religious denominations put forth their best efforts in these largest urban centers, and that more is being done for the people religiously and morally in these centers than perhaps for any other portion of the world's population.

Proposed Remedies for the Evils of City Life.—The proposed remedies for the evils of city life are well worth attention, not only that we may understand the problem of the city better, but also that we may understand social conditions in general better. Of the remedies which we shall discuss it may be said that four are foolish and two are wise. The foolish ones are those that try to check the growth of the cities; the wise ones are those that recognize that the cities are here to stay and must be dealt with as permanent and even increasingly important factors in our civilization.

(1) The first remedy is to make agriculture more attractive and remunerative. This is a good thing in itself, but, as we have seen, it will not check the growth of the cities; rather, every improvement in the conditions of agriculture in the way of making it more productive and remunerative will drive more to the cities.

(2) A second remedy, akin to the first, is to make village life more attractive. Like the first remedy, this is good in itself, but it is hardly probable that it will stop the growth of cities; rather, it might be urged that village improvement will give people a taste of the higher comforts and conveniences to be found in cities and will tend to send them to the city.

(3) The third proposed remedy is to colonize the poor of the cities in the country. This has been especially advocated by General Booth and other leaders of the Salvation Army. This plan, however, cannot do much toward helping solve the problem of the city. It is a difficult thing to get the poor in the city adjusted again to rural life, and the probability is that in many cases they would be worse off in the country than in the city. Moreover, the vacant places they left would soon be filled by others, and in general the whole plan seems to be against man's instincts as well as against the social forces of the time.

(4) Administrative decentralization may be mentioned as a plan adopted by some state legislatures to prevent the growth of cities, that is, to scatter the state institutions through the rural sections of the state instead of locating them in the cities. On the whole, this is a foolish plan. The cities will not be checked in their growth by this, while on the other hand it is the cities which most need the presence of the state institutions.

(5) The most important remedy for the cure of the evils of the cities, and one which meets these evils on their own ground, is what has been called "improved municipal housekeeping"; that is, the supervision and control by the city of all those things which are used in common by the people. The idea is that the city is not in its social conditions comparable to the rural community; rather it is more like one big household, and it is necessary, therefore, that there be collective housekeeping, so to speak, in order to keep those things which the people use in common at least in good order. This has also been called "municipal socialism." It is not socialism, however, in the strict sense, for it does not advocate the ownership in common of all capital, but rather municipal control of public utilities. We cannot enter into this large subject, upon which many books have been written; to a few of these the student will find references at the end of this chapter. Here it is only necessary to say that all of this civic improvement implies that the city must own or control adequately its sewer system, its water supply, its streets; that it must control the housing of the people, the disposal of garbage, the smoke nuisance, general sanitary and living conditions; that it must provide adequate protection against fire, an adequate park system, an adequate free school system, with public playgrounds for children, free libraries, free art galleries and museums, municipal theaters, public baths, and gymnasiums.

All of this is of course a species of socialism in the sense that it is collective control of the conditions of living together. It advocates, however, that the city should take over only those things that are used in common. The trouble with this so-called municipal socialism is that it presupposes a pretty high degree of intelligence on the part of people. Whether or not a municipality shall own and operate its own street railways, electric light and gas plants, is largely a question of the development of the social consciousness and intelligence in that particular community. In some communities such municipal undertakings have been made a success; in others they have failed. But it is evident that with a large mass of people living together the common conditions of living must be subject to intelligent collective control if human life and character are to have a proper environment in which to develop.

(6) The last remedy proposed for the evils of the city is the development of the suburbs through rapid transit. This is already being rapidly accomplished in many of our larger cities. The solution of the mechanical problem of rapid transit will probably, in other words, tend greatly to relieve automatically the present congestion which we find in many of our large cities. Probably the best form of such rapid transit is underground electric roads, or subways. Transportation upon these roads must be made cheap enough to enable workingmen to live at a distance from their labor. With the solution of the problem of rapid transit it should be possible to scatter a city's population anywhere within a radius of thirty miles. But it would be a mistake to think that rapid transit alone will solve the problems of city communities. Stringent regulation by law of sanitary and housing conditions and, as has just been said, of all the things used in common, is necessary to put order and healthfulness into that vast household which we call a modern great city.

In conclusion we would emphasize again that the era of the city is just beginning; that a larger and larger proportion of our population must come to live in the cities, and that, therefore, the city will dominate the society of the future. Hence, humanity must solve the problem of the city if social progress is to continue. And the problem is by no means insoluble. Man is not yet adjusted to city life. The city is so new even to civilized man that he has carried into it the habits which he practiced in isolated rural communities. These are the sources of trouble in our cities, and, as we have already seen, new adjustments have to be made by individuals in order to secure harmonious social relationships under the crowded conditions of the city. The city requires, therefore, a higher degree of intelligence on the part of the individual than the rural social life, and a great part of the solution of the problem of the city must come through the development of such higher intelligence and morality by means of education. At any rate, it is foolish to decry the city or to attempt to stop its growth. That is impossible and, we think, undesirable. The ideal social life of man has never been the isolated life of the rural community. The city has always been in a sense man's ideal, as is shown by the fact that nearly all attempts to depict a perfect human society have been pictures of cities. Man's ideal, as Dr. Weber says, is not the city or the country, but the city and the country blended, and this is what the city of the future should become. No doubt the time will come when present cities will be looked back upon with horror, as we look back on eighteenth-century cities. The city of the future need not present any of the hideous, disagreeable, and unwholesome aspects of our present cities. The city can be made, through science and morality, a place in which human beings may find their ideal society.

SELECT REFERENCES

For brief reading:

WEBER, *Growth of Cities in the Nineteenth Century.*
WILCOX, *The American City.*
ZUEBLIN, *American Municipal Progress.*

For more extended reading:

FAIRLIE, *Municipal Administration.*
HOWE, *The City: the Hope of Democracy.*
PARSONS, *The City for the People.*
ROWE, *Problems of City Government.*
STRONG, *The Challenge of the City.*

CHAPTER XII

POVERTY AND PAUPERISM

While the many social problems arising from the presence in society of abnormal or socially unadjusted classes, namely, the dependent, defective, and delinquent classes, cannot be discussed in this book adequately, yet they must be briefly noticed in order to correlate them with other social problems, and even more in order to call the attention of the student to the vast literature which exists concerning these problems.

Definitions of Poverty and Pauperism.—Poverty is a relative term, difficult to define, but as generally employed in sociological writings at the present it means that economic and social state in which persons have not sufficient income to maintain health and physical efficiency. All who do not receive a sufficient income to maintain the minimum standard of living necessary for efficiency are known as the "poor," or are said to live below the poverty line.

Pauperism, on the other hand, is the state of legal dependence in which a person who is unable or unwilling to support himself receives relief from public sources. This is, however, legal pauperism. The word as popularly used has come to mean a degraded state of willing dependence. A pauper in this popular sense is a person unwilling to support himself and who becomes a social parasite.

Poverty is closely related to dependence or pauperism, because it is frequently the anteroom, so to speak, to pauperism, although only a small proportion of those who live in poverty actually become dependent in any one year.

The Extent of Poverty and Pauperism in the United States.—The census reports showed that in the year 1904 there were about 500,000 dependents in institutions in the United States. While the number who received relief outside of institutions from public and private sources is not known, it is certain that it is many times the total of those in institutions. It is generally estimated that about five per cent of our population are recipients of some sort of charitable relief in a single year. In our large cities the number who receive relief from public and private sources, even in average years, is very much higher. In New York apparently the number who receive relief in an average year reaches fourteen per cent, while in Boston the number who receive relief has reached as high as twenty per cent in a single year. It seems probable, therefore, that taking the country as a whole nearly five per cent of our population have to have some sort of help every year. That would make the number who received relief in 1904 about 4,000,000, and probably this is not an excessive estimate. Upon the basis of these and other known facts Mr. Robert Hunter has estimated that the number of people in the United States living below the poverty line is about 10,000,000 in years of average prosperity. If negroes are included in this estimate of those below the poverty line, it is certainly not excessive. Probably 10,000,000, or fourteen per cent of our population, understates rather than overstates the number of persons in the United States who live upon such a low standard that they fail to maintain physical and mental efficiency.

Moreover, investigations in the countries of Europe show that the estimate of fourteen per cent of our population living in poverty is far from excessive. Mr. Charles Booth, in his *Life and Labor of the People of London*, says that about thirty per cent of the population of London live below the poverty line, and Mr. B.S. Rowntree found in the English City of York about the same proportion. While poverty is more prevalent in the old world than in the United States, it would seem that in view of our large negro population it is evidently not excessive to estimate the proportion of our people living in poverty at about fifteen per cent.

Moreover, when we extend our view in history we find that poverty has been oftentimes in the past even much more prevalent than it is at present. This question of poverty is, in other words, a world-old question and is intimately bound up with the question of material civilization—that is, man's conquest of nature—and with social organization,—the relations of men to one another. At certain times in history certain institutions like slavery have either obviated or concealed poverty, and particularly its extreme expressions, in dependence and legal pauperism. Nevertheless we can regard these questions of poverty and pauperism as practically existing in all civilizations and in all ages. This is not saying, however, that modern poverty and pauperism may not have certain peculiar foundations in modern social and industrial conditions. It is only saying that it is useless to search wholly for the causes of poverty in conditions that are peculiar to the modern world, because poverty and pauperism are not peculiarly modern problems.

The Genesis of the Depressed Classes.—So complex a problem, it might be said at once, cannot manifestly have a simple explanation, yet this has been the mistake of many social thinkers of the past. They have sought some single simple explanation of human misery, and particularly in its form of economic distress or poverty. Malthus, as we have already seen, attributed all human misery to the fact that population tends to increase more rapidly than food supply, and that it is the pressure of population upon food which sufficiently explains poverty in human society. Karl Marx offered an equally sweeping explanation when he attributed all poverty to the fact that labor is not paid a sufficient wage; that the capitalist appropriates an unjust share of the product of labor, leaving to the laborer just enough to maintain existence and reproduce. Henry George in the same spirit, in his *Progress and Poverty*, attributed all poverty to one cause,—the landlord's appropriation of the unearned increment in land values. There is, of course, some truth in all of these sweeping generalizations, but it must be said that there is not sufficient in any of them to stand the test of concrete investigation; rather these men have made the mistake of attempting to explain a very complex social phenomenon in terms of a single set of causes, which, as we have already seen, has been the bane of social science in the past. Even the theory of evolution itself fails to explain, as ordinarily stated, the genesis of the depressed classes in human society. It may explain it in part, however. As we have already seen, biological variations are always found in individuals, making some naturally superior, some naturally inferior, and in the struggle for existence we know that the inferior are more liable to go down; they are less apt to maintain a place in society, and hence more readily fall into the depressed classes. Many well-endowed persons, however, also fall into the dependent classes through accidents and causes inherent in our social organization but in no way natural. Thus, owing to our industrial system and to our laws of property, inheritance, and the like, it often happens that a superior person through sickness or other accident gets caught in a mesh of causes which bring him down to the dependent classes, and on the other hand inferior individuals, through inheritance or "social pull," oftentimes enjoy a very large economic surplus all their lives. It may be admitted, however, that slight defects in personal character or ability enter into practically all cases of dependence. This is more apt to be the case also in a progressive society like our own, where rising standards of efficiency make the economic struggle more severe all the time. Formerly, for example, any employee could drink and retain his position, but now the drinker quickly loses his position in many industries and gives place to the sober man. Oftentimes, however, such defects that give rise to dependence are not inherent but are produced by social conditions themselves, like faulty education, bad surroundings, and the like. Through the improvement of social conditions, therefore, there is no doubt that much of the present poverty of the civilized world can be wiped out. This is not saying, however, that poverty and dependence will ever be wholly eliminated. Probably, no matter how ideal social conditions might be, even under the most just social organization, there would be some accidents and variations in individuals which would produce a condition of dependence. Moreover, the elimination of poverty and pauperism is not so simple as some suppose. It is not wholly a question of the improvement of social conditions; it also involves the control of physical heredity, because many of the principal defects that give rise to dependence are inherent in heredity. But man can control to some extent even the birth of the inferior or unfit classes. This may seem, however, so far in the future that it is idle to discuss it, although, as we shall see, society is undoubtedly taking steps to prevent the propagation of the unfit. In the meantime, however, so long as humanity progresses through natural selection we shall have poverty, to some extent at least, no matter how much industrial and social conditions may be improved. Yet without the control of physical heredity or the substitution of artificial for natural selection, poverty can be undoubtedly greatly lessened, and it is the rational aim of applied social science to discover how this may be done. It would seem that the existence of 10,000,000 persons in the United States living below the poverty line cannot be justified upon either moral or economic grounds; that it represents a great waste of human life and human resources, and that much of the social maladjustment which this poverty is an expression of might easily yield to wisely instituted remedial measures. If the social maladjustment which is undoubtedly the cause of the bulk of modern poverty were done away with, it is safe to say that it would be reduced to less than one third of its present dimensions.

The Concrete Causes of Poverty.—It is necessary to inquire somewhat more minutely into the concrete conditions, social and individual, which give rise to poverty and dependence. Manifestly the poor do not constitute any single class in society. All classes, in a sense, are represented among the poor, and the causes of poverty which are manifest will depend very greatly upon the class of the poor that is studied. If, for example, we should study the causes of dependence among defective classes, naturally personal defects of various sorts would be emphasized. Again, if we should study almshouse paupers, we should expect to find the causes of their dependence different from the causes of the temporary dependence of those who are dealt with outside of institutions and largely by private societies, especially the charity organization societies of large cities. It is especially, however, this latter class of temporary dependents that we are most interested in, because they show most clearly the forces operating to produce the various classes of permanent dependents.

There are two great classes of causes of poverty: objective causes, or causes outside of the individual, that is, in the environment; and subjective causes, or causes within the individual. We shall take up first the objective causes.

The Objective Causes of Poverty. The objective causes of poverty may be again divided into causes in the physical environment and causes in the social environment. The causes in the physical environment should not be overlooked, even though to a great extent they may not be amenable to social control. Much poverty in certain regions is caused simply by the unpropitious physical environment, such as unproductive soil, bad climate, and the like. Added to these unpropitious factors in the environment we have also great natural calamities, such as tornadoes, floods, earthquakes, and volcanic eruptions. Every one is familiar with the great amount of misery which is caused, temporarily at least, by such calamities. Again, certain things in the organic environment, particularly in the way of disease-producing bacteria, are also productive of much poverty. Certain bacteria exist, we now know, plentifully in nature, such as the malaria germ, to which rightfully has been ascribed the physical degeneracy of people living in certain sections of the earth.

But the most important objective causes of poverty are undoubtedly those found in the social environment,—those which spring from certain social conditions or faults in social organization. Among these we may mention:

(1) *Economic Causes.* Defective industrial organization and economic evils of various sorts are thought by many persons to be the main productive causes of poverty and dependence in modern society, and there can be no doubt that a very large per cent of poverty may be traced directly to economic evils. This is shown by the fact that in the schedules of all charity organization societies "lack of employment" figures as the first or second most conspicuous cause of distress in the cases with which such societies deal. It is usually estimated that from twenty to forty per cent of all such cases of dependence may be attributed to lack of employment, not due to the employee. It is well known that in periods of industrial depression the number of applicants for aid in our large cities increases enormously, and local strikes and lockouts frequently have the same effect. Again, changes in methods of production through the introduction of new machinery frequently displace large numbers of workingmen, who, on account of age or other reasons, fail to get employment along new lines. Changes in trade brought about through changes in fashions have to some extent at least a similar effect. Again, fluctuations in the value of money may undoubtedly depress a debtor class to the point of dependence. Unwise methods of taxation, such as levying heavy taxes on the necessaries of life, produce a great deal of poverty and economic distress. Systems of land tenure such as prevail in England and even to some extent in the United States, may also be another economic cause of poverty. The free land which has up to the present time existed in this country has been a great aid against poverty. The employment of women and children in factories is another cause of poverty which needs to be mentioned under this head. As we have already seen, this breaks up the home, and in the case of the employment of children stops the development of the child. Still another economic cause of poverty is unhealthful and dangerous occupations. The disease-begetting occupations in modern industry are very numerous, such as hat making,

glass blowing, the grinding of tools, and the like—any work in which there is a great deal of dust. Among dangerous occupations must also be included those in which there are numerous accidents, such as mining and railway occupations. The accidents in mines and on railways in the United States each year cause as many deaths and serious injuries as have often resulted in many a petty war. Thus, on the railways of the United States in 1904 there was a total of 10,046 persons killed and 84,155 injured, about three fourths of those injured being employees,—one employee being killed in every three hundred and fifty-seven and one injured in every seventeen. While it is improbable that our great industries can be carried on without some sacrifice of health and life, it seems reasonable to believe that the number of those who are sacrificed at present is far greater than is necessary, and that reasonable precautions in industry might greatly increase the healthfulness of the occupations and diminish the number of accidents to employees.

On the whole, it is probable that these economic causes of poverty figure in from 50 to 80 per cent of all cases, not operating alone, to be sure, but often in connection with faults of character or physical or mental defects in the individual; for it is always to be remembered in discussing the causes of poverty that one never finds a case which can be fairly attributed to a single cause. The complexity of causes operating in the case of a single dependent family frequently makes it impossible for any one to say with certainty what is the chief and what are the contributing causes. Oftentimes what appears to be the chief cause, such as lack of employment, has back of it defects in individual character which are not apparent to the investigator. Researches along this line have shown that the number of cases of distress which may be attributed to lack of employment, for example, may be very greatly reduced when all individual defects are taken into consideration. This, however, is not an argument for regarding the economic causes of poverty as any less important than has been indicated.

(2) Unsanitary conditions of living are frequent causes of poverty. Among these unsanitary conditions may be mentioned especially the housing of the poor. The housing of the poor in badly ventilated, poorly lighted, and unsanitary dwellings greatly increases sickness and death and undoubtedly contributes greatly to their economic depression. Thus in New York city in the first ward, where there is only one house on each lot, the death rate is 29 per 1000 of the population, but where rear tenements have been erected it is 62 per 1000 of the population. The importance of public sanitation, and especially of the prevention of overcrowding and the securing of properly lighted and ventilated dwellings for the people, is so great that we need not enlarge upon it.

(3) Defects in our educational system are certainly productive of poverty. Ignorant and illiterate persons are much more liable to become dependent. In particular the lack of industrial training in our public schools is a prolific cause of dependence in our complex industrial civilization.

(4) Defects in government, permitting corruption on the one hand, or failing to check economic or sanitary evils on the other hand, are manifest causes of poverty. Indeed, inasmuch as government exists to regulate the whole social order, wherever it fails to perform this work properly some economic distress must ensue.

(5) Corruption in social institutions and customs is certainly a cause of poverty: such, for example, is the custom of social drinking, and such also the unwise and indiscriminate charity which has so often existed in the past.

(6) Unrestricted immigration, especially in our Eastern states and cities, is, as we have already seen, a prolific cause of dependence.

The Subjective Causes of Poverty are the causes within the individual. Among these must be enumerated: (1) Physical and mental defects of all sorts, especially those arising from sickness and accidents. Sickness causing temporary or permanent disability figures in from 25 to 40 per cent of all cases applying for relief in our large cities. Probably it is the most common and most important single cause of poverty with which charity workers have to deal. Back of sickness, however, are often remote causes in the environment or in personal character. We have already spoken of accident as a cause of poverty in connection with dangerous occupations. It is only necessary to add that good authorities estimate that there are over 1,000,000 serious accidents in the United States every year, in order to see that disabilities resulting from accident are prolific as causes of poverty, especially in our large industrial centers. The physical and mental defects which manifest themselves in the defective classes proper, such as the feeble-minded, the insane, the epileptics, the deaf-mutes, and the blind, do not need to be dwelt upon as causes of dependence.

(2) Next after sickness in the list of subjective causes of poverty comes intemperance. While the effect of intemperance in producing poverty has often been exaggerated, there can be no doubt that intemperance is one of the most important causes with which we have to deal. Back of intemperance, of course, may often be again causes in the social environment, or other remote causes, but these do not detract from the fact that practically one fourth of all the cases of distress with which charity organization societies have to deal are attributable, more or less, to intemperance. The Committee of Fifty who investigated this subject found that, in thirty-three cities, out of thirty thousand cases dependence was due to personal intemperance in 18.46 per cent, and due to the intemperance of

others in 9.36 per cent, making a total of 27.82 per cent of cases in which intemperance can be traced as a cause of poverty. Other investigations conducted in American cities give substantially the same results, although certain other investigations in English cities give higher percentages. It is noteworthy also that in an investigation conducted by the Massachusetts Bureau of Labor 39 per cent of the cases of poverty were attributed directly or indirectly to drink. Again the Committee of Fifty found that in the case of alms-house paupers a considerably higher per cent owed their condition to the influence of drink either directly or indirectly, the percentage being 41.55.

(3) Sexual vice is undoubtedly a prolific cause of poverty, although it is very hard to trace concretely in the study of specific cases. Dr. Dugdale, however, in his study of the Jukes family places sexual vice even ahead of intemperance as a cause of their degradation, and other similar studies of similar families have reached substantially the same results.

(4) Shiftlessness and laziness are frequently found in the lists of causes of dependence used by charity organization societies, from 10 to 15 per cent of the cases of distress being attributed more or less to these causes. It is now generally agreed, however, that in most cases these causes may be resolved into more remote causes, laziness being oftentimes attributable to a degenerate or at least undervitalized physical condition.

(5) Old age, which has not been rendered destitute by vice, drink, or other faults of character, is frequently in itself a cause of dependence. Old age seems to figure more largely as a cause of dependence in the European statistics than in American; nevertheless, even in America we frequently find old persons who have worked hard all their lives and yet come to poverty in their old age through no fault of their own. It is for this reason that many are urging old-age pensions as a means of preventing dependence among the aged.

(6) Neglect and desertion by relatives, or the disregard of family ties, in America at least, may be put down as one of the important causes of dependence. From five to ten per cent of all the cases of distress, for example, which charity organization societies in our large cities deal with are those of deserted wives. Again, it is particularly common in America for children to fail to support aged parents and even the desertion of children by parents is of frequent occurrence.

(7) Death of main support must also be mentioned as an important cause of dependence. Widows and their children always figure largely among those helped by charitable societies and institutions. Probably from 10 to 20 per cent of all cases dealt with by societies for relieving temporary distress

are cases in which the death of the breadwinner has temporarily rendered the family dependent.

(8) Crime, dishonesty, ignorance, and the like are manifest frequent causes of dependence, and as such need no discussion.

We have enumerated in detail some of the more important objective and subjective causes of poverty and dependence in order that the student may see that such causes are very complex, and, as we have already said, there rarely exists a dependent family in which three or more of these causes are not found to be active. Certain questions arise from such a brief presentation as this which we may mention but cannot hope adequately to deal with. Such, for example, is the question whether the subjective causes of poverty can all be reduced to objective causes. In our opinion this cannot be done, because the subjective causes have their roots in biological and psychological conditions, which cannot be attributed directly to causes in the environment. No doubt, however, many of the subjective causes of poverty are characteristics which have been acquired by individuals from the influence of their environment. When we attribute a certain per cent of poverty to intemperance, for example, it is probable that that particular personal defect may be ascribed almost wholly to the environment. On the other hand, there are other personal defects, such as sickness, vice, and mental deficiency, that cannot always with certainty be traced to environmental factors. It is safest to conclude that while personality is built up largely out of social influences, society is, on the other hand, also rooted in human nature, so that both objective and subjective causes combine to produce practically all social phenomena, and especially the phenomena of poverty and dependence. It is unscientific, therefore, to disregard either the subjective or the objective causes of poverty.

Another question which is frequently raised in connection with poverty or dependence is, whether it is due to misconduct or misfortune. This question really has not much meaning in it when it is analyzed. As we have already seen in practically every case of poverty, personal defects and bad environment combine. Only a few of these personal defects, however, can by any proper use of language be regarded as misconduct. The great mass of poverty, therefore, seems attributable to misfortune rather than to misconduct,—using these words in their popular sense. But such a conclusion as this necessarily rests upon a somewhat superficial examination of the causes of distress which does not enter into the remote springs of personal character and development. On the whole, it seems unwise to attempt to divide the poor into the "worthy" and "unworthy" poor, as has often been done, for no one can say who is the worthy and who is the unworthy in a moral sense. The only sense in which these words may be used scientifically in charitable work is to mean "needy" and "not needy."

Pauperism and Degeneracy. In order to see more clearly the biological roots of dependence we must notice briefly the relation of habitual pauperism to degeneracy. Studies like that made by Dr. Dugdale of the Jukes family show that unquestionably there is in many instances a close relation between habitual pauperism of various types and degeneracy. Out of 709 in the Jukes family studied by Dugdale 500 had been aided. Pauperism was 7 1_2 times as common among the Jukes as in the ordinary population. Along with the pauperism of the Jukes went prostitution, illegitimacy, crime, and physical disease and defects. Many other studies have shown the same intimate relation between physical degeneracy and habitual dependence or pauperism. There can be no doubt, therefore, that general physical degeneracy, or biological unfitness, is, as we have already asserted in the beginning, a conspicuous factor in the worst cases of chronic pauperism.

The Influence of Heredity upon Pauperism. Similar studies to those already mentioned have shown that dependence is often times hereditary in families from generation to generation. This is doubtless based upon the inheritance of physical and mental defects. Indirectly, therefore, there is such a thing as hereditary pauperism. Now we know from the labors of Weismann that acquired characteristics are not inherited, but only congenital, or inborn characteristics. It is not the characteristics, in other words, which are acquired from the influence of environment that are transmitted to offspring, but the characteristics that arise through variations in the germ, caused by forces which are not yet well understood. Defects that are acquired by the individual in his lifetime, in other words, will not be transmitted; but the defects that arise through accident or other means in the germ are transmitted. This being so, it follows that acquired pauperism or dependence is not transmitted but only the pauperism which rests upon congenital defects. This is illustrated by the case of the deaf. Deaf-mutes are of two sorts: persons who are born deaf, or the congenital deaf-mutes, and persons who become deaf-mutes through diseases affecting the ear in early childhood. These latter are styled adventitious deaf-mutes. Now when congenital deaf-mutes marry, they show a strong tendency to transmit their defect to offspring, but the children of adventitious deaf-mutes are always normal. Dr. Fay, in his investigations into the marriages of the deaf in the United States shows that only 0.3 per cent of the children born from the marriages of persons adventitiously deaf and having no deaf relatives are born deaf; while on the other hand, 30.3 per cent of the children born from the marriages of persons congenitally deaf, both parents having deaf relatives, are born deaf. In other words, the number of deaf-mutes born where both parents are congenitally deaf and have deaf relatives is one hundred times greater than where both parents are adventitiously deaf and have no deaf relatives. This is pretty conclusive proof that it is only the congenital defects which are transmissible, but these are so highly transmissible that they may express themselves in pauperism from generation to generation.

The marriage of all persons in whom there is an hereditary taint of feeble-mindedness, insanity, epilepsy, and the like ought, therefore, to be forbidden by law. But unless these defective classes were segregated in institutions, the only result of this might be to increase illegitimacy; therefore, any step in eradicating degeneracy and pauperism must look to the isolation and custodial care through life of the hopelessly defective classes. All this gives point to our conclusion that poverty and pauperism have roots which are quite independent of defects in economic conditions, and that, until heredity itself can be controlled, we cannot expect to eliminate poverty entirely.

Proposed Remedies for Poverty and Pauperism.—The scientific remedies for poverty and pauperism, that is, the scientific methods of dealing with the various dependent classes and of preventing their existence, now form the subject-matter of a great independent science, the science of philanthropy, which, as we have already seen, may be considered a branch of applied sociology. We have not room in this book to discuss adequately these remedies, but we may call the attention of the student again to the vast literature existing upon the subject, and may point out the trend of modern scientific philanthropy in developing scientific methods for removing the causes of dependence and of preventing the existence of the various dependent classes.

As we have already seen, poverty is an economic expression of biological or psychological defects of the individual on the one hand, and of a faulty social and industrial organization on the other hand. This implies that the remedies must be along the lines of the biological and psychological adjustment of the individual and of the correction of the faults in social organization.

Where biological defects of the individual are the cause of dependence, we have just implied that, unless these defects are relatively superficial, the scientific policy for treating these classes of defective individuals would be that of segregation in institutions. The feeble-minded, the chronic insane, the chronic epileptic, and other hopelessly defective persons, in other words, should be permanently kept in institutions where tender and humane care should be provided, but in such a way that they will not reproduce their kind and burden future generations. The policy of segregating the hopelessly defective is one of the most scientifically approved policies of modern philanthropy. In this way, to a certain extent, the reproduction of unfit elements in society might be lessened, and the spread of degeneracy checked. In the case of slightly defective adults, such as the congenitally deaf and the congenitally blind, it is difficult to say exactly what the policy should be. It would seem that many of these persons may be relatively adjusted to free social life, although if they marry and have offspring we know, if their defect is congenital, that a certain proportion of the offspring, according to Mendel's law, will inherit the defect.

In the case of those individuals whose dependence is due to psychological defects, or defective character, it is evident that we have a different problem. Here, in general, the wise policy would seem to be, not to segregate, but to overcome the defective character. Psychological defects, we know, are much more frequently acquired than biological defects and much more easily remedied. The work of scientific philanthropy in dealing with this class of individuals must be, therefore, a work of remedying defects in individual character. This is, perhaps, best done through personal relations between the dependent person and those who may help him. Defective character is, on the whole, therefore, best remedied by such means as education, religious influences, friendly visiting, and the like. The class of dependents whose condition is due to defective character may be on the whole, therefore, best treated outside of institutions, and probably better through voluntary private charity than through public relief systems.

There remains another class of dependents whose condition is not due either to biological nor to psychological defects in themselves, but to faulty social and industrial conditions. For these, the best method of treatment consists in remedying the faulty conditions or in removing them, if possible, from them. This means that, in many cases, society must provide pensions, insurance against accident and sickness, legislation to check social abuses, and, above all, proper facilities for education. Here comes in the need of child-labor legislation, of better housing, of industrial insurance, of industrial education, and the like.

In the light of these principles, let us review very briefly the different methods of dealing with dependent classes at the present time.

Public and Private Outdoor Relief. By outdoor relief we mean relief given to the poor outside of an institution. Usually, outdoor relief refers simply to the public relief of dependents outside of institutions, but we shall use the phrase to cover both public and private relief. It is evident from what has already been said that the class of persons to whom this form of relief is appropriate are those in temporary distress, whose condition of dependence is not a permanent one and, therefore, usually those whose condition is due either to defective personal character or to faulty social organization. If the temporary dependence is due to defective personal character, it is evident that the aid may be so given, if given wisely, as to stimulate the overcoming of the moral defect. Hence the need of carefully planned measures of relief in all such cases. Hence, also, the need of the friendly visitor, who by personal contact with such a family will help them to become socially adjusted. If, on the other hand, the temporarily dependent person is simply a victim of circumstances, there is, then, also, the need of wise charity in order to overcome those adverse circumstances without impairing the character of the individual who is helped by destroying his self-respect and the like.

It is evident that the task of relieving temporarily dependent persons outside of institutions is a delicate and difficult one, and requires carefully trained workers to do it successfully. For this reason, many have argued that outdoor relief should not be undertaken by the state in any of its branches, such as the city or county. In general, it must be admitted that the private society is, in many cases, naturally better fitted to accomplish this delicate and difficult task of restoring the temporarily dependent person. But, on the other hand, it must be said that the whole matter is simply a question of administration. Private societies may be quite as lax and unscientific in their charity as the state, and it is conceivable that the state can develop a system of outdoor relief which will be administered by experts quite as carefully as any private organization could administer it. Indeed, this is what has been practically done in Germany under the *Elberfeldt System*, which is a state system for dispensing outdoor relief to the temporarily indigent. In the United States, however, this work of relieving the temporarily dependent in their own homes has been, in our large cities, undertaken with great success by the charity organization societies, which, in general, do the work with such thoroughness as to obviate the necessity for public outdoor relief in our large cities.

State Charitable Institutions. Indoor relief, or relief within institutions, for the permanently dependent classes is probably best undertaken by the state. Originally, the only institution of this sort was the almshouse or the poor house; but with the development of our complex civilization many of the permanently dependent have been provided for in other institutions than the almshouse, and it would seem that ultimately all the permanently dependent would be cared for in specialized state institutions. Thus, the permanently dependent, through various sorts of defects, such as the feeble-minded, chronic epileptic, chronic insane, and the like, are properly cared for in institutions especially provided for the purpose by the state and manned by experts. Into the details of public care of the unfit and defective of various types it is not necessary to go further than to say that such public care should be of the most scientific character, and with the double aim of reclaiming all those that can be reclaimed, and of providing permanently tender and humane care for those who cannot be fitted for free social life. State institutions then, should be manned by experts, and their activities should be coördinated by some central board. In accordance with this principle, it would seem that the best state policy would be to provide expert commissions for the care of different classes, such as the insane, and the like, and a supervisory board to watch over the work of these commissions and the institutions.

Dependent Children. The care of dependent children is manifestly one of the most important forms of remedial philanthropic work, for it is manifest that the dependent child will make a dependent adult unless proper measures are taken to secure his adjustment to the social life. The dependent child is rarely biologically defective. The problem is, usually, in his case, the development of character under proper social conditions. For this reason, both the state and private societies have claimed the field of care of dependent children. While private societies have accomplished in this respect some of the most notable work, it would seem, however, that the work is one which properly belongs to the state in its capacity of legal guardian of all dependent children. The state, through a properly organized system of child helping, could conceivably guarantee that every neglected and dependent child should have normal opportunities to become adjusted to the social life. The system in the state of Michigan, with its Public School for Dependent Children at Coldwater, and its plan of placing these children, after a few months, in good homes, is a system which cannot receive too high commendation. In general, it is practically agreed by experts that the dependent child cannot be well adjusted to the social life by being reared in an institution, but that the better plan is to find suitable homes in which these children can be placed and reared under state supervision. In this way, practically every dependent child can be guaranteed a good chance in life. In the United States, private societies called "Childrens' Home Societies" are also doing this work with great success.

Public and Private Charity. As has already been indicated, the ordinary line to be observed between private charity and public relief is that to private charity should be given the more delicate and difficult tasks, such as readjusting the temporarily dependent persons, the care of, in some cases, dependent children and the like, while to public charity should be given the cases which need permanent relief in institutions. This is only a conventional line, however, between private charity and public relief. As has already been pointed out, the state can conceivably, also, undertake the more delicate and difficult tasks of charitable aid, and probably it should do so as rapidly as it demonstrates its fitness to undertake this work, as the state, when once it has achieved certain standards, is a more certain and reliable agency than private institutions or societies. But there is in philanthropic work, a large place for the private society or institution. There will probably always be debatable cases which may better be looked after by private agencies than by public. There is, therefore, in every well-developed community, room for both public and private agencies, although there should be close coöperation where both exist one with the other. The church, through all its history, has undertaken philanthropic work with notable success, and it would be regrettable if the philanthropic activities of the church were to cease at this time, when they are needed as never before, in spite of the large development of public philanthropy. Church charity should, however, be made as scientific as any other form of charity, and should be carefully coördinated with the work of the state and other secular agencies. Among the secular agencies we have already mentioned the charity organization society as typifying in many ways the highest type of philanthropic activity of the present. It would seem that this society, organizing as it does all the philanthropic forces and agencies of the community, could scarcely be displaced by state activity; and that there would remain to this society, as well as many other private philanthropic societies, a very large field of activity in the future. State activity in the field of charity is, therefore, to be encouraged, but it must not be supposed that such activity can take the place of private charity.

Preventive Agencies. A very large task for both private societies and the state is to be found in the field of prevention. This field is so broad, however, that we cannot attempt to even mention the many different movements alone which characterize our present social development. Such are the movements for better housing, for better sanitation, for purer food, for juster economic conditions, for the prevention of disease, and the like. The main thing to be said with respect to these movements is that they need to be guided by the larger social view, they need synthesis in order that they may work toward a common goal, and in harmony, also, with the activities of the state. In the field of prevention the state has much to do, especially in forwarding education along lines of social need and in creating juster economic conditions.

We may, perhaps, sum up this chapter by saying that it is evident that the cure of poverty is not to be sought merely in certain economic rearrangements, but in scientific control of the whole life process of human society. This means that, in order to get rid of poverty, the defects in education, in government, in religion and morality, in philanthropy, and even in physical heredity, must be got rid of. Of course, this can only be done when there is a scientific understanding of the conditions necessary for normal human social life. What some of these requirements for a normal life are will be seen in a subsequent chapter, and it is only necessary to say in conclusion that the wisest measures for removing pauperism will be directed toward the prevention of its causes rather than toward the reclaiming of those who have already been caught in its meshes.

SELECT REFERENCES

For brief reading:

WARNER, *American Charities*, Revised Edition.
DEVINE, *Misery and Its Causes*.
HUNTER, *Poverty*.

For more extended reading:

DUGDALE, *The Jukes*. DEVINE, *Principles of Relief.* HENDERSON, *Dependent, Defective and Delinquent Classes*. RUS, *How the Other Half Lives*. ROWNTREE, *Poverty: a Study of Town Life. Proceedings of the National Conference of Charities and Correction. The Survey* (formerly *Charities and the Commons*).

CHAPTER XIII

CRIME

The problem of crime is one of the great problems of social pathology. There have been developed, in order to deal with this problem scientifically, a number of subsidiary sciences, especially Criminology and Penology, which are sciences dealing with the causes, nature, and treatment of crime. We cannot therefore deal with this problem adequately in this chapter, but again must refer the student to the literature on the subject.

The Definition of Crime.—The best definition of crime and the simplest is that it is a violation of law. It is evident from this definition that crime is primarily a legal matter; and as laws vary from age to age and from country to country, so too the definition of crime varies. Nevertheless, because crime is a variable quantity that does not make it impossible of scientific treatment; for law itself is only one aspect or phase of the social life, namely, that which has to do with the control of conduct through organized social authority. Therefore, while crime is primarily a legal matter, it is also a social matter and has at the same time psychological and biological implications. While crime is an expression of social maladjustment defined by the law differently under different circumstances, it nevertheless has psychological and biological roots; and these we must take into account in a scientific study of crime.

The simplest and best definition of the criminal accordingly is a violator of the law. However, because the criminal lacks social adjustment the causes of this lack of adjustment are very often in certain psychological and biological conditions of the individual. While the criminal is defined by the law differently from age to age, he is nevertheless under all circumstances the socially peculiar and sometimes the psychologically and biologically peculiar person. Under all circumstances he is a variation from his group; and whether the causes of his variation are psychological or biological is the problem that concerns us.

But in the group of socially maladjusted persons whom we call criminals are many classes and it is necessary to note the chief of these classes before we can understand the many causes of crime.

The classification of criminals. The legal classification of criminals according to the nature of their crime is manifestly of no use for scientific purposes. What we need is a classification of criminals according to their own peculiar nature. Inasmuch as the nature and conduct of a criminal person is largely a matter of his psychology the most scientific classification of criminals must be upon a psychological basis; and a simple psychological classification can be made upon the basis of habit, that is, as to whether the habit of crime is inborn, acquired, or not yet formed. According to this classification then there are three main classes of criminals: (i) The instinctive or born criminal. This is a person in whom the tendency to crime is inborn, and this inborn tendency is always due to some congenital defect. The most common type of the instinctive or born criminal is the moral imbecile, a person only slightly mentally defective who cannot distinguish right from wrong. It is evident that in the instinctive or born criminal biological causes of crime predominate. This class is however relatively small among the general criminal class, and it is estimated by experts that it constitutes not more than from 10 per cent to 15 per cent of our prison population. (2) The habitual criminal. The habitual criminal is a normal person who has acquired the tendency to crime from his environment. The most marked type of the habitual criminal is the professional criminal, who is frequently a person above the average in ability and who deliberately chooses a career of crime, taking the risks of his calling. It is evident that the professional criminal class is the most dangerous class of criminals with whom society has to deal. A more common type of habitual criminal, however, is the occasional habitual criminal, a weak person who drifts into crime through temptation and who has not strength of character enough to throw off the habit. It is estimated that habitual criminals of both types mentioned constitute from 40 per cent to 50 per cent of our prison population. (3) The single offender. The single offender is a normal person who commits only a single crime through some sudden stress or temptation, but lives ever after a law-abiding life. The two types of the single offender are the criminal by passion and the accidental criminal. The criminal by passion is a moral, and oftentimes a conscientious, person who commits a crime through some sudden stress of passion, under great provocation. The accidental criminal, on the other hand, is the weak type of moral person who yields once through some sudden temptation, but who regrets it ever afterward. It is estimated that single offenders constitute from 40 per cent to 50 per cent of our prison population. Strictly speaking, they are only legal criminals, and not criminals in the sociological sense, being relatively moral and law-abiding citizens whose variation from the normal is confined to some single offense. Nevertheless, single offenders constitute, as we have already seen, a very considerable proportion of our prison population.

If this classification of criminals is correct, it is evident that it is very important both in studying the causes of crime and in devising practical measures for dealing with the criminal class; for the instinctive criminal, the habitual criminal, and the single offender manifestly need very different methods of treatment. One of the gravest faults of the criminal law and of penal institutions hitherto is that they have not provided for the different treatment of different classes of criminals.

The Extent of Crime in the United States.—According to the United States census there were in prisons on June 30, 1904, a total of 81,772 prisoners above the age of five years serving sentences. Of this number 77,269 were males and 4503 were females; again, 55,111 were whites, and 26,661 were colored. Classified according to the prisons in which they were found, 53,292 were in state penitentiaries, 7261 were in state reformatories, 18,544 were in county jails, and 2675 were in city prisons. These were only the persons serving prison sentences. An unknown number were in county and city jails awaiting trial and serving out fines. Again, it must be remembered that this was simply the prison population on a single day, June 30, 1904. During 1904 there were, according to the census, 149,691 persons committed to prisons to serve sentences. To all of the above we must add also the 23,034 juvenile delinquents who were found, on June 30, 1904, in the juvenile reformatories of the United States.

Unfortunately we have no figures from previous censuses with which we can compare the above, as the census of 1890 and previous censuses included prisoners awaiting trial. In 1890, however, there were, deducting the 15,526 awaiting trial and serving out fines, 66,803 persons above the age of five years serving sentences.

These prison statistics, however, give us little idea of the actual amount of crime in the United States, because they include only the persons committed to prison to serve sentences, and do not include the vast number who escape the meshes of the law or who simply receive fines, or whose sentences are suspended. It is estimated by competent authorities, basing their estimate upon the number of known convictions of crime in certain large cities, that there are not less than 1,000,000 convictions for crime, annually, in the United States—including, of course, convictions for both felonies and misdemeanors. That this is not an excessive estimate may be indicated by the fact that in the state of New York alone in 1900, a year before the custom of suspending sentence on probation came so largely into vogue, there were nearly 100,000 commitments to prison.

All these figures, however, fail to give us any very correct idea of the amount of serious crime in the United States—the prison statistics, because they understate the matter, the statistics of convictions, because they overstate. A peculiarity about serious crime in the United States, it must be remembered, is that so many persons escape through the meshes of the law, and this is particularly true in the case of the characteristic American crime of homicide. An enterprising newspaper, *The Chicago Tribune*, has for years, with the help of the Associated Press, collected statistics of homicide and suicide in the United States. While these statistics seem relatively incomplete and inaccurate for the earlier years, since 1892 they present every appearance of great accuracy, and have not been seriously impugned. According to these statistics the United States has had for the last dozen years from six to ten thousand cases of homicide annually, including all cases where one person has killed another. In 1896 the number was 10,652, in 1899, 6225; in 1900, 8275; in 1904, 8482; in 1906, 9350; in 1908, 8592. The census of 1904 showed only 2444 persons committed to prison for homicide in that year, but these figures are not in conflict with those of *The Chicago Tribune*, because the census statistics omit the vast number of persons who committed homicide but who escaped, were not convicted, were killed, or for some other reason failed to show up in the statistics of commitment. Accepting *The Chicago Tribune's* figures as relatively accurate, it may be remarked at this point that the number of homicides is far greater in the United States than in other civilized countries, with the exception of Italy, Spain, and some other countries of the Mediterranean region. England, for example, has only between three and four hundred cases of homicide annually as compared with our six to ten thousand, although England's population is about 30,000,000 as against over 80,000,000 for the United States. The greatest number of these homicides take place in the Southern and Western states, Texas leading, according to the statistics, with about one thousand homicides annually. This suggests that to some extent our high homicide rate is due to the survival of frontier conditions in a large number of the states, although it is probably even more due to American individualism and lawlessness, the tendency of every man to take the law into his own hands.

There can be no doubt that the amount of serious crime in the United States is relatively high, although there is no reason to believe that the serious crimes against property are proportionate to the serious crimes against persons.

The Cost of Crime in the United States. The Hon. Eugene Smith, a lawyer of New York city, in a paper read before the National Prison Association in 1900, estimated that the criminal population of the United States costs not less than $600,000,000 annually. He based his estimate upon the cost of crime in New York city and other large cities of the country. He found that the probable expenses of government in the United States attributable to crime, that is, the cost of police, criminal courts, prisons, and other institutions connected with the prevention and repression of crime, amounted to about $200,000,000 per year. This is the amount paid by the taxpayers for the repression and extirpation of crime annually. In addition there is the cost of the criminal class through the destruction of property, their plunder, and the like. Mr. Smith estimated that there were no less than

250,000 dangerous criminals in the United States and that each such criminal cost the people of the United States, on the average $1600 annually. Accordingly, the 250,000 criminals would cost a total of $400,000,000 annually, which, added to the $200,000,000 paid out in taxes for the repression of the criminal class and protection against crime, makes a total of $600,000,000 paid out every year by the people of the United States as the cost of supporting the criminal class. While this figure seems enormous, careful students of the matter consider that it is an underestimate rather than an overestimate of the total cost of crime. We may compare the amount with certain other figures. The cost of public education in the United States is about $350,000,000 annually; the annual value of our wheat crop is about $600,000,000, and of our cotton crop about the same. It is evident that the problem of crime is worthy of serious study even from a financial standpoint alone.

Is Crime Increasing? How we answer this question will, of course, depend upon the length of time considered. We have no statistics going back further than fifty years in this country. Moreover, it is entirely possible to hold that while crime has decreased during the historic era among civilized peoples, it has increased during the last twenty-five or fifty years. All statistics of crime in the United States seem to show that it has increased. In 1850 for example, the number of prisoners was 6737 which was one prisoner to every 3442 of the population. But the census of 1850 was seriously defective, and we would better take the census of 1860 as the basis of our comparison. In 1860 the census showed a total prison population of 19,086, which was one prisoner to every 1647 of the population. In 1890 the census showed 82,329 prisoners in the total population, which was one in every 757. In other words, between 1860 and 1890 the total population of the country just doubled, while the number of prisoners quadrupled. Inasmuch as the census of 1904 was taken upon an entirely different basis, we cannot bring the comparison down to that year.

The value of these statistics has often been questioned, but it has been questioned chiefly by people who have not taken other corroborative evidence into account. The chief corroborating evidence is to be found in the statistics of prisoners in our state prisons from 1880 to 1904. Now only those are sent to state prisons who are guilty of felonies, and the length of term of sentence in our state prisons has steadily shortened during the last twenty-five years, while within the last few years the practice of suspending sentence on probation for first felons has been largely introduced. We should expect, therefore, a decrease in the state prison population in proportion to the general population. But we find that the number in state prisons rose from 30,659 in 1880, to 45,233 in 1890, an increase of 47.5 per cent, while the general population increased only 24.86 per cent. Again the number rose in 1904 to 60,553, an increase of 33 per cent, while the general population increased about 30 per cent. Apparently, therefore, the amount of serious crime in the United States is increasing more rapidly than the population. Corroborating evidence is also found from Massachusetts statistics, which indicate that between 1850 and 1880 the prison population increased twice as rapidly as the general population. Other evidence could be cited, but the statistics of our state penitentiaries may be considered conclusive when all facts are taken into consideration. There is apparently no escape from the conclusion that serious crime between 1880 and 1904 increased more rapidly than the population.

The amount of minor offenses, every one admits, has increased. The statistics of all European countries show this, and there is no reason to suppose that the United States is an exception in this regard. England is the only country of the civilized world in which there has been apparently a decrease in proportion to population of both serious crimes and minor offenses. This decrease of crime in England may be attributed largely to England's excellent prison system, and also to the swiftness and certainty of English courts of justice.

The Causes of Crime.—The causes of crime may be classified best, as we classified the causes of poverty, into objective and subjective. Objective causes are those outside of the individual, in the environment; subjective causes are causes in the individual, whether in his bodily make-up or his mental peculiarities.

The Objective Causes of Crime. The objective causes of crime may be divided into causes in the physical environment and causes in the social environment. The causes in the physical environment are relatively unimportant, but are worthy of note as showing how many various factors enter into this social phenomenon of crime. Climate and season seem to be the two chief physical factors that influence crime; and in connection with these we have two general rules, abundantly verified by statistics; namely, crimes against the person are more numerous in southern climates than crimes against property; and again crimes against the person are more numerous in summer than in winter, while crimes against property are more numerous in winter than in summer. All this is of course simply an outcome of the effect of climate and season upon general living conditions.

The causes of crime in the social environment are of course much the most important objective causes of crime, and, many students think, altogether the most important causes of crime in general. Let us briefly note some of the more important social conditions that give rise to crime.

(1) Conditions connected with the family life have a great influence on crime; indeed, inasmuch as the family is the chief agency in society for

socializing the young, perhaps domestic conditions are more important in the production of crime than any other set of causes. We cannot enter into the discussion of the matter fully, but we have already seen in former chapters that demoralized homes contribute an undue proportion of criminals. It is estimated by those in charge of reform schools for delinquent children that from 85 to 90 per cent of the children in those institutions come from more or less demoralized or disrupted families. Illegitimate children notoriously drift into the criminal classes, while dependent children who grow up in charitable institutions are prone also to take the same course. Domestic conditions have of course an influence on the criminality or non-criminality of adults. This is best shown perhaps by the fact that the great proportion of criminals in our prisons are unmarried persons. Thus the United States prison census of 1904 showed that 64 per cent of all prisoners were single persons. Statistics from other countries are practically the same. This means that, on the one hand, the family life is a preventive of crime, and on the other that the socially abnormal classes who drift into crime are not apt to marry.

(2) Industrial conditions also have a profound influence upon criminal statistics. Economic crises, hard times, strikes, lockouts, are all productive of crime. Quetelet, the Belgian statistician, thought that the general rule could be laid down that, as the price of food increases, crimes against property increase, while crimes against persons decrease. At any rate, increase in the cost of the necessities of life is very apt to increase crimes of certain sorts.

The various industrial classes show a different ratio of criminality. In general among industrial classes the least crime is committed by the agricultural classes, while the most crime is committed by the unemployed or those with no occupation. The census of 1904 showed that 50 per cent of all prisoners that year were non-agricultural laborers or servants.

(3) The demographical conditions, conditions concerning the distribution and density of the population, have an influence upon crime. In general there is more crime in the cities than in the country districts. The statistics of all civilized countries seem to show about twice as great a percentage of crime in their large cities as in the rural districts.

(4) The influence of race and nationality seems to be marked in criminal statistics. We have already noted that the ratio of criminality among the negroes in the United States is from four to five times higher than among the whites. We have also seen that among our recent immigrants the Southern Italians have a pronounced tendency to crime, especially serious crime. Among our older immigrants the Irish on the other hand, owing largely to their love of liquor, have a pronounced tendency toward minor

offenses. Even in 1904, 36.2 per cent of the foreign-born prisoners were Irish, while the Irish constituted but 15.6 per cent of the total foreign-born population.

(5) Defects in government and law are among the most potent causes of crime. These are so numerous that we cannot attempt even to mention all. It is obvious that such things as too great leniency on the part of our judges and shortness of sentence if convicted; difficulty or uncertainty in securing justice in criminal courts; costliness of obtaining justice in our civil courts; bad prison systems in which first offenders and hardened criminals mingle; lack of police surveillance of habitual criminals; corrupt methods of appointing the police; partisanship in the administration of government, and the like, all conduce to crime. And many of these things, we may add, have been especially in evidence in America.

(6) Educational conditions have undoubtedly a great influence upon crime. While education in the sense of school education could never in itself stamp out crime, still defective educational conditions greatly increase crime. This is shown sufficiently by the fact that illiterates are much more liable to commit crime than those who have a fair education. The prison census of 1904 showed that 12.6 per cent of the prisoners were illiterate, while only 10.7 per cent of the general population were illiterate; and of the major offenders not less than 20 per cent were illiterate.

The defects in our educational conditions which especially favor the development of crime in certain classes are chiefly: lack of facilities for industrial education, lack of physical education, and lack of specific moral instruction. The need of these three things in a socialized school system need not here be more than emphasized.

The influence of the press as a popular educator must here be mentioned as one of the important stimuli to crime under modern conditions. The excessive exploitation of crimes in the modern sensational press no doubt conduces to increase criminality in certain classes, for it has been demonstrated that crime is often a matter of suggestion or imitation. When 75 per cent of the space in our daily newspapers is taken up with reports of crime and immorality, as it is in some cases, it is not to be wondered at that the contagion of crime is sown broadcast in society.

(7) The influence of certain social institutions in producing crime must be mentioned. Here comes in especially the lack of opportunity for wholesome social amusements among our poorer classes, particularly in our large cities. Lacking these, the masses resort to the saloon, gambling-houses, cheap music and dance halls, and vulgar theatrical entertainments. The influence of all of these institutions is undoubtedly to spread the contagion of vice and crime among their patrons.

(8) The influence of manners and customs upon crime cannot be overlooked. The custom in certain communities, for example, of carrying concealed weapons undoubtedly has much to do with the swollen homicide statistics of the United States. Vicious and corrupting customs, such as compulsory social drinking, and the like, undoubtedly greatly influence crime. Even the luxury and extravagance of the rich might easily be shown to have a demoralizing effect, both upon the upper and the lower classes of society.

The list of causes of crime in the social environment might be indefinitely extended until the student would perhaps think that practically everything was a cause of crime in one way or another; and it is true that everything that depresses men in society is a cause of crime. However, if the student has gained an impression of the great complexity of the causes of crime, that is the main thing.

A question may here be raised whether it is possible to reduce all the causes of crime to causes in the social environment—that is, all subjective causes to objective. Many writers have contended that this is possible, but we shall see that there are causes in heredity and causes in psychological conditions, to say nothing of some possible free will in individuals, which cannot be derived from social conditions and which would produce crime quite independent of objective social conditions, unless these subjective factors were also controlled. There is no reason to believe that a perfectly just social organization which did not attempt to control heredity and the moral character of individuals would succeed in eliminating crime. On the contrary, biological variation alone arising from influences independent of the environment would produce a certain amount of crime. Crime, in other words, is, to a certain extent, like pauperism, an expression of the elimination of the inferior variants in society, and will continue to exist as long as we allow the process of evolution by natural selection to go on.

Nevertheless, it is true in a certain sense, as Lacassagne says, that "every society has the criminals it deserves;" that is, every society could, by taking proper means, practically eliminate crime and the criminal class. This would have to be done, however, by something more radical than a mere reorganization of human society in an industrial way. Three things are necessary for society practically to eliminate crime: first, the correction of defects in social conditions, particularly of economic evils in society; second, the proper control of physical heredity by a rational system of eugenics; third, the proper education and training of every child for social life from infancy up.

The Subjective Causes of Crime. In order to see all that is involved in the above program let us study somewhat the subjective causes of crime. These may be divided into biological and psychological. Among the biological causes of crime, and one which certainly cannot be reduced to the environment, is sex. As we have already seen, crime is a social phenomenon which is chiefly confined to the male sex. In 1904, for example, 94.5 per cent of the prison population in the United States were males, and in the statistics of convictions it is estimated that ninety-one men are convicted for every nine women. The statistics for all civilized countries show practically the same conditions, although in most European countries the proportion of female prisoners is somewhat higher, owing, undoubtedly, to certain influences in the social environment.

Another subjective factor in crime, which again cannot be reduced to environment, is age. Practically all crime falls in the active period of life, and the bulk of it between the ages of twenty-one and forty years. The average of men in our state penitentiaries is frequently not above twenty-seven or twenty-eight years.

Other subjective biological conditions that cause crime may be summed up under the word "degeneracy." These abnormal conditions, however, we shall examine later.

Among the psychological conditions of the individual that give rise to crime the most common are habits, aims, and ideals. Of peculiar interest among personal habits that have an influence upon crime is intemperance, and this is such an important cause of crime that we must stop to examine it in some detail. It is often said that 95 per cent of the crime of our country results from this cause alone. The Committee of Fifty, however, investigated the cases of 13,402 convicts with reference to this matter, and found that intemperance was a cause of crime in the cases of 49.95 per cent. It was a chief cause of crime, however, only in the cases of 31.18 per cent. In the remaining cases the intemperance was that of ancestors or associates. Other investigators have found that intemperance figures as a cause of crime in from 60 to 80 per cent of the cases, but these investigations were not so full as that of the Committee of Fifty, and it is safer to conclude, for the present at least, that intemperance figures as a cause in about fifty per cent in the cases of serious crime. The wonder is that any one cause could figure in so many cases when there are so many varied influences in society depressing men. Of course intemperance can, as has already been said, in large part be ascribed to the influence of external stimuli in the environment, but it has also causes in the biological and psychological make-up of certain individuals that cannot be easily reduced to environmental factors.

Influence of Physical Degeneracy upon Crime. By degeneracy we mean, to use Morel's definition, "a morbid deviation from the normal type." That is, degeneracy is such an alteration of organic structures and functions that the organism becomes incapable of adapting itself to more or less complex conditions. Ordinary forms of degeneracy that are well recognized are feeble-mindedness, chronic insanity, chronic epilepsy, congenital deaf-mutism, habitual pauperism, and the like. Now there can be no doubt that criminality in some of its forms is related to these functional forms of degeneracy. Even ordinary people have noticed its similarity to insanity, while Lombroso has traced an elaborate parallel between criminality and epilepsy. Without accepting extreme views, it may be claimed that criminality is, in some cases, a form of biological degeneracy for the following reasons:

(1) The investigations of criminal anthropologists have established the fact that criminals as a class present a much larger number of structural and functional abnormalities than does the average man. The prisoners in our state prisons, for example, with few exceptions, could not measure up to the requirements laid down by the United States Army authorities for the enlistment of soldiers.

(2) Investigations, like that of the Jukes family by Dr. Dugdale, have established the fact that criminals, paupers, imbeciles, drunkards, prostitutes, and other degenerates frequently spring from the same family stock. A very large percentage of the prisoners in our prisons have come from more or less degenerate family stocks.

(3) Criminals more often show other forms of degeneracy than criminality than does the average population; that is, criminals often belong to one of the well-recognized degenerate classes, such as imbeciles, epileptics, and insane.

These three arguments may be considered to be conclusive proof that criminality is in some cases a manifestation of physiological degeneracy; but they do not show that the bulk of criminals come from physiologically degenerate stocks. On the contrary it is highly probable that the marks of physiological degeneracy are not to be seen in from more than 25 to 30 per cent of our criminal class. These marks of degeneracy are of course especially common among the instinctive or born criminals, and to some extent they are found among the habitual criminals also.

The Influence of Heredity on Crime. A word must be said about the influence of heredity on crime. The student will remember that, according to the modern theory of heredity, acquired characters, or characteristics, are not transmissible. Accordingly, when we find crime running in a family for generations, as in the Jukes or Zero families, we must assume either that the criminal tendency is transmitted by the social environment or that it is due to some congenital variation in some ancestor. In other words, if a person is a criminal by hereditary defect, if the criminal tendency is born in him, as it is in the instinctive criminal, he will transmit the tendency toward crime to his offspring; but if a normal person becomes a criminal by acquired habit he will transmit no tendency toward crime to his children, although his children may of course acquire the tendency from their social environment.

This is not saying, however, that in such cases as habitual drunkenness and habitual vice an impaired constitution may not be transmitted to offspring. But this, strictly speaking, is not the transmission of any specific acquired characteristic, but only a general transmission of impaired vitality which may show itself in crime and in various forms of degeneracy. The germ cells are of course a part of the body, and anything that profoundly impairs the nutrition of the body generally, such as alcoholism and constitutional diseases, would also impair the nutrition of the germ cells, and result in a weakened constitution in offspring.

Lombroso's Theory of Crime. Lombroso, and the Italian school of criminologists generally, attribute crime chiefly to atavism, that is, reversion to primitive types. They claim that the criminal in modern society is merely a biological reversion to the savage type of man; that the criminal constitutes therefore a distinct "anthropological variety"; and that there is a marked "criminal type" which can be made out even before a person has committed a crime. They say further that the criminal type is marked physically by having five or more of the stigmata of degeneration, and that it is marked mentally by having the characteristics of the savage or nature man. We cannot stop to criticize in full this completely biological theory of crime which is offered by Lombroso and his followers. Undoubtedly crime has biological roots, and these we have attempted to point out in discussing the influence of degeneracy upon crime. But to claim that the criminal constitutes a well-marked "anthropological variety" of the human species, as Lombroso argues, is to set up a claim for which there is no foundation. What Lombroso thinks are the marks of the criminal are simply the marks belonging to the degenerate classes in general. That is, they are found among the insane and feeble-minded, for example, as well as in some classes of criminals. There is then no criminal type which clearly separates the criminal from other classes of degenerates, and which will mark a man out as belonging to the criminal class even before he has committed a crime. Lombroso and some of his school have altogether overemphasized the physical and anatomical side of the study of the criminal, and slighted the sociological side of such study. Moreover, Lombroso's statements, which he makes in very general terms, apply, if they apply at all, not to criminals as a class, but only to instinctive criminals, as indeed he himself has acknowledged.

Remedies for Crime.—The remedies for crime are dealt with by the subsidiary science of penology, which may be regarded as a branch of scientific philanthropy. We can only direct the student's attention here to the vast literature on the subject and remark that the cure for crime consists not in some social panacea or in social revolution, but in dealing with the causes of crime so as to prevent the existence of the criminal class. In a general way, we have already indicated in discussing the remedies for poverty and pauperism what the steps must be to eradicate crime. In order practically to wipe out crime in society, as we have already said, three things are necessary. First, every individual must have a good birth; that is, heredity must be controlled so that only those who are physically and mentally sound are allowed to marry and reproduce. The difficulties of doing this we have already noted. Second, every individual must have a good training, both at home and at school, so as to adjust him properly to the social life. His education must fit him to take his place among other men, make him able to take care of himself, and to help others; and make him, in every possible way, acquainted with the social inheritance of the race. Last but not least, just social conditions must be provided. Everything in the social environment must be carefully looked after in order to insure the best development of the individual and to prevent his environment from being in any way a drawback to him.

These things, if it were possible to bring them about, would wipe out crime, or, at least, minimize it to the lowest terms. Of course, this cannot be done in a generation, perhaps not in many generations, but it is evident that the problem of crime is in no way an insoluble problem in human society. With time and care and scientific knowledge, crime, as well as poverty and pauperism, could be wiped out.

But curative measures are important, also, in dealing with the criminal, and each distinct class must be dealt with differently. We noted in the beginning of the chapter the three great character types in the criminal class: the instinctive criminal, in whom the tendency toward a life of crime is inborn; the habitual criminal, who acquires the habit of crime from his surroundings; and the single offender, who, while committing a single offense, never becomes a criminal in the strictest sense. These three distinct classes of criminals, whom we might style the degenerates, the derelicts, and the accidental offenders, need to be recognized in our criminal law and to be dealt with differently by our criminal courts and correctional institutions. The instinctive criminal can scarcely be adjusted to normal social life. He is, as we have already seen, essentially a defective, usually more or less feeble-minded. Reformation in the fullest sense of the word is almost out of the question in his case. The proper policy for society with reference to the instinctive criminal class, which constitutes but a small portion of our total criminal population, would be segregation for life. Practically, of course, this may have its difficulties until we perfect our means of discovering slight mental defects in individuals which make them incapable of social adjustment, but practically, also, we have found means of recognizing this type by such marks as incorrigibility, recidivism, and the stigmata of degeneracy.

The habitual criminal, who originally was a normal person, can be, at least in the early part of his career, fully reformed. Children and adolescents, even though habitual offenders, are easily susceptible of reformation, but this is difficult with the adult habitual offender past thirty years of age who has a long criminal record behind him. Like the instinctive criminal, he is scarcely capable of reformation. Hardened habitual offenders, and especially professional criminals, should, therefore, be sentenced upon indeterminate sentences, terminable only when adequate evidence of their reformation has been secured. This can best be accomplished by what is known as the "habitual criminal act," providing that persons guilty of three or four felonies shall be sent to prison for life, to be released only upon satisfactory evidence of reformation.

The single offender, who is usually a reputable citizen who commits crime through passion or through great temptation, can usually best be dealt with outside of prison walls. The young single offender, if not properly handled, may be easily transformed into an habitual criminal. On the whole, a young single offender who has had no criminal record is, perhaps, best dealt with by the system of probation which we will note later. On the other hand, certain single offenders past thirty years of age, such as bribe-givers and bribe-takers, society may have to punish in order to make an example of. Exemplary punishment is, undoubtedly, still necessary in some cases, and in the main it should be reserved for this class of mature offenders in society who have otherwise lived reputable lives. Just how far exemplary punishment should be used in society as a deterrent to crime is a disputed question among penologists. Whether, as in cases of homicide, it should ever go to the extent of capital punishment or not depends very much upon the civilization of the group. In a civilization like ours, where blood vengeance is so often demanded by mobs, it is probably unwise, for the present at least, to seek the abolition of capital punishment for murder in the first degree.

The Prison System. Every state should have at least six distinct sets of institutions to deal with the criminal class.

1. County and city jails for the detention of offenders awaiting trial.

2. Reform schools for delinquent children under sixteen years of age who require institutional treatment.

3. Industrial reformatories for adult first offenders between sixteen and thirty years of age who require institutional treatment.

4. Special reformatories for vagrants, inebriates, and prostitutes.

5. A hospital prison for the criminal insane.

6. County and state penitentiaries for incorrigible, hardened criminals.

If any one of these sets of institutions is lacking in a state, it is impossible for the state to deal properly in a remedial way with the problem of crime. All these institutions, of course, need to be manned by experts and equipped in the best possible way. The present condition of our jails, of our penitentiaries, and to some extent of our reform schools, frequently makes them schools of crime. Nothing is more demoralizing in any community than a bad jail where criminals of all classes are herded together in idleness. Again, the administration of some of our state penitentiaries with an eye to profit only, makes them places for the deformation of character rather than for its reformation. Again, the lack of special institutions to deal with habitual vagrants, drunkards, and prostitutes, is one of the great reasons why we find it so difficult to stamp out crime. Into the details of the organization, construction, and management of these institutions we cannot go in this book. It is sufficient to say that all these institutions should furnish specialized scientific treatment for the various delinquent classes with which they deal, and to do this they should aim to reproduce the conditions and discipline of free life as far as possible. These institutions, in other words, with the exception of the penitentiaries and other institutions for segregation, should aim at overcoming defective character in individuals. Their work is mainly, therefore, a work of remedying psychical defects in the individual which prevent his proper adjustment to society. In the case of penitentiaries, however, the work is one mainly of segregation, of providing humane care under such conditions as least to burden society, and at the same time give such opportunity as there may be for reformation.

Substitutes for Imprisonment. We have already noted that some classes of offenders may be reformed outside of prison walls. This is especially true of children, of the younger misdemeanants, and of those who have committed their first felony. It has been found that by suspending sentences in such cases, giving the person liberty upon certain conditions, and placing him under the surveillance of an officer of the court who will stand in the relation of friend and quasi-guardian to him, that reformation can, in many cases, be easily accomplished. This is known as the probation system. It has been characterized as "a reformatory without walls." Originating in Massachusetts, it has been increasingly put into practice of recent years in many states with much success. The system, however, will not work well without trained probation officers to watch over those who are given conditional liberty. The practice of placing upon probation without probation officers is a questionable one and is liable to bring in disrepute the whole system. Probation is not mere leniency, as some suppose, but is rather a system of reformation in line with the most scientific approved methods.

Coupled with probation should often go fines and restitution to injured parties. In such cases, when the person is placed upon probation, the fine or restitution may often be paid in installments, and it has been found to have a decidedly reformatory effect upon the character of the offender. Fines without probation are, however, but little more than retribution, or exemplary punishment.

Delinquent Children. The treatment of delinquent children constitutes a special problem in itself. It has recently come to be well recognized that criminal tendencies nearly always appear in childhood, and that if we can overcome these tendencies in the delinquent child, we shall largely prevent the existence of an habitual criminal class. Strictly speaking, of course, the child is a presumptive rather than a real criminal. The delinquent child is socially maladjusted and is scarcely ever to be considered an enemy of organized society. Delinquent children should be dealt with, therefore, as presumptive rather than as genuine criminals. In general, therefore, they should not be arrested, should not be put in jail with older offenders, and should be tried by a special court in which the judge representing the state plays the role of a parent. For the most part, delinquent children may be dealt with, as we have already seen by putting them upon probation under the care of proper probation officers. When the home surroundings are not good, such children may often be placed in families and their reformation more easily secured than if placed in institutions. In any case, they should never be sent to the reform school except as a last resort. The parent or guardian, also, should be held responsible for the delinquency of the child if he is contributory thereto by his negligence or otherwise.

We may sum up this chapter, then, by repeating that the problem of crime is in no way an insoluble problem in human society, though, perhaps, a certain amount of occasional and accidental crime will always exist. The solution of the problem, as we have seen, only demands that man should secure the same mastery over his social environment and over human nature that he has already practically achieved over physical nature; and the gradual development of the social sciences will certainly make this possible some time in the future.

SELECT REFERENCES

For brief reading:

ELLIS, *The Criminal.*
WINES, *Punishment and Reformation.*
BOIES, *The Science of Penology.*

For more extended reading:

BARROWS, *The Reformatory System in the United States.*
BARROWS, *Children's Courts in the United States.*
DRAHMS, *The Criminal.*
FERRI, *Criminal Sociology.*
MORRISON, *Crime and Its Causes.*
MORRISON, *Our Juvenile Offenders.*
PARMELEE, *Anthropology and Sociology in Relation to Criminal Procedure.*
TRAVIS, *The Young Malefactor.*

CHAPTER XIV

SOCIALISM IN THE LIGHT OF SOCIOLOGY

There have been many "short-cuts" proposed to the solution of social problems. Among these the various schemes for reorganizing human society and industry, brought together under the general name of "socialism," have attracted most attention and deserve most serious consideration. In criticizing the most conspicuous of these schemes of social reconstruction, the so-called "scientific socialism," it should be understood at the outset that there is no intention of questioning the general aims of the socialists. Those aims, as voiced by their best representatives, are in entire accord with sound science, religion, and ethics. That humanity should gain collective control over the conditions of its existence is the ultimate and highest aim of all science, all education, and all government. No student of sociology doubts that human society has steadily moved, though with interruptions, toward a larger control over its own processes; and no sane man doubts that such collective control over the conditions of existence is desirable. These general aims, which the socialists share with all workers for humanity, are not in question. What is in question are the specific means or methods by which the socialists propose to reconstruct human society—to gain collective control over the means of existence. In order to criticize socialism we must see a little more narrowly what socialism is and what it proposes to do.

Socialism Defined.—As a recent socialist writer has declared, socialism, like Christianity, is a term which has come to have no definite meaning. It is used by all sorts of people to cover all sorts of vague and indefinite schemes to improve or revolutionize society. [Footnote: It has been said that the word "socialism," as currently used, has four distinct meanings: (1) Utopian socialism, i.e., schemes like More's Utopia; (2) the socialist party and its program, i.e., "the socialization of the instruments of production;" (3) The Marxist doctrine of social evolution, i.e., "the materialistic conception of history;" (4) a vague body of beliefs of the working classes, more or less derived from (2) and (3). It is of course only socialism in the second and third senses which is discussed in this chapter.] Such a vague conception would, of course, be impossible of scientific criticism. But fortunately the word historically has come to have a fairly clear and definite meaning. It has come to stand for the social and political program of a party, the Social-Democratic party of Germany and other European states. Karl Marx and his associates were the founders of this party, hence historical socialism is synonymous with Marxian socialism, and we shall so use the word. The cardinal tenet or principle of the socialist party is the public ownership of all capital, that is, of the means of production. Certain other things are, however, involved in this, and we may define the full program of Marxian socialism by saying that it proposes: (1) the common ownership of the means of production (abolition of private property in capital); (2) common management of the means of production (industry) by democratically selected authorities; (3) distribution of the product by these common authorities in accordance with some democratically approved principle; (4) private property in incomes (consumption goods) to be retained.

It is evident from this outline of "orthodox" or Marxian socialism that it is primarily and dominantly an economic program. It is true that it emphasizes democratic forms of government, but this is only incidental to its main purpose of securing a just distribution of economic goods. Strictly speaking, in a correct use of scientific terms, Marxian socialism should be called "economic socialism."

The Theoretical Basis of Marxian Socialism.—Marx's socialism is frequently called scientific socialism, because its followers believe that it rests upon a scientific theory of social evolution. This theory is best stated in Marx's own words, as he gives it in his *Critique of Political Economy*, namely, that "the method of the production of material life determines the social, political, and spiritual life process in general." We find it stated in other words, though in substance the same, by Engels, Marx's friend and coworker. Engels says, "In every historical epoch, the prevailing mode of economic production and exchange, and the social organization *necessarily* following from it, form the basis upon which is built up, and from which alone can be explained, the political and intellectual history of that epoch." In other words, according to Marx and his followers, the economic element in human society determines all other elements; if the other elements cannot be fully derived from the economic, their form and expression is at least determined by the economic. This is the so-called "materialistic conception of history" upon which Marxian socialists believe their program to have a firm scientific foundation. [Footnote: In several utterances of his later years Marx qualified considerably his "materialistic conception of history," but the more radical or revolutionary wing of his followers have always adhered to the extreme form of the theory.] The followers of Marx, indeed, declare that with this principle Marx explains social evolution quite as fully as Darwin explained organic evolution through natural selection; and they do not hesitate to compare Marx's work in the social sciences with Darwin's work in the biological sciences.

It may certainly be agreed that this social philosophy which we have already said is best characterized as "economic determinism," is the logically necessary foundation of economic socialism. If the change of the economic or industrial order of human society is going to work such wonders as the socialists claim, then it must follow that the economic element is the fundamental and determining element in the social life. If what is wrong with human society is chiefly wrong economic conditions, then the changing of those conditions should, of course, change the whole social superstructure. It would seem, therefore, that the dominantly economic program of Marxian socialists must stand or fall with the economic interpretation of social organization and evolution which Marx proposed. If it can be shown that Marx's philosophy of human society is essentially unsound, then the proposition to regenerate human society simply by economic reorganization is also unsound. Let us see whether the positions of the economic socialists are tenable in the light of the sociological principles which have been emphasized in the previous chapters of this book.

Criticism of Marxian Socialism.—The student has already been told that human society is a complex of living organisms, responding now this way, now that, to external stimuli in the environment. These stimuli in the environment we have roughly, but inaccurately, spoken of as causes, though they are not causes in a mechanical sense. The responses which are given to these stimuli by individuals and groups vary greatly according to heredity, instincts, and habits,—the inner nature, in other words, of the organisms composing society. Now, the stimuli in the environment which give rise to the activities of individuals and societies, though not in any mechanical way, may be classified into several great groups, such as the economic, the reproductive, the political, the religious, and so on. The economic stimuli would be those that have to do with the processes of production, distribution, and consumption of wealth; that is, the economic stimuli are those which are concerned with economic values. Now, while the student has not been even introduced to the psychological theory of human society, he perhaps knows enough of individual human nature to see that there is no reason in the nature of things why one's responses to economic stimuli, those connected with economic values, should determine his response to all other stimuli; and this is what scientific sociology and scientific psychology exactly find; namely, that there is no reason for believing that economic stimuli determine in any exact way or to any such extent, as Marx thought, responses to other stimuli. It is true that our habits of response to a certain class of stimuli affect to a certain extent our habits of response to all other classes. Thus it follows that the economic phase of human society affects to a very great degree all other phases of human society. But this is simply the doctrine of the unity of personality and the interdependence of all phases of the social life, and it is very different from Marx's theory that the economic determines all the other phases; for under the doctrine of social interdependence we can see it is quite as reasonable to state that the religious and political phases of the social life determine the economic as it is to state that the economic determines the political and religious.

Let us bring the discussion down to more concrete terms. The student has seen that in every social problem there are a multitude of factors or stimuli (causes) at work, and that in no problem is the economic factor so all important that it may be said that the other factors are simply subsidiary. On the contrary, in such a problem as crime the methods of production and distribution of material goods, while important factors in the problem of crime, in no way determine that problem; and ideal conditions of the production and distribution of wealth would in no way solve the problem of crime. So, too, the negro problem is hardly touched by the question of the forms of industry or the economic organization of society. We might go on with a whole list of social problems and show that in every case the economic factor is no more important than many other factors, and that the economic reorganization of society would in some cases scarcely affect these problems at all. *The social problem, therefore,—the problem of the relations of men to one another,—is not simply nor fundamentally an economic problem; rather it is fundamentally a biological and psychological problem,*—if you please, a moral problem.

This brings us to a second criticism of socialism, namely, that it proposes to reorganize human society upon an economic basis, not upon a biological basis. The program of the socialist looks forward to the satisfaction of economic needs, but it has failed to take into account the biological requirements for existence. It would be far more scientific to reorganize society upon the basis of the needs of the family than to reorganize it simply upon the basis of industry. The reproductive process which the economic socialists ignore, or leave unregulated almost entirely, is far more important for the continued existence of human society than all its economic processes,—if by the reproductive process we mean the rearing as well as the birth of offspring; and if by the economic process we mean merely the forms and methods of the production and distribution of material goods.

In other words, the socialistic program leaves the future out of account, and aims simply to satisfy the present generation with a just distribution of material goods. If it could be shown that a just distribution of material goods would insure the future of the race and of civilization, then, of course, the socialist plea would be made good. But this is just what is doubtful. On the whole, it must be said that the socialist program is based upon the wishes and desires of the adult, not upon the needs of the child or of the race.

The extreme emphasis which Marxian socialism throws upon economic and industrial conditions in human society is, therefore, not justified by the scientific facts which we know about collective human life. Rather it must be said that this is the vital weakness of Marxian socialism,—that it over-emphasizes the economic element. Of course, we are not saying that control over economic conditions is not necessary to collective control over the general conditions of existence, which society is undoubtedly aiming at, but it is saying that conceivably collective control over the social life process might be upon some other basis than the economic. It might emphasize, for example, the health and continuity of the race, or individual moral character, far more than the distribution of economic values. Modern economic socialism proposes simply to carry a step further our already predominatingly economic social organization by frankly recognizing the economic as the basis of all things in the social life. Modern economic socialism is, therefore, rightfully judged as materialistic. It is really an expression of the industrial and commercial spirit of the present age. When the perspective of life becomes shifted again to the more important biological and spiritual elements in life, socialism will lose its prevailingly economic character, or it will cease to exist.

It must be emphasized here that all the material and economic progress of the modern world has not added greatly to the happiness or betterment of man. It is true that material progress is important, yes, necessary for spiritual progress. But material progress alone does not lead to spiritual progress, and therefore mere material progress can never add anything to the real happiness and social betterment of the race. On the contrary, it is possible to conceive of a society in which every one has an economic surplus,—a society rolling in wealth, approximately equally divided, and yet one in which human misery in its worst forms of vice and crime, pessimism and self-destruction, prevail. It is an old truth that making men "better-off" does not necessarily make them "better," and one which cannot be too often emphasized, but one which the modern socialist gets angry at when it is mentioned to him. It is therefore a matter of comparative indifference, from the standpoint of the happiness and ultimate survival of the race, whether economic goods are distributed relatively evenly in human society or not. We say comparative indifference, because, of course, no one can be indifferent to the material needs of life, inasmuch as they are the basis of its higher development. But after a certain minimum is assured it is extremely doubtful whether a surplus will be of benefit or not, and this minimum necessary for the higher spiritual development of the social life can be secured through the reform of present society without trying the doubtful social revolution which the socialists advocate.

This brings us to a third criticism of Marxian socialism. Traditionally Marxian socialism has been revolutionary socialism. The vast mass of the socialist party to-day look forward to some revolution which will, as they say, "socialize the instruments of production," that is, transfer capital from private ownership and management to public ownership and management. Probably rightly, many socialists hold that such a wholesale transfer from private to public ownership would be the only way in which a socialistic regime could be successfully inaugurated. But if this revolution were accomplished it is evident that it is highly uncertain whether its results would be permanent. For all that we have learned concerning human society leads us to say that social organization at any particular time is very largely a matter of habit. Now collective habits are less easily changed than individual habits, because any change in collective habits practically necessitates the consent of all the individuals who make up the social group. We know also that even in individual life old habits are not easily supplanted by new ones and that there is always a tendency to revert to the old. All historical evidence shows that revolutions are always followed by periods of reaction, and that this reaction is usually proportionate to the extent and suddenness of change in social organization.

Some modern socialists have argued from de Vries's mutation theory in biology that in social evolution we must expect mutations also, and that, therefore, the great changes in human society are normally accomplished by means of revolution. But this argument rests wholly on analogy, and arguments from analogy in science are practically worthless. It may be asserted, on the other hand, that all the great changes in human society which have been desirable have come about only after prolonged preparation and after a series of gradual steps which led up to the final change. The Greco-Roman world, for example, was becoming ripe for Christianity before Christianity finally appeared and became triumphant. The centuries from the fourteenth to the sixteenth had prepared for the protestant reformation in the countries of modern Europe before the reformation became an established fact.

Thus, radical reconstruction of the social life by means of revolution is scarcely possible. The instincts and habits of individual human nature upon which the social order rests cannot be easily changed by revolutionary programs in legislation or in institutions. The only probable result of such an attempt would be the collapse of the new social order, because it would have insufficient foundations in individual character upon which to rest. The idea of ushering in the social millennium through some vast social revolution is therefore chimerical.

It is not the place in this book to take up the practical objections to economic socialism. These practical objections are for the most part of a political and economic nature, and they accordingly can be better dealt with in treatises on politics and economics than in one on sociology. It is perhaps sufficient to say that the political and economic objections to socialism are not less weighty than the sociological objections. Government, for example, exists in human society to regulate, and not to carry on directly, all social activities. If the state were in its various forms called upon to own and manage all productive wealth in society, it is extremely probable that such an experiment would break down of its own weight, since the state would be attempting that which, in the nature of things, as the chief regulative institution of society, it is not fitted to do. But it is not our purpose, as has just been said, to go into the political and economic objections to economic or Marxian socialism. To understand these the student must consult the leading works on economic and political science.

Substitutes for Economic Socialism.—Certain steps sociology and all social sciences already indicate as necessary for larger collective control over the conditions of social existence. These steps, however, aim not at instituting a new social order, but at removing certain demonstrated causes of social maladjustment which exist in present society; and as in the solution of special social problems we have seen reason to reject "short-cuts" and "cure-alls," so in a scientific reconstruction of human society we have good reason to reject the social revolution which the followers of Marx advocate, and to offer as a substitute in its stead some social reforms which will make more nearly possible a normal social life.

Perhaps the necessary steps for bringing about such a normal social life have never been better summed up than by Professor Devine in his book on *Misery and its Causes*. Rather than offer a program of our own we shall, therefore, give a brief resume of the conditions which Professor Devine names as essential to normal social life, believing that these offer a program upon which all sane social workers and reformers can unite. Professor Devine names ten conditions essential to a normal social life: (1) the securing of a sound physical heredity, that is, a good birth for every child, by a rational system of eugenics; (2) the securing of a protected childhood, which will assure the normal development of the child, and of a protected motherhood, which will assure the proper care of the child; (3) a system of education which shall be adapted to social needs, inspired by the ideals of rational living and social service; (4) the securing of freedom from preventable disease; (5) the elimination of professional vice and crime; (6) the securing of a prolonged working period for both men and women; (7) a general system of insurance against the ordinary contingencies of life which now cause poverty or dependence; (8) a liberal relief system which will meet the material needs of those who become accidentally dependent; (9) a standard of living sufficiently high to insure full nourishment, reasonable recreation, proper housing, and the other elementary necessities of life; (10) a social religion which shall make the service of humanity the highest aim of all individuals.

It is sufficient to say, in closing this chapter, that if these ten essentials of a normal social life could be realized—and there is no reason why they cannot be—there would be no need to try the social revolution which Marxian socialism advocates.

There can be no question that the ultimate aim of the social sciences is to provide society with the knowledge necessary for collective control over its own life processes. Sociology and the special social sciences are aiming, therefore, in an indirect way to accomplish the same thing which political socialism aims at accomplishing through economic revolution. There would seem to be no danger in trusting science to work out this problem of collective control over the conditions of existence. There are no risks to run by the scientific method, for it proceeds step by step, adequately testing theories by facts as it goes along. The thing to do, therefore, for those who wish to see "a humanity adjusted to the requirements of its existence" is to encourage scientific social research along all lines. With a fuller knowledge of human nature and human society it will be possible to indicate sane and safe reconstructions in the social order, so that ultimately humanity will control its social environment and its own human nature even more completely than it now controls the forces of physical nature. But the ultimate reliance in all such reconstruction, as we will try to show in the next chapter, must be, not revolution, nor even legislation, but education.

SELECT REFERENCES

For brief reading:

ELY, *Socialism and Social Reform.*
SPARGO, *Socialism.* Revised edition.
GILMAN, *Socialism and the American Spirit.*

For more extended reading:

HUNTER, *Socialists at Work.*
KIRKUP, *History of Socialism.*
SCHAEFFLE, *Quintessence of Socialism.*
WELLS, *New Worlds for Old.*

CHAPTER XV

EDUCATION AND SOCIAL PROGRESS

As has just been said, the ultimate reliance in all social reform or social reconstruction must be upon the education of the individual. Social organization can never be more complex or of a higher type than the individual character and intelligence of the members of the group warrants. At any given stage of society, therefore, the intelligence and moral character of its individual members limits social organization. Only by raising the intelligence and character of the individual members of society can a higher type of social life permanently result.

Another fact to which the student needs his attention called is that all progress in human society, it follows, from what has just been said, depends upon the relation between one generation and its successor. Only as new life comes into society is there opportunity to improve the character of that life. If at any given time intelligence and character limit the possibilities of social organization, then it is equally manifest that only in the new individuals of society can that intelligence and character be greatly improved.

There are, of course, two possible ways of bringing about such improvement:—first, through the selection of the hereditary elements in society, eliminating the unfit and preserving the more fit; but, as we have repeatedly pointed out, such a scheme of artificial selection is far in the future, and in any case its inauguration would have to depend upon the *second* method of improving individual character, which is through education and training. As we have insisted, not only may the natural instincts and tendencies of individuals be greatly modified by training but through education the habits and hence the character of individuals can be controlled. Therefore the main reliance of society in all forward movements must be upon education, that is, upon artificial means of controlling the formation of character and habit in individuals.

The finality of education in social betterment can be, perhaps, further illustrated by reconsidering for a moment some of the social problems which we have just studied. Take for example the problem of crime. There are only three possible means, as we have already seen, of eliminating crime from human society:—first, through changes in individual human nature, brought about by biological selection, that is, through a system of selective breeding, eliminating all who show any criminal tendencies. This method would, perhaps, eliminate certain types of criminals as we have already seen, namely, those in whom the hereditary tendency to crime is dominant. A second means of attacking the problem of crime would be by improving social and economic conditions by means of the interference of the organized authority of society in the form of the state. Legislation and administration directed to social ends might accomplish much in reducing the temptations and opportunities for crime in any group. The correction of evils in social and industrial organization would, no doubt, again greatly lessen crime but it is entirely conceivable, from all that we know of human nature and human society, that crime might still persist under a just social and industrial organization. Crime could be completely eliminated only through a third means, namely, the careful training of each new individual in society as he came on the stage of life, so that he would be moral and law-abiding, respecting the rights of others and the institutions of society. Moreover, neither selective breeding nor governmental interference in social conditions could accomplish very much in eliminating crime unless these were backed by a wise system of social education.

Now what is true of crime is equally true of all social problems. They may be approached from either of three sides:—first, from the biological side, or the side of physical heredity; second, from the side of social organization, or the improvement of the social environment; third, from the side of individual character, or the psychical adjustment of the individual to society. As Professor Ward and many other sociologists have emphasized, it is this latter side which is the most available point of attack on all social problems; for when we have secured a right attitude of the individual toward society all social problems will be more than half solved. Thus, as we said at the beginning of this book, education has a bearing upon every social problem, and every social problem also has a bearing upon education. Just how important this reciprocal relationship between education and social life is, we can appreciate only when we have considered somewhat more fully the nature of social progress.

The Nature of Social Progress.—Social progress has been defined in many ways by the social thinkers of the past. Without entering into any formal definition of social progress, we believe that it will be evident to the reader of this book that social progress consists, for one thing, in the more complete adaptation of society to the conditions of life. We regard those changes as progressive whether they be moral, intellectual, or material, which bring about a better adaptation of individuals to one another in society, and of social groups to the requirements of their existence. Social progress means, in other words, the adaptation of society to a wider and more universal environment. The ideal of human progress is apparently adaptation to a perfectly universal environment, such an adaptation as shall harmonize all factors whether internal or external, present or remote, in the life of humanity. Social progress means, therefore, greater harmony among the members of a group. It means also greater efficiency of those members in performing their work. Finally, it means greater ability on the part of the group to survive. Social progress includes, therefore, the ideals of social harmony, social efficiency, and social survival. Things which do not ultimately conduce to these ends can scarcely be called progressive.

Now it is evident that adaptation on the part of individuals and groups to the requirements of life may be in part accomplished by biological selection, that is, by eliminating the least adapted. But selection is, after all, a very clumsy and imperfect instrument for securing the highest type of adaptation. Again, it is evident that a certain degree of adaptation can be secured through the constraint of government and law; but only a relatively low type of adaptation can be secured in such an external way. It is finally evident, therefore, that the highest type of adaptation in either individual or social life can be secured only by training the intelligence and moral character of individuals so that they will be sufficient to meet the requirements of existence.

Another feature of social progress which we have not yet mentioned in this chapter, though we have noted it repeatedly in earlier chapters, is the increased complexity of social organization. This increased complexity is in part due to the mere increase in numbers. It is also due to the various processes themselves by which wider and more universal adaptation is brought about in society. Thus, while every useful mechanical invention aids man to conquer nature, it at the same time increases the complexity of social life. Now in a more complex society there is more opportunity for conflicts of habit between individuals, more opportunity for social maladjustment, and therefore more opportunity for the failure of some part or all of the group in achieving a social life characterized by harmony, efficiency, and capacity for survival. Hence, the adaptation of individuals in the large and complex groups of modern civilized societies becomes a greater and greater problem. The regulative institutions of society, such as government, law, religion, and education, have to grapple with this problem of adjusting individuals to the requirements of an increasingly complex social life. No doubt religion, government, and law have a great function to perform in increasing social regulation, but they can only perform it effectively after they enlist education on their side.

The Social Function of Education.—We are now prepared to understand the meaning of educational systems in civilized society and to see what the true function of education is. Education exists to adapt individuals to their social life. It is for the purpose of fitting the individual to take his place in the social group and to add something to the life of the group. Educational systems exist not to train the individual to develop his powers and capacity simply as an individual unit, but rather to fit him effectively to carry on the social life before he actively participates in it. In other words, the social function of education is to guide and control the formation of habit and character on the part of the individual, as well as to develop his capacity and powers, so that he shall become an efficient member of society. This work is not, at least in complex civilizations like our own, one which we carry on simply in order to achieve social perfection, but it is rather something which is necessary for the survival of large and complex groups. Otherwise, as we have pointed out, the conflicts in the acquirement of habit and character on the part of individuals would be so great that there would be no possibility of their working together harmoniously in a common social life. Just so far as the system of education is defective, is insufficient to meet social needs, in so far may we expect the production of individuals who are socially maladjusted, as shown in pauperism, defectiveness, and crime.

Education is, then, the great means of controlling habit and character in complex social groups, and as such it is the chief means to which society must look for all substantial social progress. It is the instrument by which human nature may be apparently indefinitely modified, and hence, also, the instrument by which society may be perfected. The task of social regeneration is essentially a task of education.

Education as a Factor in Past Social Evolution.—Does past social history justify these large claims for education as a factor in social development? It must be replied that the history of human society undoubtedly substantiates this position, but even if it did not, we should still have good ground for claiming that education can be such an all-powerful factor in the social future. The sociological study of past civilizations, however, shows quite conclusively that all of them have depended in one way or another upon educational processes, not only for continuity, but largely, also, for their development. As we have already seen, the life history of a culture or a civilization is frequently the life history of a religion. But religious beliefs, together with the moral and social beliefs, which become attached to them, were effectively transmitted only through the instruction of the young. The religious element did scarcely more than afford a powerful sanction for the moral and social beliefs upon which the social organization of the past rested; hence, when we ascribe great importance to the religious factor in social evolution, we also ascribe, at the same time, great importance to education, because it was essentially the educational process, together with religious sanction, which made possible most of the civilizations and social progress of the past.

Indeed, we have no record of any people of any very considerable culture that did not employ educational processes to the largest degree to preserve and transmit that culture from generation to generation. Culture has been passed down in human history, therefore, essentially by educational processes. These educational processes have controlled the formation of habits and character, of ways of thinking and ways of acting, in successive generations of individuals. The educational processes have had much more to do, therefore, with the civilizations and social organization of the past than industrial conditions. Industrial conditions have been rather relatively external factors in the social environment to which society has had to adapt itself more or less. In the same way, political authority has rested on, and been derived from, the social traditions rather than the reverse. It is therefore not too much for the sociologist to say, agreeing with Thomas Davidson, that education is the last and highest method of social evolution. The lowest method of evolution was by selection, and *that*, as we have already emphasized, cannot be neglected. The next method of social evolution apparently to develop was the method of adaptation by organized authority, and, as we have already seen, organized authority in society, or social regulation by means of authority, must indefinitely persist and perhaps increase, rather than diminish; but the latest and highest method of social evolution is not through biological selection nor through the exercise of despotic authority, but through the education of the individual, so that he shall become adjusted to the social life in habits and character before he participates in it. Human society may be modified, we now see, best through modifying the nature of the individual, and the most direct method to do this is through education.

The Socialized Education of the Future.—If what has been said is substantially correct, then education should become conscious of its social mission and purpose. The educator should conserve education as the chief means of social progress, and education should be directed to producing efficient members of society. The education of the future must aim, in other words, not at producing lawyers, physicians, engineers, but at producing citizens. Education for citizenship means that there must be radical reconstruction in the educational processes of the present. The education of the nineteenth century aimed at developing largely power and capacity in the individual as such. Its implicit, and oftentimes its avowed, aim was individual success. The popularity of higher education in the nineteenth century especially rested upon the cult of individual success. It became, therefore, largely commercialized, and emphasized chiefly the professions and occupations which best assured the individual a successful career among a commercial and industrial people.

It is needless to say that the individualistic, commercialized education of the latter years of the nineteenth century very often failed to produce the good citizen. On the contrary, with its ideal of individual power and success, it frequently produced the cultured freebooter, which our modern industry has so often afforded examples of. Education, instead of being a socializing agency and the chief instrument of social regeneration, became an individualizing agency dissolving the social order itself.

Very slowly our educators are becoming conscious of the fact that this type of education is a social menace, and that our educational system needs reformation from bottom to top in order to become again equal to the social task imposed upon it by the more complex social conditions of the twentieth century. Hence the demand for a socialized education, which is proceeding, not only from sociologists and social workers, but from the progressive leaders of education itself. What this socialized education of the future shall be is not the province of this book to discuss, but a few of its essential characteristics may be noted. As has already been said, such education will aim, first of all, at producing the citizen before it aims at producing the lawyer, the engineer, the physician, or any other professional or occupational type. No doubt, this means, for one thing, that all individuals shall be taught to be good fathers and mothers, good neighbors and members of communities, even more than they are taught the accomplishments of life. No doubt, also, the socialized education of the future will emphasize the adjustment of the individual to the industrial order of society, because it is necessary that individuals shall be producers if they are to be efficient citizens. The necessity and value of industrial training in our system of education has already been emphasized in discussing other social problems. Such training has its place and that place, as we have already seen, is a very important and fundamental one; but it must not be forgotten that the relations of men to one another are more important than the relations of men to nature. In industrial training, the element which is apt to be emphasized is the relations of the individual to the physical facts and forces of nature; but this is only a beginning of the training for citizenship, because good citizenship consists essentially in harmonious and efficient functioning in the social group. Therefore, the study of the relationships of men to one another must be the final and crowning element in a system of social education. Such studies as history, government, economics, ethics, and sociology must occupy a larger and larger place in the education of the future if we are to secure a humanity adjusted to the requirements of its existence. Historical and sociological instruction should lead up, moreover, to direct ethical instruction. If the industrial element in the social life is important, the moral element is even more so, since it is, as we have already said, the ideal aspect of the social. In some way or another, our public schools, from the kindergarten up, must make a place for social and ethical instruction of a direct and explicit character.

In the higher education, the social sciences must be especially emphasized, because it is those who receive higher education who become the leaders of society, and it is important, no matter what occupation or profession they may serve society in, that they understand the bearings of their work upon social welfare. They must know their duties as citizens and understand how society may best be served. In other words, our higher education should put to the front the ideal, not of individual power and success, but of social service; and this means that, in addition to the technical or professional education which the more highly educated are giving, there must be a sufficient knowledge of social conditions and of the laws and principles of social progress given them to enable them to serve society rightly. Intelligent social service cannot exist without social knowledge.

All this implies that the older idea that education can be given regardless of content is, from the social point of view, a great mistake. Social knowledge is necessary, as we have just said, for efficient social service, and a socialized education can have no other end than social service. Therefore, sociological knowledge in the broadest sense should be required in the education of every citizen, and particularly those who are to become social leaders. Professor Ward has ably argued that if sufficient information of the facts, conditions, and laws of human society could be given to all, that alone would bring about in the highest degree social progress. Whether we agree or not that the mere giving of information will of itself lead to progressive or dynamic action in society, it must be admitted that right social information is indispensable for right social action. As Professor Cooley has said, "We live in a system, and to achieve right ends, or any rational ends whatever, we must learn to understand that system." Hence, the commanding place which sociology and the social sciences should occupy in the education of all classes, and especially in the training of the teacher himself.

It is not unreasonable to believe that the development of the social sciences will show us the way to remove many, if not all, social evils; and it is also not unreasonable to believe that the knowledge which these sciences will furnish will stimulate in the vast mass of individuals an impetus to remove these evils. Moreover, training in the social sciences will check many of the most menacing tendencies of our present civilization. For one thing, training in the social sciences will lessen the practical materialism of modern civilization, for it will throw the emphasis on the relations of men to one another rather than on the relations of man to nature. The social sciences, aiming at the control of the social conditions and of social progress, necessarily emphasize the higher life of man, and they therefore set before the student as the goal, not material achievement or individual success, but the service of man. Again, training in the social sciences will check the exaggerated individualism, which, as we have already seen, is one of the most menacing tendencies of our time; for the social sciences show the solidarity of the society and the interdependence of its parts. They show that no individual lives to himself, and that his acts evidently affect the whole of society. Finally, training in the social sciences will insure the development of true moral freedom in our social life, for these sciences involve a searching but impersonal criticism of social institutions and public policies. Now the very breath of life of a free society is intelligent public criticism of its institutions and policies. Without this, there can be no change, no progress. But intelligent criticism implies scientific criticism, that is, criticism based upon adequate scientific knowledge and without personal bias. This means the scientific study of institutions and social organization. If the American people are to perfect their institutions, they must maintain and develop their moral freedom; and to maintain true moral freedom, they must encourage the scientific study of social conditions and institutions. To secure an unbiased attitude toward social and political problems, to train every citizen for social service, to reconstruct social organization along scientific lines, it is necessary, therefore, to give the social sciences an honored place in the education of all classes and professions.

SELECT REFERENCES

For brief reading:

WARD, *Applied Sociology*, Chaps. VIII-XII.
WARD, *Dynamic Sociology*, Vol. II, Chap. XIV.
HORNE, *The Philosophy of Education*, Chaps. IV and V.
DEWEY, *The School and Society*.

For more extended reading:

DAVIDSON, *History of Education.*
GRAVES, *History of Education.*
MONROE, *History of Education.*

Milton Keynes UK
Ingram Content Group UK Ltd.
UKHW011122180424
441376UK00004B/159

9 789357 962612